Midwest
GARDENER'S
Handbook

Jan Riggenbach

Cover design: Bill Kersey
Page design: Christa Schoenbrodt
Illustrations: Marta Drayton
Project production: S.E. Anderson

Midwest Gardener's Handbook / Jan Riggenbach
p.   cm.
Includes index.
ISBN 1-888608-13-7

First printing 1999
Printed in the United States of America
10 9 8 7 6 5 4 3 2 1

IntegraColor Publishing
3638 Executive Blvd.
Mesquite, TX 75149

Contents

The year was 1919. World War I had just ended. The Eighteenth Amendment to the Constitution passed, prohibiting the sale of alcohol. Huge backyard vegetable gardens were standard fixtures for Midwest families. And in Shenandoah, Iowa, a young man by the name of Earl May printed his first seed and nursery catalog.

Earl May Catalog, 1922

A farm boy from Nebraska, May had met his future wife, Gertrude Welch, while pursuing a law degree at the University of Nebraska. After their marriage, they moved to Shenandoah, Gertrude's hometown. Shenandoah was also the home of Mount Arbor Nursery. Owned by Gertrude's father, E.S. Welch, it was one of the largest wholesale nurseries in the world. May became fascinated and, with financial backing from his father-in-law, abandoned a career in law to launch his own seed and nursery business.

Competition was stiff, and at first catalog orders came in at a trickle. But May was a natural-born salesman. He traveled 60 miles northwest to Omaha, Nebraska, to broadcast monthly from radio station WOAW. One of the first to advertise by radio, May was so successful that he soon decided to build his own radio station in Shenandoah.

KMA Radio opened as a department of May Seed and Nursery in 1925, with May himself often at the microphone. Catering to the rural population, broadcasts included early-morning newscasts, so farmers could hear the news before they left for their fields. Within two years, the Shenandoah station had become one of the best-known stations in America, and—in a 1926 Radio Digest poll—May was voted the world's most popular radio announcer.

Earl E. May, Founder

Meanwhile, the station was serving its original purpose: Selling its products to gardeners across the Midwest. Earl May became a household name, and his plants a backyard staple.

In 1930, May opened a second retail store, in Lincoln, Nebraska. Five years later, more stores dotted the region. The pace continues today, with Earl

May garden centers now spanning the region from Sioux City to Kansas City, North Platte to Iowa City.

When May died in 1946, his son Ed and son-in-law J.D. Rankin took over the business.

Earl May Seed Company, 1919 Shenandoah, Iowa

They bought more radio stations and also added some television stations to the family's holdings. Though many of these

Earl May in the Rose Garden

holdings were sold in the mid 1980s, the seed and nursery business remained in family hands. Earl May's granddaughter—Betty Jane Shaw—has been at the helm since 1989. Under her guidance, the number of stores has grown to more than 50, with many of the older stores renovated as new ones are built.

Much has changed since the early days, when Earl May sold everything from baby chicks to radios along with his seeds and plants. Today's big sellers are perennials, shrubs, and other ornamental plants. The days of the huge backyard garden, counted on to produce all of a family's vegetables and fruits for the year, are largely gone. Despite that, you'll still find a large selection of vegetable seeds and fruiting plants at the company's stores. Earl May knows that food gardens, though now grown more for pleasure than necessity, are still important to Midwest gardeners.

Betty Jane Shaw, Owner
Granddaughter of Earl E. May

Gone is the spring seed and nursery catalog. Today's customers prefer to come see the plants before they buy, so the company has turned its full attention to retail stores. In place of bare-root plants shipped directly to the customer in early spring, most plants are now grown in containers displayed at the store. That's a big boon to gardeners, who can plant container-grown trees, shrubs, and flowers throughout the entire growing season.

Gone, too, are the Earl May Display Gardens in Shenandoah that were popular after World War II. The baby chicks have been replaced by pet departments. A popular new attraction: Water garden displays. A large selection of wildflowers has been added to satisfy Midwest gardeners' new appreciation of native plants. Landscape departments at each store assist customers in planning improvements to their yards.

But one thing hasn't changed. Betty Jane Shaw still runs the company on the philosophy that built her grandfather's business: "Have the merchandise people want, when they want it, and at a price they want to pay."

Gardening in the Midwest

When Earl May Seed & Nursery opened its doors in 1919, Shenandoah was already a mecca for seed and nursery companies. Besides Mount Arbor Nursery, the southwest Iowa community was home to David S. Lake's Shenandoah Nurseries, Henry Field Seed Co., and others.

The rich prairie soil that made Shenandoah attractive to so many seed and nursery companies back then is what makes most of the Midwest ideal for gardening today.

Nevertheless, gardening in this region is often a challenge. To survive, our plants must be able to withstand wildly variable weather: bitter cold, blistering heat, drying wind, drought, and excessive rain. Fortunately, there are many plants that can meet the challenge. In this book, you'll find descriptions of hundreds of the best, along with tips to help them thrive in your Midwest garden. Many of the plants are accompanied by icons that indicate some of the plant's special features:

 Attracts Butterflies

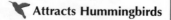 Attracts Hummingbirds

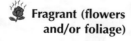 Fragrant (flowers and/or foliage)

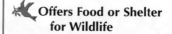 Offers Food or Shelter for Wildlife

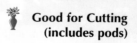 Good for Cutting (includes pods)

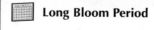 Long Bloom Period

 Fall Color

 Offers Winter Interest

An illustrated Appendix presents practical gardening techniques.

Our Midwest Climate

Temperature dictates almost everything a gardener does: when to plant, what to plant, when to harvest, when to fertilize, when to check for certain pests and diseases, and much more.

If you're a new gardener, the first step to a successful Midwest garden is to learn what to expect. First, turn to the USDA Hardiness Zone Map on page 12 to determine your zone. Then, before you buy a perennial, shrub, or tree, check the plant tag or the zone information in this book to be sure the plant is winter-hardy where you live. For example, if the map shows your location is in zone 5, you can feel confident buying any plant rated hardy to zone 5 or lower but avoid a plant rated as hardy only to zone 6.

Next, check the first map on page 13 to determine an important date on which much spring planning advice is based: your average last spring frost. But remember, this is an average. So, if the instructions say to plant "after danger of frost," you should add about two weeks to your average date.

Equally important is the date of the average *first* frost in the fall. After you find your date on page 13, you can determine the timing for such things as planting vegetables for fall harvest or protecting cold-sensitive tropical plants.

As anyone who lives in the Midwest soon discovers, our region is sometimes too wet, sometimes too dry. For the most successful garden, it pays to

Hardiness Zone Map

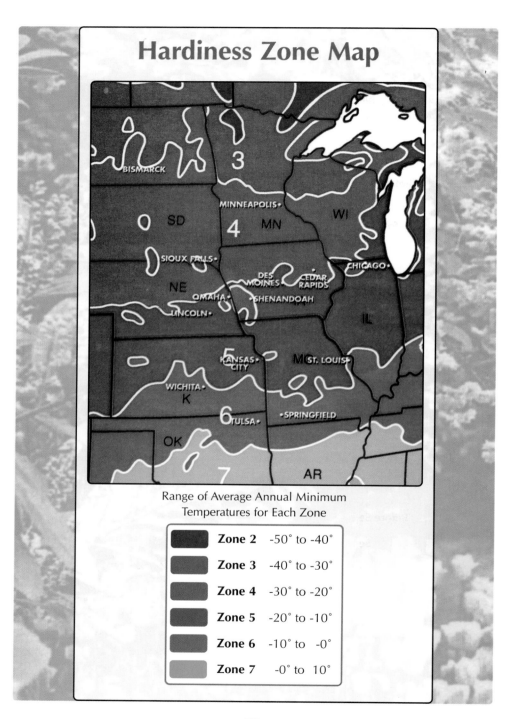

Range of Average Annual Minimum
Temperatures for Each Zone

	Zone 2	-50° to -40°
	Zone 3	-40° to -30°
	Zone 4	-30° to -20°
	Zone 5	-20° to -10°
	Zone 6	-10° to -0°
	Zone 7	-0° to 10°

Average Dates–Last Spring Frost

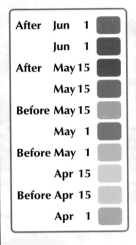

After Jun 1
Jun 1
After May 15
May 15
Before May 15
May 1
Before May 1
Apr 15
Before Apr 15
Apr 1

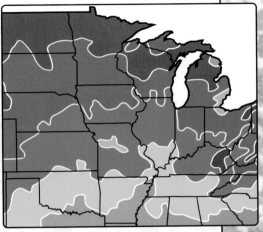

Average Dates–First Autumn Frost

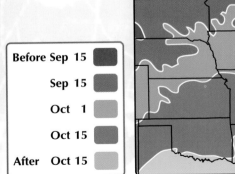

Before Sep 15
Sep 15
Oct 1
Oct 15
After Oct 15

Data Source: National Climatic Data Center (NCDC)
Co-operative station data 1951-80

hedge your bets by planting some plants that like "wet feet" and others that like it dry.

Choosing only drought-tolerant plants—a landscaping technique called xeriscaping—works well in Colorado where the idea originated. In the Midwest, though, a better idea is to group drought-tolerant plants together in one part of your yard. That way, you can reduce your use of water without risking a yard full of drought-lovers to an unusually wet growing season.

Another excellent technique to reduce water use is mulching. A blanket of shredded bark or other mulch spread on the ground not only conserves soil moisture but also keeps most weeds from sprouting.

If you use an automatic watering system to reduce the work of caring for plants in dry weather, be careful not to overwater. Drought-tolerant plants are easily drowned if planted in the path of an automatic sprinkler. Other plants may be harmed as well if you allow your system to continue operating in rainy weather.

Soil Secrets

In the excitement of planting, it's easy to forget the part of the garden that lies beneath the surface. The soil, although not glamorous, is the most important component of a successful garden.

Although Midwestern gardeners don't have to cope with many of the serious soil problems found in other regions, not all of our soils are perfect. In new neighborhoods, the topsoil may have been removed or compacted during construction. Some areas have soil that is too sandy or too "clayish." The

14

soil may be too alkaline or, less frequently, too acid for certain plants to thrive. But you don't have to be a soil scientist to fix any of these problems. One magic ingredient, humus, helps solve them all. Even if your soil is nearly perfect, more humus can help keep it that way.

Where do you find humus? It comes from plant and animal wastes, such as grass clippings, small prunings, shredded bark, wood chips, or manure. Before you plant, cover the ground with several inches of these or other organic materials, then dig the materials into the soil. They'll turn into humus as they decay.

For more humus, start a compost pile. Put in the pile just about any plant waste such as grass clippings, weeds, leaves, eggshells, sawdust, coffee grounds, and wood ashes. Make sure all grass clippings and other materials are disease-free and are not contaminated with weed-killer. Top each 6- to 8-inch layer with a sprinkle of nitrogen fertilizer or compost starter, then a 1-inch layer of garden soil. Repeat the layers until your compost container is full. Keep the pile slightly moist, and mix the materials now and then to speed up decomposition. When the pile's contents look like a heap of dark, crumbly soil, the compost is ready to use to enrich the soil.

Mulches also help improve the soil, adding humus as they slowly decay.

Fertilizing Basics

A humus-rich soil meets all the nutritional needs of some plants, but most need additional fertilizer for peak performance. Once you've been gardening for a while, you can probably tell just by looking at your plants what your soil needs. If the leaves are lush but the plants produce few flowers or fruits, the plants probably need more phosphorus. If growth is poor and the leaves are small and pale, they need more nitrogen. If the edges of the older leaves are brown and new growth dies, you may need to add more potassium.

Rather than seeking a quick fix, choose slow-release fertilizers that make nutrients available over a long period. Most organic fertilizers are naturally slow-release. If you prefer, you can buy slow-release chemical fertilizers.

Plants in containers are an exception: Because nutrients are constantly washed away by frequent watering, container plants require regular supplemental feeding. Stir a liquid or powdered plant food into the watering can every second or third time you water. Plants, like people, thrive on frequent, small meals, so use half the strength recommended on the fertilizer package.

Preventing Plant Problems

You can eliminate most pests and diseases simply by choosing resistant varieties and by matching each plant to the site it prefers. Also make time for some easy cultural practices, such as thinning plants for good air circulation and cleaning up plant debris in the fall.

If pests do attack, most are easily controlled with simple measures, such as a forceful spray of water from the garden hose, or handpicking.

The reasons we garden have changed

some, since 1919. So have some of the ways

we garden. Yet the basics remain the same:

Build your soil. Choose the right plants

for your site. Make sure they're well-fed

(and watered, when necessary). Prune,

pick, and provide pest-control, as needed.

*But most of all, **enjoy**! That's what*

Midwest gardening is all about.

Annuals

With only a single season to live their whole lives, annuals are programmed to bloom their hearts out. That makes them the ideal choice for planting in containers and in other places where you want non-stop color, though color isn't all these plants have to offer. Some, such as alyssum, fill the air with a sweet fragrance. Lantana is a magnet for butterflies. Red salvia blossoms are a favorite of hummingbirds. Lisianthus is unsurpassed as a cut flower.

Pinks, coleus, and other old-fashioned annuals are once again popular choices for Midwest gardens. Many gardeners get a kick out of also experimenting with a few newly introduced varieties every year. If you find the array of new offerings confusing, just remember that you can't go wrong with All-America Selections award winners. These plants have proven themselves in extensive independent tests, and chances are they'll be winners in your garden, too.

If you normally fill your flower beds with bedding plants, you owe it to yourself to check out the seed racks as well. You'll discover many annuals that are seldom offered as bedding plants. Nasturtiums and bachelor's buttons, for example, are best grown from seeds because their roots don't like to be disturbed. On the other hand, some annuals are available only as bedding plants because growers produce them from cuttings. Fan flower and most varieties of New Guinea impatiens fit that category.

For an "instant" garden, you can buy annuals that are already blooming, though you'll get the best performance from marigolds, snapdragons, and many others if you purchase plants without flowers. If you do buy plants in bloom, force yourself to cut off the flowers when you plant. The plants will thank you later with a superior performance.

Most annuals look better and bloom more if you cut off all their fading flowers, a practice called "deadheading." If it sounds more time-consuming than you can manage, choose plants that take care of the job by themselves. The flowers of wax begonias, impatiens, and vinca are all "self-cleaning." Other flowers—including cup flower and moss rose—produce so many blooms that it would be an impossible task to cut off each one. Instead, use grass clippers to give the plants a light shearing. You'll be rewarded with a fresh flush of blooms in about two weeks.

Read on for descriptions of many delightful annuals, along with tips to help them thrive in your Midwest garden.

Ageratum

Ageratum houstonianum

BLOOM TIME: June to frost

BLOOM COLOR: Blue, pink, violet, or white

LIGHT REQUIREMENT: Sun or partial shade

HEIGHT × WIDTH: 6 to 15 inches × 6 to 15 inches

Special Features

Though ageratum's fuzzy flower clusters come in other colors, blue-flowered ageratum provides one of the best blues for the summer garden and continues to rank first among ageratums with most gardeners. Butterflies find the flowers appealing, and the taller, long-stemmed varieties are good for cutting. Ageratums are exceptionally easy to grow. They make a beautiful edging for a garden path and add a colorful touch to containers.

How to Grow

Transplant bedding plants in the garden after the danger of spring frost. Space plants 6 to 12 inches apart according to the mature size of the variety you select. You can also grow ageratums from seed. Start seeds indoors 6 to 8 weeks before the last frost. Press the seeds firmly onto the soil surface but don't cover them with soil.

Care and Maintenance

Ageratums thrive with neglect; water only in dry weather, and don't fertilize. Avoid overhead watering, which increases the chance of disease. Cut off old flower clusters as they brown to keep the plants looking better and blooming more. If there are a lot of brown flower clusters, you can renew the plants in a jiffy with a light shearing. You'll have a new flush of blooms in about 2 weeks. Allow a few seedheads to remain in the garden to self-seed. Volunteer plants are easy to transplant in spring; put them wherever you'd like a touch of blue.

GARDEN TIP

♦ Despite the similarity in looks, the perennial ageratum (*Eupatorium coelestinum*) is not related to the annual. This hardy ageratum is twice as tall and is often invasive. The plants spread by rhizomes and also self-seed with abandon.

Recommended Varieties

Short varieties, such as 'Blue Mink', are often available as bedding plants. They grow about 10 inches tall and look nice at the front of a flower border. 'Hawaii' hybrids grow only 6 to 8 inches tall and come in white and two shades of blue. Taller ageratums, like the 2-foot-tall 'Blue Horizon', are most often grown from seeds.

'Blue Horizon'

Alyssum
Lobularia maritima

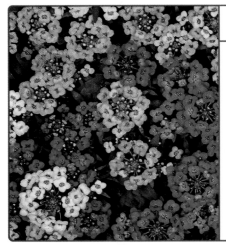

OTHER COMMON NAMES:
Sweet Alyssum, Snowdrift

BLOOM TIME: Late spring
to late fall

BLOOM COLOR: Pink,
purple, rose, violet, or white

LIGHT REQUIREMENT:
Sun or partial shade

HEIGHT × WIDTH: 3 to
10 inches × 5 to 12 inches

Special Features

Spreading mounds of gray-green foliage bloom for months in the garden. The tiny, sweet-scented blossoms smell like honey. Cut some sprigs for a miniature bouquet and you can enjoy the fragrance in the house, too. Alyssum can withstand light frosts and makes a wonderful edging for flower beds or containers. The blossoms are excellent for pressed-flower crafts.

How to Grow

Alyssum is easy to grow from seeds. Sow the seeds outdoors in spring, or give them a 6-week head start indoors. To sow, sprinkle the seeds on the surface of the soil. Alyssum is also available as bedding plants in the spring. Set plants in the garden after the last spring frost, spacing them 6 to 8 inches apart. They'll bloom best if you plant them in full sun, but they will also tolerate partial shade.

Care and Maintenance

If plants stop blooming or look shabby in midsummer, shear off the top inch of growth to renew their good looks. Pests and diseases are seldom a problem with these easy-care plants.

Recommended Varieties

'Carpet of Snow', a long-standing favorite, covers itself for months with sweet-smelling,

GARDEN TIP

♦ Alyssum readily self-seeds. Once you plant it, you can expect to enjoy volunteer plants year after year.

white blossoms. So does new 'Snow Crystals', which has bigger flowers that are more likely to keep blooming in hot weather. Other popular varieties include purple 'Royal Carpet', and the 'Wonderland' series, which produces purple, rose, or white flowers.

'Royal Carpet'

'Wonderland'

'Carpet of Snow'

Bachelor's Button

Centaurea cyanus

OTHER COMMON NAME: Cornflower

BLOOM TIME: Spring and early summer

BLOOM COLOR: Blue, pink, red, rose, white, or bicolored

LIGHT REQUIREMENT: Sun

HEIGHT × WIDTH: 12 to 36 inches × 8 to 10 inches

Special Features

Long a favorite of Midwest gardeners, bachelor's buttons grow and bloom best in cool weather. Sometimes called "ragged sailors" by old-timers, the 1-inch flowers are indeed somewhat ragged or tattered in appearance, which adds to their old-fashioned charm. The gray-green leaves provide an attractive contrast. Plants are drought tolerant and easy to grow, and the flowers are excellent for cutting or drying.

How to Grow

Bachelor's buttons do best in well-drained soil that is neutral to slightly alkaline. Sow seeds outdoors in fall or early spring so plants will have plenty of time to bloom before the weather turns hot.

Care and Maintenance

Thin bachelor's buttons to allow about 8 inches between plants. Remove spent flowers to encourage continued blooming, but leave a few to produce seeds. When the seeds mature, collect them to sow in fall or, better yet, allow them to sow themselves.

When older plants succumb to summer's heat and humidity, it's nice to have some young volunteers to take their place. Provide twiggy branches or other light supports for taller varieties to lean on.

Recommended Varieties

'Polka Dot' is a dwarf mix that produces blue, lilac, rose, or white blossoms on 15-inch plants. 'Frosted Queen' grows twice as tall. Its blooms come in a mixture of pretty bicolors, including lilac with dark-blue and red with pink. 'Blue Boy' is another tall variety and has a striking blue color.

> ## GARDEN TIP
>
> ◆ Bachelor's buttons are easy to dry: Cut the flowers when they first open. Secure small bundles together with a rubber band and hang them upside-down to dry in a cool, dry place out of direct sun.

Related Species

Some plants in the same genus, or group, are perennials. *C. montana*, sometimes called mountain bluet, has open, spidery blossoms that are blue with pink centers. They're easy to grow from seeds or transplants, but watch where you put them: plants self-seed readily and can be invasive. *C. macrocephala* has large yellow flowers. Persian cornflower, *C. dealbata*, has pink flowers and silvery leaves. All three are hardy to zone 3.

C. macrocephala

Mountain Bluet

Begonia

Begonia semperflorens-cultorum hybrids

OTHER COMMON NAMES:
Fibrous Begonia, Wax
Begonia

BLOOM TIME: Summer
to frost

BLOOM COLOR: Pink,
rose, red, or white

LIGHT REQUIREMENT:
Full or partial shade

HEIGHT × WIDTH: 8 to
12 inches × 8 to 12 inches

Special Features

Small, bushy plants are loaded with 1- to 2-inch clusters of single
or double flowers that bloom throughout the summer. The foliage
may be green or bronze, but it's always shiny. Begonias are ideal
for growing in windowboxes or other containers, and they also
look great when used as a flowering ground cover in the dappled
shade beneath a tree.

How to Grow

Many begonias actually do well in sun if the soil is moist, but
begonias are most valuable for their ability to bloom profusely
in the shade. Garden centers offer a wide selection of plants
in spring. Add compost to the soil before you plant. It will help
soak up excess moisture and protect the roots from soil that is too
wet or too dry. Plant begonias after danger of frost, spacing them
6 to 10 inches apart. You can also start begonias from seeds,
though it's a challenge—seeds are very tiny and must be started
indoors in January, or February at the latest. Sow the seeds on top

of moist soil, then cover the container with clear plastic to hold in the moisture. Seeds require a temperature of at least 70 degrees Fahrenheit in order to sprout.

Care and Maintenance

Water in dry weather. Mulch to help keep roots cool. Begonias are self-cleaning, so no deadheading is necessary. If leaf spots appear, hand-pick the affected leaves.

GARDEN TIPS

♦ Rescue a fibrous begonia or two before fall frost. If given sufficiently bright light, they make ideal houseplants and bloom throughout the winter.

♦ If buds drop without opening, the cause is most likely either soil that is too wet or too dry, or prolonged hot temperatures.

Recommended Varieties

'Varsity' begonias bloom early and produce an abundance of large flowers. Choose from bronze- or green-leafed varieties with flowers of pink, rose, scarlet, or white.

Related Species

Tuberous begonias (*B. × tuberhybrida*) produce large, showy flowers in a variety of shapes, with some that resemble camellias or carnations. Some are upright, like the 'Non-Stop' series and 'Pin-up® Flame', a 1999 All-America Selections winner with unique yellow and orange blooms. Others, such as the 'Illumination' series, are trailers that look wonderful in hanging baskets. You can buy young plants in spring or start

Tuberous Begonia

your own from tubers in late winter. Dried tubers are easily stored over winter at a temperature of about 50 degrees Fahrenheit.

Browallia

Browallia speciosa

BLOOM TIME: Summer

BLOOM COLOR: Blue-purple or white

LIGHT REQUIREMENT: Partial shade

HEIGHT × WIDTH: 8 to 12 inches × 8 to 12 inches

Special Features

Browallia is a wonderful plant for containers or shady borders. It produces masses of delicate-looking, trumpet-shaped flowers all summer. The bushy mounds of lush foliage are attractive, too.

How to Grow

Transplant bedding plants to the garden after the danger of frost, spacing plants 8 to 10 inches apart. Browallia does best in moderately rich, well-drained soil in partial shade. It also grows well in full sun as long as the soil never dries out. If you prefer to grow browallia from seeds, start 6 to 8 weeks before the last frost. Sow seeds indoors on the surface of moist potting soil; do not cover.

Care and Maintenance

Mulch to conserve soil moisture, and water when necessary to keep the soil moist. You can probably skip pinching out growing tips to produce bushier plants; the improved varieties most often offered today are more compact than older versions. If you see aphids on the leaves, knock the tiny insects off with water from the garden hose, or spray plants with insecticidal soap. Problems with other pests or diseases are unlikely.

Recommended Varieties

'Blue Bells' grows 8 to 12 inches tall and produces prolific blue-purple blossoms.

GARDEN TIP

♦ At the end of the growing season, pot up a browallia plant and bring it inside. It will bloom all winter on a sunny windowsill.

'Blue Bells'

'Silver Bells'

Cockscomb

Celosia argentea var. *cristata*

BLOOM TIME: Midsummer to frost

BLOOM COLOR: Orange, red, rose, or scarlet

LIGHT REQUIREMENT: Sun

HEIGHT × WIDTH: 12 to 24 inches × 8 to 12 inches

Special Features

One look at cockscomb, and you'll see where it gets its name: the flowers, which grow up to 10 inches long on some varieties, resemble a rooster's comb. Cockscomb is not for everyone, however; some gardeners love the flowers, and others find them grotesque. Either way, they are long-lasting in the garden. If you cut them before the seeds ripen and hang them by their stems to dry, the flowers will last indefinitely.

How to Grow

Buy young plants that have not yet grown tall and spindly, or grow cockscomb from seeds. Sow seeds directly in the garden or start them indoors in individual pots 6 weeks before the last expected frost. Move plants to the garden when the weather is warm and settled and nighttime temperatures are consistently above 50 degrees Fahrenheit. Allow 8 inches between dwarf varieties and 12 inches between larger varieties. Cockscomb does best in rich, moist soil.

Care and Maintenance

Cockscomb is an easy-to-grow plant that is tolerant of both heat and drought. Water only when the soil is extremely dry. Provide support if the weight of heavy flower heads threatens to topple the plants. Pests and diseases seldom require control.

GARDEN TIP

♦ Unless you want hundreds of volunteer plants, remove cockscombs before the tiny seeds imbedded in their "throats" turn brown.

Recommended Varieties

'Prestige Scarlet', a 1997 All-America Selections winner, is a "multiflora" cockscomb, producing many more but smaller flowers than most other varieties. The 3-inch red flowers are spectacular in the garden, and their size makes them more versatile in arrangements. Despite the heavy load of flowers, the 18-inch plants are strong enough to stay upright without stakes.

Related Species

Plumed celosia (*C. plumosa*) is topped with feathery plumes. Plants in the 'Century' series grow 2 feet tall and produce one extra-large plume flanked by many smaller plumes on the side. Colors include cream, red, rose, and yellow.

Plumed Celosia

'Prestige Scarlet'

Coleus

Coleus species and hybrids

FOLIAGE COLOR:
Multicolored

LIGHT REQUIREMENT:
Shade or sun

HEIGHT × WIDTH: 10 to
20 inches × 10 to 20 inches

Special Features

This tropical plant boasts colorful leaves that are as showy as any flower. Beloved by Victorians but then nearly forgotten, coleus is now coming back strong. Some old favorites can be found in garden centers along with spectacular new varieties. Coleus leaves can be smooth or frilly, big or little, plain or deeply-cut.

How to Grow

You can grow coleus from seed started indoors in February, but the most unusual color combinations are usually available only in purchased plants. Plant them any time after the danger of spring frost has passed. Coleus is at its best when massed under a tree or planted in a container.

Care and Maintenance

Water as often as necessary to keep the soil moist, particularly if your plants are growing in the sun. If seedheads form, pinch them out. Pinch off growing tips as often as necessary to keep your plants the size and shape that suits you. If aphids or whiteflies attack, control them by spraying plants with insecticidal soap.

Recommended Varieties

Most gardeners prefer to choose coleus by leaf color rather than by named variety. The color choices are gorgeous, including yellow with red flecks, plum with splashes of pink, and green with reddish-purple markings. 'Wizard', a seed variety, is an excellent foot-tall dwarf that comes in a rainbow of colors.

GARDEN TIP

◆ If you want to overwinter your coleus plants inside, bring them in before nighttime temperatures dip below 50 degrees Fahrenheit. You can also save coleus by taking 4- to 6-inch cuttings. Pinch off the lower leaves of the cuttings and stand the cut stems in a container of water. Change the water regularly, and plant the cuttings in individual pots after ample roots grow.

'Wizard'

Cosmos

Cosmos bipinnatus

BLOOM TIME: Summer to frost

BLOOM COLOR: Crimson, pink, rose, or white

LIGHT REQUIREMENT: Sun

HEIGHT × WIDTH: 24 to 60 inches × 18 to 24 inches

Special Features

Three-inch daisylike flowers hover on long, graceful stems above the feathery foliage of cosmos. These plants thrive on neglect. With blossoms that last five days or more in a bouquet, cosmos makes an excellent cut flower—and there's no danger of running out: the more you cut, the more they bloom.

How to Grow

If you have rich garden soil and like to coddle your plants, forget trying to grow cosmos: the plants won't bloom for you. They need well-drained soil but no fertilizer. Sow seeds outdoors after the danger of frost has passed. When plants are several inches tall, thin them to stand 18 inches apart.

Care and Maintenance

Shear off spent flowers to promote continued blooming and improve the appearance of the plants. Cosmos flowers best in dry soil, so don't water unless the plants are wilting. Stake plants, particularly tall varieties grown on windswept sites. Pests rarely require control. Cosmos are generally free of disease, too, as long as they have good air circulation. If leaf spots or powdery mildew occur, simply remove infected branches. Toward the end of the season, allow some of the spent flowers to remain to set seed. Collect the seed when it's dry to plant the following spring, or allow the plants to self-seed.

GARDEN TIP

♦ Don't rush to clean up cosmos after the plants are killed by frost. If you leave them standing, their seeds will attract birds to your garden.

Recommended Varieties

'Sensation' is a beautiful mix that produces pink, purple, or white blossoms on 4- to 5-foot-tall plants. 'Sonata' plants grow only 2 feet fall and have pink, red, rose, or white blossoms. 'Seashell' has unique, quilled petals of cream, pink, red, or rose. Plants grow about 3 feet tall.

Related Species

Yellow cosmos (*C. sulphureus*) is shorter, with varieties from 1 to 3 feet tall. Blooms are orange, red, or yellow. One of the best-known varieties is 2-foot-tall 'Sunny Red', which won a 1986 All-America Selections award.

'Sensation'

'Sunny Red'

Cup Flower
Nierembergia hippomanica

BLOOM TIME: Summer to frost

BLOOM COLOR: Purple, blue, or white

LIGHT REQUIREMENT: Sun or partial shade

HEIGHT × WIDTH: 4 to 6 inches × 12 inches

Special Features

This dainty little plant grows in a low mound and is perfect for edging flower beds. It's also a good choice for planting in containers, where you can enjoy the 1-inch, cup-shaped flowers all summer long.

How to Grow

Purchase cup flower plants in spring, or grow your own plants from seed. Start seeds indoors 2 to 3 months before the last expected spring frost. Barely cover the seeds with soil. After the last spring frost, transplant cup flowers in the garden, spacing plants 8 to 10 inches apart in soil enriched with a slow-release fertilizer.

Care and Maintenance

Water in dry weather, and mulch to conserve soil moisture. Cup flower is extremely easy to grow and is seldom bothered by pests or diseases.

Recommended Varieties

'Purple Robe' is an outstanding dark-purple variety. 'Mont Blanc', a 1993 All-America Selections award winner, produces pure-white flowers and stands up particularly well to both heat and drought.

'Purple Robe'

'Mont Blanc'

Fan Flower

Scaevola aemula

OTHER COMMON NAMES:
Australian Fan Flower, Blue
Fan Flower

BLOOM TIME: Summer to
frost

BLOOM COLOR: Blue

LIGHT REQUIREMENT:
Sun or partial shade

HEIGHT × WIDTH: 8 to
12 inches × 36 to 48 inches

Special Features

Fan flower is a bushy, trailing plant that's ideal for planting where it can tumble over the sides of a hanging basket or rock wall. By midsummer, dozens of blue-violet, fan-shaped flowers cover the lobed leaves. Fan flower is native to a hot, dry climate and looks better the hotter it gets.

How to Grow

Combine fan flower with other annuals in a large container, or plant two or three in a 10-inch basket of their own. Don't move the plants outside until nighttime temperatures are consistently above 50 degrees Fahrenheit.

Care and Maintenance

Fan flower is drought tolerant and thrives on neglect. If it gets straggly, just pinch off the growing tips as you would a petunia. Avoid overwatering; it may cause the stems or roots to rot. If whiteflies are a nuisance, spray the plants with insecticidal soap.

Recommended Varieties

'New Wonder', which is a Proven Winner® variety, has dense foliage and prolific blooms.

GARDEN TIP

◆ Rabbits seem to be inordinately fond of fan flower. If hungry bunnies frequent your neighborhood, it may be best to plant this annual in containers that are out of reach.

'New Wonder'

Flowering Tobacco

Nicotiana alata

BLOOM TIME: Summer to hard frost

BLOOM COLOR: Lime, pink, purple, red, rose, or white

LIGHT REQUIREMENT: Partial shade

HEIGHT × WIDTH: 1 to 4 feet × 1 to 2 feet

Special Features

An old-fashioned favorite, flowering tobacco is covered with masses of star-shaped trumpet flowers all summer long. Hybrids offer the gardener a choice of short varieties that look beautiful in containers. Unlike the originals, many newer types feature blossoms that stay open during the day, though this improvement often comes at the expense of the fine fragrance.

How to Grow

Flowering tobacco is easy to grow from seed, but don't cover it; the seeds need light to sprout. You can plant seeds outdoors after the last frost, or give them a head start indoors 6 weeks earlier. Plants perform best when protected from the hot afternoon sun, but they will tolerate full sun if they have adequate moisture. Space them 1 to 2 feet apart, depending on the size of the variety you've chosen.

Care and Maintenance

Once planted, flowering tobacco usually requires little attention. Occasionally, it suffers from some of the same problems as tomatoes, which are members of the same family. If you notice large, jagged holes in the leaves, take a close look. You may discover a tomato hornworm munching away. Because the large worms blend into their surroundings, they're hard to detect. Once you see them, though, they're easy to handpick. If flea beetles are

GARDEN TIP

◆ Plant a dwarf variety of flowering tobacco in your windowbox. If you're lucky, hummingbirds will add to the view.

riddling the leaves with small holes, dust the plants with rotenone.

Recommended Varieties

'Nicki' hybrids feature bushy plants that stand about 20 inches tall and come in lime, pink, rose, red, or white. The 'Havana' series produces plants that grow 12 to 14 inches high and have blossoms of lilac, lime, purple, red, rose, or white. The series also includes 'Havana Appleblossom', a beautiful pink and white variety that won Europe's Fleuroselect Gold Medal in 1995. 'Domino' is another compact, foot-tall series that comes in many colors and is known for its heat resistance.

Related Species

Woodland tobacco (*N. sylvestris*) grows 5 to 6 feet tall and has pure-white blossoms that hang limp during the day. In the evening, blossoms perk up and fill the air with a sweet perfume that attracts hummingbird moths.

Woodland Tobacco

Geranium

Pelargonium hybrids

BLOOM TIME: Spring to frost

BLOOM COLOR: Lavender, pink, rose, red, salmon, white, or bicolored

LIGHT REQUIREMENT: Sun

HEIGHT × WIDTH: 12 to 18 inches × 12 to 18 inches

Special Features

The National Garden Bureau calls the geranium "one of the easiest, prettiest, and most adaptable flowering plants you can grow." Red is still the favorite, though pastel-colored varieties, which glow in the evening light, are gaining in popularity. There are many types of tender geraniums. Zonals, named for the horseshoe-shaped band of color on their leaves, are the type we all know best. They come in many colors and bicolors, and produce single or double flowers. Our summer nights are too hot for Regal, or Martha Washington, geraniums; the same is true of ivy geraniums, those beautiful trailing types with leaves that look like true ivy. When hot weather arrives, they often stop blooming. More dependable bloomers for hanging baskets in our region include cascade geraniums, alpine ivies, and floribundas. Scented geraniums don't have much going for them flower-wise. But their leaves smell wonderful, producing the fragrance of rose, orange, apricot, apple, nutmeg, or almost any other pleasant scent you can think of.

How to Grow

You'll find a wide assortment of geraniums at garden centers. Most varieties are produced by cuttings, not seeds, and should be purchased as started plants. Plant them outdoors after the danger of spring frost has passed. Be sure to plant in well-drained soil; geraniums won't tolerate "wet feet."

Care and Maintenance

Allow soil to dry to the touch before watering geraniums. Add fertilizer diluted to half the recommended strength every second or third time you water container plants. Regularly pick off yellow leaves and dead flowers to keep your plants looking their best. This will also help thwart botrytis, a potentially serious fungus disease. If blossoms dry up before they open, suspect tiny insect pests called thrips. Pull open a bud and examine it for tiny insects at the base of the petals. To control thrips, pick off and destroy old flowers and dried up buds, then spray the plants with insecticidal soap. Low humidity can also cause geranium buds to dry up, but our humid Midwest climate usually eliminates that worry for outdoor plants. To save geraniums in fall, move whole plants indoors if space allows. If not, take 4- to 6-inch cuttings and root them in damp sand.

GARDEN TIP

♦ If plants don't bloom, a likely cause is too little light. Geraniums need full sun for at least half of the day. Blooming may also cease temporarily when the weather is very hot. Look forward to better blooms as soon as the nights cool down.

Recommended Varieties

There are many outstanding varieties of geraniums. You may prefer to pick yours out by color rather than by name. 'Pinto', 'Maverick', and 'Ringo 2000' are three well-known series of compact, sturdy zonal geraniums that can be counted on for good performance. All three come in a full range of colors. 'Minicascade' is an alpine ivy variety that produces lavender, pink, or red flowers.

Globe Amaranth

Gomphrena globosa

BLOOM TIME: Midsummer to frost

BLOOM COLOR: Pink, purple, red, or white

LIGHT REQUIREMENT: Sun

HEIGHT × WIDTH: 6 to 18 inches × 6 to 12 inches

Special Features

Round flowers that look something like clover blossoms grow on upright, spreading plants. Globe amaranth's bright color persists for months after the flowers are cut and dried, making it one of the best of the everlastings.

How to Grow

Although dwarf varieties are sometimes available as bedding plants in the spring, globe amaranth is usually grown from seed. The easiest way to get seeds to sprout is to sow them in the garden in late fall or early spring. Barely cover seeds with soil. To start seeds indoors, begin 6 to 8 weeks before the last frost and soak the seeds overnight before planting. Wait until after the last spring frost to transplant bedding plants. Space dwarf varieties 6 to 8 inches apart; space other varieties a foot apart. Average, well-drained soil works best.

Care and Maintenance

Globe amaranth is an easy-to-grow plant that is tolerant of both heat and drought. Water only when the soil is extremely dry. Pests don't usually bother the plants, and diseases will not be a problem as long as you allow plenty of room for good air circulation and grow the plants in full sun. Some gardeners like to pinch out the growing tips early in the season to make the plants more compact with more plentiful flowers. Others prefer to allow the plants to retain their natural shape.

GARDEN TIP

♦ Allow some flowers to dry and shatter in the garden. It's easier than starting seeds inside, and you'll never be without plenty of volunteer plants to combine with your other flowers.

Recommended Varieties

'Strawberry Fields' produces plentiful true-red flowers and is one of the best of the globe amaranths. 'Lavender Lady' has lilac blossoms. Both grow about 2 feet tall. 'Buddy' is a dwarf that grows only 6 to 9 inches tall and has magenta flowers. 'Gnome' mix produces pink, purple, or white blossoms on dwarf plants.

'Strawberry Fields'

'Buddy'

Heliotrope

Heliotropium arborescens

OTHER COMMON NAME:
Cherry Pie Plant

BLOOM TIME: Summer to frost

BLOOM COLOR: Lilac, purple, or white

LIGHT REQUIREMENT: Sun

HEIGHT × WIDTH: 10 to 36 inches × 12 to 36 inches

Special Features

Heliotrope is an old-fashioned favorite with dense flower clusters that often serve as landing pads for monarchs and other butterflies. Even before blooming begins, the stout, bushy plants are handsome, with textured, dark-green leaves. Tall varieties with pale flowers usually have the most fragrance; dwarf varieties are ideal for planting in containers.

How to Grow

Move bedding plants to the garden after the soil has thoroughly warmed in late spring. You can also grow heliotrope from seeds, but you'll need to start them indoors in February. The plants grow best in rich, moist soil.

Care and Maintenance

Water in dry weather. Unless you're growing a dwarf variety, pinch back young plants to encourage a bushy shape. Cut off spent flowers. Pests and diseases are seldom a problem.

Recommended Varieties

'Hybrid Marine' has dark-purple blossoms on 18-inch plants. 'Dwarf Marine' grows about a foot tall.

GARDEN TIP

◆ To enjoy the sweet fragrance of heliotrope in winter, bring a potted plant indoors in early fall. Keep the pot in a sunny window in a cool room. In late winter, you can root cuttings to plant in the garden in spring.

'Hybrid Marine'

Impatiens

Impatiens walleriana

OTHER COMMON NAME:
Bizzy Lizzie

BLOOM TIME: Summer to frost

BLOOM COLOR: All except true blue

LIGHT REQUIREMENT: Full or partial shade

HEIGHT × WIDTH: 8 to 20 inches × 8 to 20 inches

Special Features

As easy to grow as they are beautiful, impatiens bloom profusely in spots too shady for most other annuals. They come in every color of the rainbow (except true blue) and some bicolors. Leaf color may be bright green or dark bronze. Flower form varies from single, to semi-double, to fully double flowers.

How to Grow

Garden centers carry a good selection of young plants in the spring. Plant them outside after the danger of spring frost. Space plants 8 to 12 inches apart. The distance between them affects their height, with plants growing taller the closer together you put them. Impatiens need a spot protected from sun. They bloom best in filtered shade, such as that beneath a tree with high branches. Add compost to the soil before planting but avoid nitrogen fertilizers, which produce more height and less flowers. Impatiens are also easy to grow from seeds but require a head start indoors. Plant the seeds in containers 8 to 10 weeks before the last expected frost.

Care and Maintenance

Water as often as necessary to keep the soil moist. No other care should be needed. Plants are self-cleaning and do not require deadheading.

Recommended Varieties

Choosing which kinds of impatiens to grow is often more complicated than grow-

> ### GARDEN TIP
>
> ◆ If you want to plant impatiens under a mature tree, plant the flowers in containers first, then sink the containers into the ground. That way, the impatiens won't have to compete with the tree's roots for water and nutrients.

ing them. The choice of colors, sizes, and forms is rapidly expanding. 'Super Elfin' and 'Accent' impatiens form the lowest mounds and are some of the most popular. Both come in a wide range of colors. The blossoms of 'Mosaic' have a unique textured look; colors include lilac and rose. 'Seashell' impatiens have unusual blossoms that resemble cupped shells. They come in many colors, including bright yellow, which is rare in impatiens.

Related Species

New Guinea hybrid impatiens are known for their large flowers and colorful leaves. The plants grow and bloom best in our region with morning sun and afternoon shade. Most New Guinea impatiens are produced from cuttings because their seeds are sterile. 'Java' and other seed-grown types are usually less expensive and often not as vigorous.

'Super Elfin'

New Guinea

Lantana

Lantana hybrids

BLOOM TIME: Summer to frost

BLOOM COLOR: Orange, pink, red, white, or yellow

LIGHT REQUIREMENT: Sun

HEIGHT × WIDTH: 1 to 3 feet × 1 to 3 feet

Special Features

Lantana's beautiful multicolored flower clusters are a magnet for butterflies. The bright-green foliage always looks just as fresh at the end of the summer as at the beginning of the season. Most gardeners enjoy the fragrance of the leaves and flowers, although it is offensive to some. Shrubby forms are ideal for planting in a flower border or in a large container. Trailing forms look great cascading from a windowbox or over a rock wall. For a special treat, plant a lantana in a container right outside your window and enjoy a close-up view of visiting swallowtails.

How to Grow

Potted lantanas are available at garden centers in spring or summer. Don't set them outside until nights are consistently above 60 degrees Fahrenheit; chilled plants often take a long time to start blooming again. Lantana performs best if planted in rich soil that has been amended with compost or other organic materials

Care and Maintenance

Lantana is one of the easiest plants you can grow. It stands up to heat and drought, requires no deadheading, and rarely suffers from any pests or diseases. You can cut it back in any amount, at any time, to keep it from outgrowing its space.

Recommended Varieties

The 'Patriot'™ series is outstanding. Developed by Jack Roberson of American Daylily & Perennials in Missouri, this group of lantanas includes

both mounding and weeping forms in many color combinations. 'Patriot Rainbow'™, winner of the 1994 Florastar Award, has a compact, self-branching habit that requires no pinching. It displays a parade of multicolored florets from chiffon yellow to orange to fuchsia.

'Patriot Rainbow'

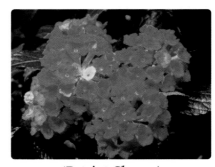

'Patriot Cherry'

'Patriot Firewagon'

'Patriot Hot Country'

Lisianthus

Eustoma grandiflorum

OTHER COMMON NAMES: Prairie Gentian, Prairie Rose

BLOOM TIME: July to September

BLOOM COLOR: Blue, pink, (almost) red, white, or yellow

LIGHT REQUIREMENT: Sun

HEIGHT × WIDTH: 8 to 30 inches × 6 to 12 inches

Special Features

With buds shaped like rosebuds opening to silky flowers shaped like poppies, lisianthus is a show stopper. The blossoms are exceptionally lovely in a bouquet and last up to two weeks after cutting. This Southwest wildflower has no trouble surviving the hot temperatures of a Midwest summer.

How to Grow

Well-drained soil is a must for lisianthus, so a raised bed or berm makes an ideal site. Add compost before you plant to provide the rich soil these plants prefer. Set out young plants after the danger of frost has passed, spacing them 6 to 12 inches apart. You can also grow lisianthus from seed, but it's not easy. Start indoors by mid-February at the latest, pressing the tiny seeds firmly on the surface of damp potting soil. Don't cover the seeds with soil, but do cover the container with plastic and set it in a warm spot (70 degrees Fahrenheit).

Care and Maintenance

GARDEN TIP

♦ Don't worry if your plants don't seem to grow much at first. Once hot summer weather arrives, they'll put on a growth spurt and begin to bloom.

Water as necessary to keep the soil moist until the plants are established. Try not to get the leaves wet during watering. Once the plants are growing, water only when the soil is completely dry. Pinch off growing tips several times early in the season to make the plants bushier. If aphids congregate on the leaves or buds, spray with insecticidal soap.

Recommended Varieties

'Heidi' hybrids produce sprays of big blossoms on long stems that make them perfect for cutting. Plants grow 20 to 28 inches tall. 'Mermaid', a dwarf lisianthus that grows only 8 inches tall, is a good size for planting in a windowbox and requires no pinching.

'Heidi' Hybrids

Lobelia

Lobelia erinus

BLOOM TIME: Spring to frost

BLOOM COLOR: Blue, lilac, rose, white, or bicolored

LIGHT REQUIREMENT: Partial shade

HEIGHT × WIDTH: 4 to 6 inches × 12 to 18 inches

Special Features

Lobelia is an old-fashioned flower that has once again become a favorite, thanks to the masses of small flowers it produces. Blue varieties are especially popular. Some lobelias are trailers that are ideal for draping over the edges of hanging baskets or other containers. Other lobelias grow in upright mounds and are often used for edging paths and flower beds.

How to Grow

Set bedding plants out after the danger of spring frost, spacing them 6 to 8 inches apart. You can also grow lobelia from seeds started indoors in January or February. Press the seeds firmly against the surface of moist potting soil but don't cover them. The ideal soil for lobelia is rich, moist, and well drained.

Care and Maintenance

Don't let plants dry out; they often don't recover. If lobelia gets leggy in midsummer, give it a light shearing; plants will soon be covered with new blooms.

Recommended Varieties

'Crystal Palace' has deep-blue flowers and bronze leaves. The flowers of 'Riviera' are blue or lilac and splashed with white. Both varieties are upright and grow 4 to 5 inches tall. 'Cascade' lobelias are trailers in blue, lavender, or rose.

GARDEN TIPS

◆ Lobelia is usually grown in partial shade in our region, but it will also thrive in full sun as long as the soil never dries out.

◆ Don't worry if your lobelia stops blooming in the heat of summer. Flowering resumes as soon as temperatures cool down.

'Crystal Palace'

'Riviera'

Marguerite Daisy

Argyranthemum frutescens

BLOOM TIME: Summer to frost

BLOOM COLOR: White or yellow

LIGHT REQUIREMENT: Sun

HEIGHT × WIDTH: 1 to 2 feet × 1 to 2 feet

Special Features

Through summer's heat, bright daisies on strong stems cover the fernlike foliage of these shrubby plants. This florist's favorite produces blossoms that are long-lasting and beautiful in bouquets. Try planting marguerite daisies in containers or massed in a sunny flower bed.

How to Grow

After the danger of spring frost has passed, transplant daisies outside in rich, well-drained soil. Add a slow-release fertilizer before you plant. Space the plants 1 to 2 feet apart depending on the variety. Adequate space for good air circulation will help keep plants free of disease.

Care and Maintenance

Water plants often enough to keep them from wilting, but not so often that the soil stays wet. Remove spent flowers regularly to promote continued flowering and improve appearance. Fertilize lightly every second or third time you water daisies that are growing in containers.

Recommended Varieties

Two varieties, both with the Proven Winners® label, bloom heavily throughout the summer and stand up exceptionally well to heat: 'Butterfly Yellow', 18 inches tall with yellow daisies, and 'Sugar Baby', a foot-tall variety that has white daisies with yellow centers.

'Sugar Baby'

'Butterfly Yellow'

Marigold

Tagetes hybrids

BLOOM TIME: Midsummer to frost

BLOOM COLOR: Gold, orange, red, white, yellow, or bicolored

LIGHT REQUIREMENT: Sun

HEIGHT × WIDTH: 6 to 36 inches × 12 to 36 inches

Special Features

When the weather is hot, Midwest gardeners can count on marigolds to splash their gardens with the bright colors of the sun. Heat- and drought-resistant once established, marigolds are an excellent choice for containers or a sunny border. They also make long-lasting cut flowers.

How to Grow

Transplant bedding plants in ordinary, well-drained garden soil after the danger of spring frost. Space plants 12 to 36 inches apart, depending on the size of the variety you choose. Marigolds are also easy to grow from seed: sow the seeds of small varieties directly in the garden; start large marigolds indoors 6 to 8 weeks before the last expected frost.

Care and Maintenance

Once they're established, marigolds don't need coddling; in fact, plants bloom best without much fertilizer or water. Though normally trouble-free, marigolds do occasionally suffer from a few pests and diseases in the Midwest. Spider mites suck sap from the leaves in hot weather, leaving the plants looking pale and lifeless.

Look closely and you may see some tiny webs. Discouraging these tiny pests is easy: just hose the plants off with water every day or two for several weeks.

If spots and mold cover the leaves, stems, and decaying flowers, gray-mold fungus is to blame. This disease is most likely to show up late in the season, when the weather is cool and damp. To prevent it, remove dead flowers regularly. If a marigold has yellow leaves and looks stunted, pull it out and dispose of it. Aster yellows is to blame; once infected, the plant can't be cured. Removing the plant stops leafhoppers from spreading the infection to healthy plants. If the leaves of a marigold wilt, then yellow and die, the trouble is root rot. Remove any plant that shows symptoms, and plant your marigolds in a different part of the garden the next time.

GARDEN TIPS

◆ So far, research hasn't backed up marigold's reputation for repelling pests, with one exception: There's proof that marigolds produce chemicals that are toxic to nematodes, microscopic worms that live in the soil.

◆ If you don't like the odor of marigolds when you bring in a bouquet, try adding a little sugar to the water.

Recommended Varieties

'Bonanza Bolero', winner of a 1999 All-America Selections award, is a 12-inch-tall French variety that blooms in just fifty days. Its bicolored gold-and-red flowers grow to 2 or more inches across. 'First Lady', an American marigold, has remained a favorite since it won an All-America Selections award in 1968. The sturdy 20-inch plants bloom profusely with double, clear-yellow blooms measuring 3 inches or more.

Related Species

Signet marigolds (*T. tenuifolia*) are charming 10-inch plants with dainty single blossoms. Their lacy foliage smells like lemons, and their edible flowers are a delightful addition to salads.

Moss Rose

Portulaca grandiflora

OTHER COMMON NAMES:
Rose Moss, Sun Moss,
Sun Rose

BLOOM TIME: Summer
to frost

BLOOM COLOR: All but blue

LIGHT REQUIREMENT:
Sun

HEIGHT × WIDTH: 6 to
8 inches × 12 to 16 inches

Special Features

Thick, needlelike leaves give moss rose excellent drought tolerance. These short spreading plants create a colorful carpet with single or double flowers in every bright or pastel color you can imagine. Most varieties open on sunny days and close at night or when it's cloudy. Moss rose is perfect for planting along borders or in containers and is at its best in places where nothing else will grow.

How to Grow

Don't be too kind to moss rose: plants prefer to grow in poor or sandy soil. You can set out bedding plants after the last spring frost, or sow seed either indoors or out. Seeds are tiny, so mix them with a little sand before you plant; do not cover. When plants are up and growing, thin them to 8 inches apart.

Care and Maintenance

Water plants growing in containers sparingly; do not water plants in the ground at all. If moss rose begins to look straggly in midsummer, shear it back to about 2 inches. Plants will be blooming beautifully again in a matter of weeks. Moss rose often self-seeds, which is a pleasure if you've planted it in a difficult spot where nothing else would grow.

Recommended Varieties

> ### GARDEN TIP
>
> ◆ Moss rose is a close relative of purslane. Its leaves, like the weed it's related to, are edible, so toss some in your salad if you're feeling adventurous.

'Sundial Peach', winner of a 1999 All-America Selections award, has frilly peach-colored blossoms nearly 2 inches across. Other colors available in the 'Sundial' series include cream, fuchsia, gold, orange, pink, scarlet, and yellow.

'Sundial Peach'

'Sundial Fuchsia'

'Sundial Yellow'

Nasturtium

Tropaeolum majus

BLOOM TIME: Summer to frost

BLOOM COLOR: Orange, red, or yellow

LIGHT REQUIREMENT: Sun or partial shade

HEIGHT × WIDTH: 1 to 10 feet × 1 to 10 feet

Special Features

Nasturtium's large, five-petaled flowers perk up the garden with their bright, sunny colors. The delicate fragrance is also a delight. Plants produce bright-green leaves and come in your choice of sizes: dwarfs to grow in containers, trailers for hanging baskets, and old-fashioned climbers that can scale a fence or serve as a pretty ground cover. Because they're exceptionally easy to grow from large, easy-to-handle seeds, nasturtiums are ideal for a child's first garden.

How to Grow

Nasturtiums don't take readily to transplanting, so it's best to start by planting seeds where you want them to grow. Plant the seeds outside after the last spring frost. Choose a spot with poor to average soil and good drainage. Don't fertilize; if you do, you're apt to get lush foliage but no flowers. Plants grow best in full sun but will tolerate light shade.

Care and Maintenance

Water as often as needed to keep the soil moderately moist. Avoid overhead watering in order to prevent the spread of foliage diseases. Aphids love nasturtiums; if you see the small, soft-bodied insects clustered on the leaves, spray with insecticidal soap. Leaf miners sometimes tunnel inside the leaves, creating a trailing design. Pick off and destroy affected leaves. Remove and discard any foliage infected with leaf spot, a fungus disease that sometimes develops in humid weather.

GARDEN TIP

- ◆ To serve a salad as pretty as those prepared in gourmet restaurants, just toss in some nasturtium petals, or even a few whole flowers. Toss in some leaves, too. Along with an extra dose of vitamin C, nasturtiums add a spicy, peppery flavor.

Recommended Varieties

Popular dwarf varieties include the foot-tall 'Whirlybird', and 'Jewel', which has large, semi-double blooms that stand out above the 18-inch-tall foliage. Both come in a choice of colors. 'Gleam' is a semi-trailer type that's ideal for hanging baskets. Its large, scarlet or gold flowers are double or semi-double. Both colors won All-America Selection awards when they were introduced in 1935, and they're still popular today.

Nasturtium Mix

Ornamental Sweet Potato

Ipomoea batatas

FOLIAGE COLOR: Purple, chartreuse, or green with pink and white markings

LIGHT REQUIREMENT: Sun or partial shade

HEIGHT × WIDTH: 8 to 12 inches × 36 to 48 inches

Special Features

Grown not for flowers but for their colorful leaves, ornamental sweet potatoes look beautiful cascading down the sides of large containers. Combine them with vertical annuals, such as melampodium and purple fountain grass, and you'll have a dynamite combination that will thrive in a hot, sunny spot. These ornamental vines are as easy to grow as sweet potatoes in the vegetable garden and come in a virtual rainbow of colors that are always in "bloom."

How to Grow

Set out bedding plants in late spring after the weather is warm and settled. Plants thrive in poor, sandy soil.

Care and Maintenance

Trim the vines to maintain the desired length and to encourage the plants to branch. Water as often as necessary to keep vines from wilting. Pests and diseases seldom require control. If tiny whiteflies are a nuisance, spray the plants with insecticidal soap.

If grasshoppers or other chewing insects munch on some of the foliage, simply pick off the damaged leaves.

Recommended Varieties

Choose the colors that combine best with your other flowers: 'Blackie' has deep-purple, lobed leaves; 'Marguarita' is a bright chartreuse; and 'Pink Frost' and 'Tricolor' are variegated with splashes of green, pink, and white.

GARDEN TIP

♦ Like their vegetable counterpart, ornamental sweet potatoes produce tuberous roots, but they're smaller and not as tasty.

'Pink Frost'

'Blackie'

Pansy

Viola × wittrockiana

BLOOM TIME: Early spring to late fall

BLOOM COLOR: Blue, lavender, orange, pink, purple, red, white, yellow or bicolored

LIGHT REQUIREMENT: Partial shade

HEIGHT × WIDTH: 6 to 10 inches × 8 to 12 inches

Special Features

In bright colors or pastels, with traditional "faces" or plain, pansies brighten containers and flower beds a month or more before it's warm enough to plant most other annuals in spring. Undaunted by cold, they do the same in autumn, lasting long after frost has turned most other flowers to mush. But there's more: Not only are the new hybrids more cold-hardy than ever, their large and sturdy root systems help them stand up to summer's heat, too. Thanks to work by plant breeders, it's easy to have pansies blooming in your Midwest garden from April through November, and often longer.

How to Grow

Pansies require a site with excellent drainage. In the Midwest, they perform best with morning sun and afternoon shade. Set plants in the garden in early to mid-spring, spacing them 6 to 10 inches apart. Thanks to improved varieties, you can also plant pansies in your Midwest garden in autumn and enjoy those same pansies again in spring, just like southern gardeners. The key to pansies' winter survival is to choose a hardy variety (see recommendations below) and plant them in a well-drained spot. If a fall freeze pushes newly planted pansies out of the ground, just push them back down, with no harm done. A light blanket of shredded leaves or other mulch pulled up snug around the plants will help protect them from cold temperatures and frost heaving.

Care and Maintenance

Water in dry weather and mulch to preserve soil moisture. To lessen the chance of fungus diseases, avoid getting the leaves wet when you water. Add fertilizer to the water every second or third time you water pansies growing in containers. Snip off faded flowers to promote continued blooms. If plants get leggy and stop blooming in summer, shear them back to about 2 inches and add fertilizer; healthy plants will rebound in cool weather.

> ## GARDEN TIPS
>
> ◆ When a cold snap hits, pansies may lie down on the ground and look dreadful. But once warmer weather returns, they stand up again, unscathed, and merrily resume blooming.
>
> ◆ Pansy blossoms are not only pretty, they're edible, too. For an elegant touch, try them in your salads or as a garnish.

Recommended Varieties

'Delta' produces large, early flowers on short, strong stems that don't flop. Flowers come in more than a dozen different colors, and the plants stand up well to both heat and cold. 'Majestic Giants' have stood the test of time: winner of two All-America Selections awards in 1966, they are still prized by gardeners for their huge, 4-inch blossoms. Varieties with medium-sized flowers are more likely to survive the winter than those with giant blossoms. In overwintering trials at Michigan State University, the 'Skyline' (with traditional "faces") and 'Sky' (single-colored) pansies outperformed all others. One variety, 'Skyline Yellow', won a perfect score, rating best among nearly 200 contenders. 'Maxim' and 'Universal Plus' also have a good track record for overwintering in the Midwest.

Petunia

Petunia × hybrida

BLOOM TIME: Summer to frost

BLOOM COLOR: Blue, coral, pink, purple, red, white, yellow, or bicolored

LIGHT REQUIREMENT: Sun or partial shade

HEIGHT × WIDTH: 6 to 12 inches × 6 to 48 inches

Special Features

There's a petunia of the right size and habit for any pot or plot. New varieties include petite petunias you can grow in a bowl, ground cover types that quickly carpet large areas, and trailers that are ideal for hanging baskets and windowboxes. Blooms are single or double, plain or ruffled, big or small, and come in every color of the rainbow, often accompanied by a heavenly fragrance.

How to Grow

Petunias adore sun; the more they get, the more they bloom. They also need good drainage in order to prevent stem rot. Transplant bedding plants outside in spring. Petunias are more tolerant of cold than many annuals and can shrug off a light frost if given the chance to toughen up gradually after coming home from the greenhouse.

Care and Maintenance

Water when the soil is dry to the touch. For best appearance and continued bloom, pinch off and remove faded flowers. Most kinds of petunias have a tendency to get "leggy" as the summer wears on. You can renew plants by cutting them to half their height;

they'll be blooming again in a matter of weeks. Better yet, pinch back a few of the longest stems every week or two so you can enjoy continuous color while gradually grooming the plants. If the leaves turn abnormally light, the petunias are probably announcing their need for fertilizer. You can give them a

GARDEN TIP

♦ Petunias look bedraggled after a rain, but don't worry: most kinds recover their good looks quickly after they dry. The bigger the blossom, though, the longer recovery takes.

quick fix by adding a dose of liquid or powdered plant food when you water. If a petunia develops spindly and yellowed foliage, leaf spots, or mottling, it's best to remove and destroy the suffering plant before the disease infects the others.

Recommended Varieties

Ground cover petunias won the admiration of gardeners with the introduction of 'Purple Wave', a 1995 All-America Selections winner. Since then, the 'Wave' series has expanded to include lilac, pink, and rose, with more colors to come. All are great in hanging baskets and as ground covers. 'Fantasy' hybrids are miniature petunias called "millifloras." They are little more than half as big as most petunias and look charming in small containers. 'Surfinia' petunias come from Europe. These cascading petunias are a natural in windowboxes and baskets. The leaves are dark-green and rounded, and the flowers have distinctive veining. 'Dream' and 'Supercascade' are lovely grandiflora petunias that produce huge, showy flowers. Plant them in containers where you can enjoy them at close range. In the garden, 'Carpet', 'Celebrity', and 'Primetime' might be better choices: their blossoms are smaller but more abundant, and the plants stand up better to the stresses of weather and diseases.

Pinks

Dianthus chinensis

OTHER COMMON NAMES: China Pink, Annual Carnation

BLOOM TIME: Late spring through early summer

BLOOM COLOR: Crimson, pink, scarlet, violet, white, or bicolored

LIGHT REQUIREMENT: Sun

HEIGHT × WIDTH: 6 to 12 inches × 6 to 12 inches

Special Features

Pinks produce charming 1-inch flowers that often have fringed petals and a spicy fragrance that helped make them an old-fashioned favorite. The gray-green leaves contrast beautifully with the pink or red flowers. If conditions are just right, pinks sometimes behave more like a short-lived perennial and may survive a winter or two. The small plants make a colorful edging for a flower bed and also perform well in containers.

How to Grow

Although pinks like sun, they don't like heat. In the Midwest, a spot that's shaded in the heat of the afternoon is often the best place for them. A rich, moist soil that is neutral to alkaline is ideal; good drainage is essential. After danger of spring frost, set plants 6 to 10 inches apart. You can also grow pinks from seed started indoors 8 to 10 weeks before the last expected frost.

Care and Maintenance

To help prevent disease, thin as much as necessary to allow good air circulation around each plant. Mulch to keep the roots cool, being sure to keep the mulch away from the base of the stems. Discard any plant that shows signs of disease. Deadhead regularly to keep the plants blooming. When blooming ceases in midsummer, cut the plants back by half.

GARDEN TIP

♦ Pinks have so many blooms that picking off the old blossoms can be time consuming. If you have a lot of plants, simply give them a light shearing with the grass clippers to make fast work of the job.

Recommended Varieties

'Ideal Violet' is a 1992 All-America Selections winner that stands up well to both heat and cold. Similar varieties in the 'Ideal' series come in an array of colors, including crimson, pearl, rose, carmine, and cherry. All grow about 10 inches tall. The 'Telstar' series is also compact and dependable. 'Strawberry Parfait' and 'Raspberry Parfait' are both bicolored with red "eyes." They grow about 6 inches tall and have been bred for heat tolerance and longer flowering.

Related Species

Sweet William (*D. barbatus*) is an old-fashioned favorite that usually behaves as a biennial, blooming the second year after planting. Other closely related plants are hardy perennials; see cheddar pinks in the perennial chapter.

Sweet William

Salvia

Salvia splendens

OTHER COMMON NAME:
Scarlet Sage

BLOOM TIME: Summer
to frost

BLOOM COLOR: Burgundy,
purple, red, and white

LIGHT REQUIREMENT:
Sun or partial shade

HEIGHT × WIDTH: 10 to
30 inches × 10 to 15 inches

Special Features

Although salvia comes in other colors, it is the fiery red spikes for which this annual is best known. Hummingbirds seek out the red flowers as well. Bright green leaves add to the plant's attraction. Tall varieties massed in a bed of their own look smashing, and dwarf varieties are ideal for growing in containers.

How to Grow

Salvias do best in moist, rich soil that is well drained. After danger of frost has passed, transplant bedding plants outside, spacing them 10 to 12 inches apart. You can also grow salvia from seed started indoors 8 to 10 weeks before the last expected frost.

Care and Maintenance

Water plants in dry weather, and mulch to conserve soil moisture. You can make tall varieties bushier by pinching off their growing tips while plants are young. Dwarf varieties do not require pinching. Remove faded spikes before they set seed; this will improve the plants' appearance and promote continued blooms.

Recommended Varieties

'Flare' grows 18 inches tall and has extra-long spikes of bright red. 'St. John's Fire' is a foot-tall dwarf with scarlet-red spikes.

GARDEN TIP

◆ The bright color of scarlet sage fades when flowers are dried, but blue salvia retains its color and is a favorite for drying.

Related Species

Blue salvia (*S. farinacea*) blooms for months, but its blue spikes are especially welcome after the first fall frosts, when other annuals have given up. Try 'Victoria', a classic blue, or 'Strata', a unique blue-and-white bicolor variety that won an All-America Selection award in 1996. Texas sage (*S. coccinea*) grows 2 to 3 feet tall and produces loose red spikes. Hummingbirds adore this plant and prefer it over scarlet sage if given a choice. An outstanding variety is 'Lady in Red', winner of a 1992 All-America Selections award.

'Victoria'

'Lady in Red'

Snapdragon

Antirrhinum majus

BLOOM TIME: Spring to frost

BLOOM COLOR: Crimson, lilac, orange, pink, purple, rose, scarlet, white, yellow, or bicolored

LIGHT REQUIREMENT: Sun or partial shade

HEIGHT × WIDTH: 6 to 36 inches × 6 to 12 inches

Special Features

If you ever squeezed snapdragon blossoms to open and shut the "dragon" mouths when you were a child, chances are you still have a soft spot for these old-fashioned favorites. The colorful florets bloom from bottom to top on vertical stalks. Tall varieties are great for bouquets: the more you cut, the more they bloom.

How to Grow

Snapdragons prefer to grow in loamy or sandy soils. If your soil is clay, add organic materials such as compost before you plant. Good drainage is essential to prevent root rot. Space bedding plants 6 to 12 inches apart in spring. You can also grow snapdragons from seeds sown in the garden in early spring as soon as the soil can be worked. For a head start, plant seeds indoors, pressing them firmly against damp potting soil. Do not cover the seeds with soil.

Care and Maintenance

Avoid overwatering snapdragons; it encourages root rot. If your plants are growing in containers, be sure to fertilize regularly;

snapdragons require more nutrients than many other annuals. You can make plants bushier by pinching off their growing tips when the plants are young. To keep plants blooming, remove faded blooms before they have a chance to set seed. Stake tall varieties. Snapdragons bloom best when the weather is cool, so don't be surprised if yours take a rest in midsummer. Mulch to keep the roots cool. The caterpillar stage of the buckeye butterfly may nibble on the foliage of snapdragons. If you love butterflies, the small amount of damage is tolerable.

GARDEN TIP

♦ Though not as cold-hardy as pansies, snapdragons can take light frosts. Use dwarf varieties such as 'Floral Showers' to provide welcome color in containers in spring and fall.

Recommended Species

'Floral Showers' includes dwarf plants in many colors and bicolors. The 6- to 8-inch-tall plants are early to bloom and hold up well in heat. 'Bright Butterflies'—a 1966 All-America Selections winner that is still popular today—is a colorful mix of tall, open-faced snapdragons. They have no jaws for snapping, but their long stems make them ideal for cutting. 'Lampion Appleblossom' has pink blossoms and a cascading form that makes it perfect for growing in a hanging basket.

Spider Flower

Cleome hassleriana

BLOOM TIME: Summer to frost

BLOOM COLOR: Pink, purple, rose, or white

LIGHT REQUIREMENT: Sun or partial shade

HEIGHT × WIDTH: 36 to 48 inches × 24 to 36 inches

Special Features

Spider flowers always seem to draw plenty of "oohs" and "ahs." The tall, dramatic plants produce masses of large, airy flowers that are beautiful in the garden or in a bouquet. Spider flowers are great for planting at the back of the flower border, where they will thrive regardless of heat or drought.

How to Grow

You can sow seeds in the garden in fall, or give them a head start indoors: Ten weeks before the last expected spring frost, fill a plastic bag with damp sphagnum moss. Add the seed and put the bag in the refrigerator. After several weeks of refrigeration, plant the seeds by pressing them firmly against the surface of damp potting soil. Do not cover with soil. You can also purchase spider flowers as young bedding plants in the spring. Avoid buying any that have grown too tall and straggly, as they're apt to be permanently stunted. After the last frost, move the plants to the garden. They'll do best in a well-drained soil in full sun, though they'll also tolerate light shade.

Care and Maintenance

Water if the soil is dry. When you cut a bouquet, don't worry if the plants seem a bit gummy—the leaves are naturally sticky. Diseases and pests are seldom a problem.

GARDEN TIP

♦ Be careful when you clean up the garden in autumn. The stems of mature spider flower plants are thorny.

If you don't want plants to self-seed in your garden, pick off seed pods before they split open.

Recommended Varieties

'Pink Lace' produces pink flowers that are large and lacy. 'Helen Campbell' has huge, pure-white flowers.

'Pink Lace'

Verbena

Verbena × hybrida

BLOOM TIME: Summer to frost

BLOOM COLOR: Blue, lavender, pink, purple, red, white, or bicolored

LIGHT REQUIREMENT: Sun

HEIGHT × WIDTH: 4 to 12 inches × 12 to 24 inches

Special Features

Verbena's large, flat clusters of small flowers are a butterfly's delight and a bright spot in the summer garden. Plants can be either upright or trailing. The versatile trailing forms are gorgeous in hanging baskets or windowboxes. When used as a ground cover, they quickly blanket the ground with a carpet of flowers. Upright verbenas are fine for planting in containers or along the front border of flower beds.

How to Grow

After the danger of spring frost has passed, transplant bedding plants 12 to 18 inches apart in rich, well-drained soil. To grow verbena from seeds, start indoors 8 to 10 weeks before the last expected frost. Scatter the seeds on moist potting soil, then cover the container with black plastic to exclude light until the seeds sprout.

Care and Maintenance

Water in dry weather. Mulch to help keep the roots cool. Remove the spent flowers on upright types to promote continued blooming. If trailing types stop blooming in hot weather, shear them lightly. Verbena is prone to mildew and can develop white powdery patches that cover the foliage before it yellows and dies. Remove infected stems and destroy severely infected plants. Help prevent mildew by allowing plenty of room between plants for good air circulation.

Recommended Varieties

'Imagination' began the trailing verbena trend. It was a 1993 All-America Selections winner that can be grown from seeds, producing violet-blue flowers. Trailing verbenas available as bedding plants rather than seeds include 'Temari' and 'Tapien', both Proven Winners®, and 'Babylon', a 1999 introduction. All three come in a choice of colors. Outstanding upright verbenas are 'Romance', which grows 6 inches tall and has extra-early flowers, and 'Quartz', which grows into vigorous, 10-inch plants. Both series come in a variety of colors, many with colorful centers, or "eyes."

GARDEN TIP

♦ If you're using a trailing verbena as a ground cover, arrange each stem in the direction you want it to grow. Place a small mound of soil over a middle portion of the stem to hold it in place. Each stem will then send out new roots under the soil mound, creating a new plant.

'Tapien'

'Quartz'

Vinca

Catharanthus roseus

BLOOM TIME: Summer to frost

BLOOM COLOR: Pink, rose, white, or bicolored

LIGHT REQUIREMENT: Sun or light shade

HEIGHT × WIDTH: 6 to 14 inches × 10 to 12 inches

Special Features

Vinca is one of the most carefree annuals for the sunny garden. The glossy, dark-green leaves make a handsome background for the simple but lovely flowers, some of which have contrasting center "eyes." Vinca thrives where it's hot and dry, making it the perfect plant for a sun-baked container.

How to Grow

Vinca thrives in any well-drained soil. Wait until spring weather is warm, with nights consistently above 50 degrees Fahrenheit, to set the plants outside. Vinca planted in cool weather will just sit there and sulk. Space plants 10 to 12 inches apart. To grow vinca from seeds, start them indoors in February.

Care and Maintenance

Vinca suffers from few problems and needs little care. Water only in dry weather. Yellowing leaves are vinca's signal that the soil is too wet. Plants are difficult to grow only if the summer is cool or wet; they thrive in the hot, dry weather typical of the Midwest in July and August.

Recommended Varieties

Blooms blanket the bushy plants of 'Cooler' vincas. The series come in a wide range of colors, including pastel pink, orchid, strawberry, peppermint (white with a red eye), and grape (pink with a rose eye).

GARDEN TIP

♦ If you know impatiens but don't know vinca, think of vinca as the "impatiens for sun." The flowers and plant habit are so similar that you might have to look at the leaves to tell the difference. Both plants share another important feature for busy gardeners: they're self-cleaning. Blossoms drop off by themselves and require no deadheading.

'Cooler'

Zinnia

Zinnia elegans

BLOOM TIME: Summer to frost

BLOOM COLOR: Cream, gold, lavender, orange, pink, rose, scarlet, white, or yellow

LIGHT REQUIREMENT: Sun

HEIGHT × WIDTH: 8 to 30 inches × 6 to 24 inches

Special Features

Zinnias are natives of Mexico, and they like it hot and dry. They are perfect candidates for an area that is baked by summer's heat or a container in a hot, sunny spot. Zinnia plants come in heights to fit any garden and with blossoms that range from small button size to huge flowers 6 inches in diameter. Bloom types vary: some are simple daisies, while others are double, with overlapping rows of petals. Some look like dahlias, and others are more like cactus flowers, with almost tubular petals. There are ruffled and striped varieties, too. Zinnias are wonderful for colorful, long-lasting bouquets. The more you cut, the more they bloom.

How to Grow

Zinnias have large, easy-to-handle seeds and are one of the simplest flowers to grow from seed sown directly in the garden. Plant them outside after danger of spring frost. Thin when plants are several inches tall to allow 6 to 18 inches between plants, depending on the size of the variety you planted. You can also buy short varieties as bedding plants in the spring.

Care and Maintenance

Cut off fading flowers to promote new blooms. Two fungus diseases, powdery mildew and alternaria blight, sometimes cut zinnias down in their prime. Fortunately, there are several ways to head off the problem: Begin by thinning plants to ensure plenty of room for good air circulation. Avoid overhead sprinkling. The variety you grow makes a big difference: large-flowered zinnias are usually more susceptible than those with small flowers. Disease-resistant varieties are also available (see recommendations below).

> ## GARDEN TIP
>
> ◆ Butterflies may pass by ruffled or fancy-shaped zinnias; the simple, daisy-like types are more to their liking.

Recommended Varieties

'Thumbelina' grows only 6 inches tall and produces miniature blooms. It's a good choice for windowboxes or other containers. 'Peter Pan' zinnias won many All-America Selections awards in the 1970s and 1980s. This foot-tall variety produces abundant 3-inch flowers and is still one of the best. The 1999 All-America Selections Gold Medal went to 'Profusion Cherry' and 'Profusion Orange' for their outstanding disease resistance. These spreading plants bear 2- to 3-inch, daisylike flowers. New leaves hide spent flowers and plants continue to bloom without deadheading.

Related Species

Z. angustifolia—a disease-resistant relative of the common garden zinnia—offers excellent resistance to disease. Superb named varieties include 'Crystal White', a 1997 All-America Selections winner, and the 'Star' series, which produces flowers in gold, orange, or white. All have simple, daisylike blooms.

Bulbs, Corms, and Tubers

The plants in this chapter are diverse. Some are hardy flowers that grow from bulbs planted in the fall: harbingers of spring such as daffodils and tulips, or summer-blooming beauties like lilies and alliums. Others are tender plants, such as caladiums and dahlias, that must be dug up in the fall and stored indoors if they are to survive the winter.

Some of these plants grow from structures we call bulbs, but they aren't really bulbs at all. Crocus and gladiolus grow instead from solid structures called "corms," though it's hard to tell the difference just by looking. Caladiums grow from tubers, dahlias grow from tuberous roots, and cannas grow from rhizomes. But the plants in this chapter have two things in common: All grow from some kind of underground storage structure. And all prefer to grow in well-drained soil so that the storage structure won't rot.

If your soil isn't well-drained, plant a few of these beauties in an elevated area, such as a berm or raised bed. Or try planting some in a pot. Caladiums, dahlias, and small varieties of cannas are all excellent plants for containers.

Spring bulbs don't need a spot of their own in the garden. Pair them with perennials that seldom need dividing, such as peonies or Siberian iris, or with annual bedding plants such as geraniums or impatiens. After the bulbs' blossoms fade and their leaves begin to wither, their growing companions will conceal the dying foliage.

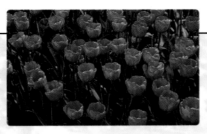

The most difficult step in growing spring-flowering bulbs is remembering to plant them in autumn. By the time hyacinths and tulips are blooming in other gardens, it's too late to plant them in your own. If you buy some bulbs in the fall and forget to plant them before the ground freezes, try to plant them as soon as the ground thaws in spring. Chances are you won't get any flowers for another year, but the bulbs won't survive till fall unless they're in the ground.

If your garden soil is poor, dig compost or other organic material into the soil before you plant. In future years, a sprinkle of slow-release bulb fertilizer on the soil surface in autumn will give hardy bulbs the nourishment they need to bloom and prosper in the coming year.

Mulch beds of hardy bulbs with a 2-inch blanket of shredded leaves, bark, or other mulch. In addition to preventing weeds and preserving soil moisture, mulch will help keep spring flower buds from emerging so soon that they get zapped by a late spring freeze.

It's just as easy to grow the tender plants in this chapter as it is to grow other annuals. The only thing left to learn is when to bring them inside and where to store them.

Caladium

Caladium × hortulanum

OTHER COMMON NAME:
Fancy-Leaved Caladium

ZONES: Tender

LIGHT REQUIREMENT:
Partial to full shade

HEIGHT × WIDTH: 8 to
24 inches × 12 to 24 inches

Special Features

Caladium's color comes not from its insignificant flowers, but from its colorful heart-shaped foliage. The bold, tropical leaves are variegated with white, red, pink, and green markings. You can count on caladiums to provide summer-long color in shady borders. These plants thrive in containers, too, and they love the Midwest's humid summers.

How to Grow

Caladiums grow from tubers. You can buy them already growing in pots in spring, or start your own tubers indoors in February or March. Cover the tubers with an inch of soil, then water; wait until the plants start growing to water again. Caladiums are easily chilled, so set their pots where the temperature is 70 degrees Fahrenheit or warmer. After the danger of spring frost has passed and night temperatures cease to dip below 50 degrees Fahrenheit, transplant your caladiums outdoors. Space the plants 12 to 18 inches apart in the garden, preferably in soil that is rich, moist, and well-drained. A site protected from harsh winds is best.

Care and Maintenance

GARDEN TIP

♦ Instead of planting caladiums directly in the ground, sink their pots up to the rims in the soil. In fall, bring the pots inside. Withhold water and let the plants die down; then store the tubers still in their pots. In February or March, repot the tubers in fresh soil and proceed as described.

Water as often as needed to keep the soil moist. If your caladiums are growing in containers, add a water-soluble or liquid fertilizer at half the recommended strength every second or third time you water. Caladiums are seldom bothered by any pests or diseases. The greatest difficulty you're apt to encounter is in getting the plants through the winter indoors. Before the first frost, when the leaves start to die down, dig up the plants and bring them inside. Allow the tops to die down, then cut off the dried tops and store the tubers in a container filled with vermiculite or peat moss. A storage place that stays about 60 degrees Fahrenheit is ideal.

Recommended Varieties

Try a white-and-green garden to light up a shady corner. Both 'White Christmas', which has green veins against a white background, and 'Candidum', which has white leaves and green margins, are particularly eye-catching in the shade. Outstanding pink-and-green varieties include 'Carolyn Wharton', which has pink leaves, green margins, and rose veins; and 'Pink Beauty', which has green leaves with pink-and-rose markings. 'Blaze' has splashes of bright red.

Blaze

'Candidum'

Canna

Canna hybrids

OTHER COMMON NAME:
Canna Lily

ZONES: Tender

BLOOM TIME: Midsummer
to frost

BLOOM COLOR: Fuchsia,
orange, pink, red, rose,
or yellow

LIGHT REQUIREMENT:
Sun or partial shade

HEIGHT × WIDTH:
18 inches to 7 feet × 12 to
30 inches

Special Features

Once popular on Victorian estates, cannas are riding a new wave of popularity in the Midwest. With new varieties small enough to grow in a pot, you no longer have to own an estate to enjoy canna's colorful flower spikes and bold, tropical foliage. Varieties with striped, multicolored leaves are sought after, as well as those with bronze, burgundy, or green leaves. Tall cannas are finding their way into more gardens, too, as gardeners discover that big cannas make a quick and handsome privacy screen.

How to Grow

After the last spring frost, cut canna rhizomes into sections that each have two or three "eyes," or buds. Mix a shovelful of compost into each planting hole, then plant the rhizomes 2 to 3 inches deep. Space dwarf varieties a foot apart; space taller cannas 18 to 24 inches apart.

Care and Maintenance

Water in dry weather, and mulch to conserve soil moisture. Snip off spent flowers and seed pods to improve the cannas' appearance. After the first fall frost, clip off the foliage near ground level and dig up the rhizomes. Let them dry a day or two, then pack the rhizomes upside down in cardboard boxes, leaving a little soil on each clump to help protect it from drying out. Store in a cool, frost-free place like the basement.

GARDEN TIP

- If you'd rather not bother digging and storing canna roots every winter, try 'Tropical Rose', a 1992 All-America Selections winner, or its sister 'Tropical Red'. Both are seed-grown dwarfs that are so quick to flower, you can grow them as annuals. You can also buy instant color with the large, potted cannas now sold at garden centers.

Recommended Varieties

Some popular dwarf cannas include 'Miss Oklahoma', which has pink flowers and deep-green leaves; 'Black Knight', which produces deep-red flowers and burgundy leaves; and 'President', which has scarlet flowers and glossy, dark-green leaves. Tropicanna™ has orange flowers and leaves with burgundy, red, pink, yellow and green stripes. An outstanding tall variety is 'Red King Humbert', which has orange-red flowers and bronze-red foliage.

'Miss Oklahoma'

'President'

Crocus

Crocus vernus

ZONES: 3 to 8

BLOOM SEASON:
Late winter

BLOOM COLOR: Pink,
purple, red, white, yellow,
or bicolored

LIGHT REQUIREMENT:
Full sun or partial shade

HEIGHT × WIDTH: 3 to
6 inches × 1 to 2 inches

Special Features

With their small, brightly-colored blossoms peaking through the snow, bunches of crocuses are a welcome sight in late winter. The blossoms last about two weeks, but if you plant an assortment of varieties you can have crocuses in bloom for a month or more. Plant them along the walk or near the door so you won't miss this early show.

How to Grow

Plant crocus corms in fall in well-drained soil. They'll look best in spring if you plant them in large drifts, or groups. Space corms about 2 inches apart and cover with 2 to 3 inches of soil.

Care and Maintenance

Allow the foliage to die down naturally after the blooms fade. Fertilize every fall by sprinkling a slow-release bulb fertilizer on the ground; top with a fresh layer of mulch. If squirrels or other animals dig up your crocuses, lay a piece of welded wire or poultry netting on the ground over newly planted bulbs. You can also plant a groundcover, such as creeping myrtle, over the bulbs to make damage from animals less likely. Crocuses spread gradually, but they rarely get crowded enough to require division.

Recommended Varieties

Choose crocus varieties for the colors you want. Some popular large-flowered Dutch hybrids include white 'Jeanne d'Arc', purple 'Remembrance', lilac-striped 'Pickwick', and 'Yellow Mammoth'. For a longer-lasting show, include varieties with smaller, earlier blossoms, such as 'Blue Ribbon', 'Goldilocks', or 'Tricolor'.

Related Species

Fall-flowering crocus (*C. speciosus*) blooms in September and has violet-blue flowers.

GARDEN TIPS

◆ If your lawn is planted with a slow-to-green, warm-season grass such as buffalo or zoysia, plant crocus bulbs in the lawn for some early color. The crocuses will bloom before the grass begins to grow, and the withered flowers and foliage will be unharmed by mowing.

◆ Autumn crocus (*Colchicum* species) is not a crocus at all, but it has similar blooms. Plant autumn crocus in late summer and you'll have flowers in just a few weeks. If you delay planting, though, they'll bloom in the sack!

'Pickwick'

'Remembrance'

Daffodil

Narcissus hybrids

ZONES: 3 to 9

BLOOM TIME: Early to mid-spring

BLOOM COLOR: Orange, pink, white, yellow, or bicolored

LIGHT REQUIREMENT: Sun

HEIGHT × WIDTH: 10 to 18 inches × 4 to 12 inches

Special Features

Daffodils announce spring with their trumpet-shaped flowers. They are one of the showiest and most popular of spring bulbs. Unlike many other bulbs, which eventually fizzle out, daffodils multiply. This makes them excellent candidates for naturalizing in a woodland garden. If deer, squirrels, gophers, or other animals often dine on your tulips, you'll find daffodils particularly rewarding. They're seldom bothered by pests of any type.

How to Grow

Plant daffodil bulbs in fall at about the same time autumn leaves begin to fall. Choose a spot with well-drained soil and place the bulbs pointed end up. Plant 6 to 12 inches apart and 6 to 8 inches deep. Daffodils need sun to thrive, but that doesn't mean you can't plant them under a tree. By the time the tree's leaves are fully expanded, early-blooming varieties of daffodils will have already finished.

BULBS, CORMS, AND TUBERS

Care and Maintenance

Spread a slow-release fertilizer over the daffodil bed every fall, then top with a fresh layer of shredded bark or other mulch. Snip off faded flowers but allow the foliage to die back naturally before removal. Resist the temptation to braid the leaves or tie them together in neat clumps; daf-

> **GARDEN TIP**
>
> ◆ Stand cut daffodils in 6 to 8 inches of lukewarm water for several hours before you mix them in a bouquet with tulips. Discard the water to get rid of daffodils' toxic sap, then make your arrangement without recutting the stems.

fodil foliage needs to soak up as much sun as it can. Rarely, daffodils may stop blooming, and you may need to dig up and divide crowded clumps. You can do the job in early summer, while the plants' dying leaves are still visible, or you can mark the location of the bulbs with golf tees and divide the clumps in fall.

Recommended Varieties

The best way to select daffodils is to study pictures of the varieties offered at the garden center and choose your favorite colors. One popular, large-cupped variety is 'Ice Follies', a white daffodil that is excellent for naturalizing. 'Pink Charm' and the golden-yellow 'Carlton' are other favorites.

Related Species

Wild daffodil bulbs are smaller than the cultivated kind, often growing no larger than the tip of your little finger. Their charming, miniature blooms top petite plants that grow only 5 to 6 inches tall. Plant these tiny bulbs 3 to 4 inches deep. The paper-white narcissus—popular for forcing indoors in winter—is best discarded after it blooms. It is hardy only to zone 9 and won't survive if transplanted outdoors in a Midwest garden.

Dahlia

Dahlia hybrids

ZONES: Tender

BLOOM TIME: Midsummer to frost

BLOOM COLOR: Bronze, lavender, maroon, pink, purple, white, or bicolored

LIGHT REQUIREMENT: Sun

HEIGHT × WIDTH: 1 to 6 feet × 1 to 3 feet

Special Features

It's hard to get bored with dahlias. No other flower comes in so many different sizes, colors, and shapes. Flowering continues until hard frost, providing plenty of bright color for the end-of-the-season garden. Dahlias are long-lasting as cut flowers, and they are as popular in indoor bouquets as they are in the garden. Luckily, the more you cut, the more they bloom.

How to Grow

You can start dahlias from seeds or plants, or from tuberous roots that look like sweet potatoes. If you decide to grow seeds, give them a head start indoors so that they'll bloom the first year. Dwarf varieties, which are ideal for planting in containers, are often sold as annual bedding plants. For a good selection of large varieties, however, purchase tuberous roots. Cut the roots into sections with a sharp knife, being sure that each section has at least one white bud and a piece of the previous year's stem. After the danger of spring frost has passed, plant each root section in the garden and cover with 4 inches of soil. A sunny site with rich, moist, well-drained soil is ideal. Fertilize at planting time with a slow-release fertilizer. If you're growing a tall variety, pound in stakes at the same time to avoid damaging the roots later. Allow plenty of room for good air circulation to help prevent mildew. Space dwarf varieties a foot apart; space tall varieties 2 to 3 feet apart.

GARDEN TIP

♦ To grow a blossom the size of a dinner plate, pinch out lateral shoots and buds, allowing only one flower to form on each stalk.

Care and Maintenance

Dahlias require moist soil when they're actively growing, so get out the garden hose if it doesn't rain. Mulch to conserve soil moisture and to keep the roots cool. Expect your plants to bloom best when cool fall temperatures replace summer's hot, humid weather. Spider mites sometimes attack in hot, dry weather. You can thwart them by spraying the plants regularly with water from the garden hose. After frost blackens the tops of dahlias, clip the foliage back to about 4 inches and dig up the roots. Leave each clump upside down for 2 hours to allow excess moisture to drain from the stem. Then shake off loose soil and sandwich the clumps upside down between layers of sand or vermiculite in a box. Store the box in a basement closet or another cool, frost-free spot.

Recommended Varieties

There are hundreds of named varieties, and choosing which dahlia to grow can be daunting. Visit public gardens or local dahlia shows to help you decide which ones you like best. Blossoms range from marble-sized to giants as big as a dinner plate. Some are rounded like pompons, while others have a cactus-type flower with long, quill-shaped petals. There are also double and semi-double dahlias, which have extra rows of petals.

Gladiolus

Gladiolus × hortulanus

ZONES: Tender

BLOOM TIME: Summer

BLOOM COLOR: Cream, pink, purple, red, yellow, or bicolored

LIGHT REQUIREMENT: Sun

HEIGHT × WIDTH: 15 to 60 inches × 8 to 24 inches

Special Features

Hummingbirds love these tall spikes of funnel-shaped flowers. Blossoms can be plain or ruffled and are a favorite for cutting. Even the sword-shaped foliage is a garden asset.

How to Grow

Enrich the soil with compost before planting. After the last spring frost, plant gladiolus corms with the pointed ends up, 8 to 12 inches apart, and 5 to 6 inches deep. This deep planting helps ensure that the plants won't topple over in the wind. Sprinkle a slow-release fertilizer on the ground after planting. For continuous flowers, you can make successive plantings every 2 weeks; but most gardeners find it easier to plant a mixture of early and late varieties all at the same time.

Care and Maintenance

Water whenever necessary to keep the soil moist, and mulch to conserve moisture. Stake tall varieties. When you cut a flower stalk, take as little foliage as possible. The more you leave, the more vigorous next year's corm will be. Cut any flowers left in the garden as soon as they fade so that the corms won't waste any energy producing seeds.

Distorted blossoms and browning foliage are a sign of an infestation of tiny insects called thrips. To control them, remove affected flowers and spray the plants with insecticidal soap every 3 days for 2 weeks. If a gladiolus develops spots on its leaves, stems, and

GARDEN TIP

♦ Drop a mothball in each sack of stored gladiolus corms to prevent damage from mice and kill over-wintering thrips.

petals, remove the affected plant and spray the remaining glads with a fungicide. If leaves and flowers are mottled or streaked and blossoms fail to completely open, a virus disease spread by aphids is the likely cause. There is no cure, so remove and destroy the affected plant. Control the aphids on remaining plants with insecticidal soap.

In early fall or immediately after the first frost, dig up the corms. Cut off the foliage 1 to 2 inches above the corm, then spread the corms out in a single layer to dry for several weeks in the garage or basement. Separate each new corm from the old corm on top. Discard the old corms as well as any new ones that show signs of rotting. Store the healthy new corms in a sack in the basement or another cool, frost-free place.

Recommended Varieties

There are hundred of different kinds of glads. Miniature varieties are best for table bouquets, while tall ones look particularly elegant in the garden. Selecting the colors you like best is usually easier than hunting for a named variety.

Grape Hyacinth

Muscaria armeniacum

ZONES: 4 to 9

BLOOM TIME: April and May

BLOOM COLOR: Purple or blue

LIGHT REQUIREMENT: Full sun or partial shade

HEIGHT × WIDTH: 4 to 8 inches × 2 to 4 inches

Special Features

One of the longest blooming of the hardy spring bulbs, grape hyacinth's blossoms last three weeks or more. The sweetly scented flowers look like upside-down clusters of purple grapes. Grape hyacinth clumps multiply over the years, making it an excellent choice for naturalizing. Plant grape hyacinths in drifts under trees and shrubs, or along the walk. They also make a breath-taking display when combined with daffodils or early tulips.

How to Grow

Grape hyacinths are so eager to grow, they're nearly fizzle-proof. Plant the bulbs pointed end up in early fall, 3 inches deep and 3 inches apart. Any well-drained soil will do. Grape hyacinths are also one of the easiest bulbs to force successfully indoors.

Care and Maintenance

Once you plant them, these little bulbs will take care of themselves. They don't require extra water or any fertilizer. They will occasionally self-sow, so plant them where they can spread into adjacent areas without crowding other spring flowers.

Grape hyacinths are perfect for naturalizing in the lawn, provided you're willing to wait until the bulbs' leaves shrivel and die before you mow.

Recommended Variety

'Blue Spike' is prized for its bright-blue, double flowers.

Related Species

Italian grape hyacinth (*M. botryoides* var. *album*) has fragrant, dense, white spikes. The bulbs are exceptionally hardy, thriving even in zone 2.

GARDEN TIP

◆ For an early taste of spring, plant the bulbs 2 inches apart and 2 inches deep in a pot filled with potting soil. Water, then set the pot in a cool (35 to 50 degrees Fahrenheit), dark spot for 6 to 10 weeks. When the shoots are 1½ inches tall, move the pot into bright, indirect light. The blooms will last longest if you set the pot where the temperature is about 60 degrees Fahrenheit.

Italian Grape Hyacinth

Hyacinth

Hyacinthus orientalis

OTHER COMMON NAME:
Garden Hyacinth

ZONES: 4 to 7

BLOOM TIME: Mid-spring

BLOOM COLOR: Blue,
ivory, pink, purple, rose, or
white

LIGHT REQUIREMENT:
Sun or partial shade

HEIGHT × WIDTH: 8 to
12 inches × 4 to 8 inches

Special Features

The heavenly fragrance of hyacinths makes them a favorite, indoors and out. The single or double flowers are tightly packed in thick clusters 6 to 8 inches tall, giving hyacinths a somewhat formal appearance.

How to Grow

Plant hyacinth bulbs in fall, pointed end up, in rich, well-drained garden soil. Water soon after planting if there is no rain. Space bulbs 6 inches apart and cover with 4 to 5 inches of soil. Lay a piece of welded wire or poultry netting on the ground over newly planted bulbs to protect them from squirrels and other animals.

Care and Maintenance

If the weather is dry, water in spring when hyacinths are blooming. Mulch to preserve soil moisture and for winter protection. Sprinkle a slow-release bulb fertilizer on the ground in fall; top with a fresh layer of mulch. Cut off faded flowers to keep bulbs from wasting their energy on seed production. To ensure blooms the following year, allow the leaves to remain until they're completely dry; surround the bulbs with other garden flowers to cover the dying hyacinth foliage.

Recommended Varieties

'Delph Blue' has medium lilac-blue flowers and is one of the best-known hyacinths. Other favorites are 'Pink Pearl', light blue; 'L'Innocence', deep pink; 'Wedgewood', ivory-white; 'Lady Derby', rose-pink; and 'Blue Jacket', navy-blue with a darker stripe.

GARDEN TIPS

◆ After the first year, hyacinth blossoms gradually get smaller and looser. Some gardeners prefer these less formal-looking flowers; others choose to dig up the bulbs after flowering and plant new bulbs in the fall.

◆ To reduce the time needed to force hyacinths into bloom indoors, you can buy pre-treated bulbs in a kit which includes instructions for forcing.

'Blue Jacket'

'Pink Pearl'

Lily

Lilium hybrids

ZONES: 4 to 9

BLOOM TIME: Summer

BLOOM COLOR: Gold, orange, pink, red, white, or yellow

LIGHT REQUIREMENT: Sun or partial shade

HEIGHT × WIDTH: 24 to 72 inches × 6 to 10 inches

Special Features

With their showy, trumpet-shaped blossoms, lilies are the aristocrats of the perennial garden. The flowers are beautiful and long-lasting in bouquets, and some are fragrant. Even if your garden is small, it's easy to squeeze in a few lilies. Though most types are tall, they are also skinny, so they fit into small spaces between other plants.

How to Grow

Plant lilies in rich, well-drained soil. It's best to plant lily bulbs in fall as soon as they are available. Buy plump bulbs that show no signs of shriveling or sprouting. Dig each planting hole two or three times as deep as the bulb. Bulbs can also be planted in spring, though they may not bloom well the first season. A third, but more expensive, option is to buy potted lilies, which can be planted any time during the growing season.

Care and Maintenance

Lilies love to have their heads in the sun and their feet in the shade, so keep the ground around them covered with mulch, or surround lilies with low-growing perennials or ground covers.

Fertilize lilies every spring when they emerge with a complete, slow-release bulb fertilizer. Stake tall varieties. As soon as blossoms fade, clip off the entire seedhead, but leave the stalk and leaves to help build a bigger bulb for next year. After a killing fall frost, remove the stems to prevent disease. When an established patch becomes crowded, dig up and divide the bulbs in autumn.

GARDEN TIPS

♦ Lily bulbs lack the hard, protective coat that keeps other hardy bulbs from drying out, so plant them as soon as you get them.

♦ Lilies are one of gophers' favorite foods. If your garden has been visited by gophers in the past, you'll need to protect your bulbs by planting them in a raised bed lined with fencing fabric.

Recommended Varieties

Asiatic lilies, the best choice for beginners, are early bloomers that usually range from 2 to 4 feet tall. They come in the most color choices but often have little or no fragrance. All varieties are easy to grow, so just pick your favorite colors. Oriental lilies bloom a bit later and fill the air with their sweet perfume. 'Casa Blanca', one of the most popular, produces huge white flowers with a strong, sweet fragrance on plants 4 to 5 feet tall.

Related Species

Madonna lily (*L. candidum*) bulbs—an exception to the rule—should be planted only 1 inch deep in August. Plants grow 3 to 4 feet tall and will bloom in late June or July the summer after planting, producing fragrant, pure-white blossoms. The regal lily (*L. regale*) is another fragrant classic; its white blooms open a bit later on plants 4 to 6 feet tall. Martagon lilies (*L. martagon*) are the earliest of the lilies to bloom and are also one of the few that thrives in shade. The plants grow 3 to 6 feet tall and have waxy blossoms that nod from long stems.

Ornamental Onion

Allium species

OTHER COMMON NAME:
Flowering Onion

ZONES: 4 to 8

BLOOM TIME: Spring or summer

BLOOM COLOR: Blue, pink, purple, white, or yellow

LIGHT REQUIREMENT: Sun or partial shade

HEIGHT × WIDTH: 6 to 40 inches × 6 to 24 inches

Special Features

Ornamental onions—the flowering cousins of onions, chives, and garlic—range from petite dwarfs ideal for the rock garden to tall varieties that are just right for the back of the border. Their showy flower clusters come in two styles: Some form a dense sphere, and others are arranged in a loose collection. Some clusters are only an inch wide, while others grow to as much as a foot in diameter. All are displayed on sturdy flower stalks and make excellent, long-lasting cut flowers.

How to Grow

Ornamental onions are easy to grow and thrive even in poor or dry soils. Their only requirement: the soil must be well-drained. Dig a 2-inch layer of compost into the bed before planting the bulbs. Plant in fall. Space small bulbs about 4 inches apart and cover with 4 inches of soil. Plant large varieties 6 inches deep and 8 to 12 inches apart. Sprinkle a slow-release bulb fertilizer on the ground, then add a layer of shredded bark or other mulch. You can also grow ornamental onions from small plants; look for them in the garden center in spring displayed with other perennials.

Care and Maintenance

Stake tall varieties, especially if your garden is located in a windy site. Snip off faded blossoms but allow the foliage to remain until it is completely dead. Combine ornamental onions with phlox, salvia, or other garden flowers to hide the dying foliage. Sprinkle a slow-release bulb fertilizer on the ground every fall and top it with a fresh layer of mulch. Mice, squirrels, and other animals that feast on many kinds of bulbs need no control; they won't bother flowering onions. When the number of blooms declines, dig and divide crowded clumps and replant as before.

GARDEN TIPS

◆ Don't worry that your alliums will make your garden smell like onions. You'll notice a faint onion scent only if you bruise the leaves.

◆ 'Ozawas' (*A. thunbergii*) breaks the rule and waits until fall to produce its rosy-purple flowers. And that's not the end of the show: its reddish-bronze leaves are attractive into winter.

Recommended Species

Persian onion (*A. christophii*) grows 24 to 30 inches tall and produces giant 8- to 12-inch, violet spheres. The flowers of *A. caeruleum* are daintier, with clusters measuring two inches or less on 20-inch-tall plants. Lily leek, or society garlic (*A. moly*), is a hardy species that thrives through zone 3 and has bright yellow flowers on 12-inch plants. Giant onion (*A. giganteum*) is the tallest member of the family, with 5-inch, purple blossoms in midsummer. This species is not quite as hardy as most, thriving only through zone 5.

Tulip

Tulipa hybrids

ZONES: 3 to 8

BLOOM TIME: Mid- to late spring

BLOOM COLOR: Orange, pink, purple, red, white, yellow, or bicolored

LIGHT REQUIREMENT: Sun

HEIGHT × WIDTH: 10 to 36 inches × 6 to 12 inches

Special Features

Too well-known to need description, tulips perk up spring with their splash of bright colors. The blossoms are most at home in a formal garden and are excellent for cutting.

How to Grow

Tulips require well-drained soil. The best time to plant in the Midwest is in October, after the soil has had a chance to cool. Place the bulbs, pointed end up, 8 to 12 inches apart in holes 8 inches deep.

Care and Maintenance

Snip off faded flowers to keep plants from wasting their energy on seed production, but allow the withering foliage to remain until it's completely dead. Sprinkle a slow-release fertilizer over tulip beds every autumn and top with a fresh layer of mulch. Protect tulip bulbs from squirrels, gophers, and other small animals by laying a piece of welded wire or poultry netting over the bed after you plant. Unfortunately, there is no good way to protect emerging tulips from deer. If deer frequent your area, you'll have better luck with daffodils.

Recommended Varieties

Choose tulips from several different groups so you can stretch the season of bloom over a month or more. Waterlily hybrids (*T. kaufmanniana*) such as scarlet-red 'Cherry Orchard' or yellow 'Stresa' are some of the first to bloom. The large blossoms of Greigii hybrids, which open next, are accented by unusual mottled foliage. 'Donna Bella'—cream-colored inside and on the edges of the carmine-red outer petals— is one of the best. 'Red Riding Hood' is another popular Greigii tulip. Darwin hybrids have giant, mid-season flowers and bloom year after year, instead of fizzling out like many other kinds of tulips. Some pretty ones to try are salmon-pink 'Big Chief' and scarlet-red 'Dover'. Parrot tulips are late bloomers with exotic-looking, fringed flowers. 'Black Parrot' is one of the most eye-catching, producing velvety, purple-black flowers.

> ## GARDEN TIP
>
> ◆ Don't skimp on digging 8-inch-deep holes to plant tulips. Shallow planting is one of the reasons tulips may fail to bloom after one or two seasons.

Related Species

Species tulips, unlike their fancy hybrid cousins, tend to bloom and multiply for years. With a delicate look that belies their tough performance, most kinds grow less than 8 inches tall, fitting easily into nooks and crannies in even the smallest garden. Many species tulips bloom earlier than large-flower hybrids, some opening even before the first daffodil. *T. tarda* has yellow-and-white, star-shaped flowers that grow five or six to a stem. The plants grow only 4 inches tall. *T. batalinii* produces fragrant flowers on stems 5 to 6 inches tall. Two popular varieties, 'Red Jewel' and 'Yellow Jewel', have the classic tulip shape.

The Food Garden

Ask a Midwest gardener how his or her garden is doing, and you'll likely hear about a *vegetable* garden. To many people in this region, the word "garden" still means a place to raise food crops. The food garden has always been important to Midwest people, who in the past often depended on the food they raised to feed their large families.

Times have changed. Food is plentiful and relatively inexpensive at the nearby super-market. But many of us are still growing our own. Why? The number one reason is because it tastes so good! There's nothing like vine-ripened tomatoes or sun-warmed berries that have been picked at the peak of perfection.

There are other reasons, too: We like the challenge. We appreciate the quality. We want to grow crops that are difficult to find at the store. We want produce that hasn't been sprayed with chemicals. We want a ready sup-ply of fresh herbs to spice up our cooking. And . . . we're having fun!

It doesn't take a lot of space to grow a lot of food. It doesn't even take a formal vegetable garden. Some crops, like peppers and colorful lettuces, are pretty enough to tuck into flower beds. New varieties, such as 'Small Miracle' broccoli and 'Spacemiser' zucchini, make it possible to grow just about anything in a con-tainer. Dwarf fruit trees and berry bushes can do double duty as an edible landscape.

What food gardens *do* require is sun. While there are plenty of flowers and shrubs that will thrive in the shade, there are very few vegetables and fruits that will. A food garden also requires that the gardener pay special attention to soil fertility. Because we're constantly taking away as we harvest, we must do more to replenish the soil. Composting plant wastes and returning them to the soil is a good start. An annual application of a slow-release fertilizer will do the rest.

To keep disease and insect problems to a minimum, fall cleanup is important. So is rotating crops (to avoid constantly growing the same kind of plant in the same place) and choosing disease-resistant varieties. Controlling pests and diseases of fruit trees is particularly challenging.

In this chapter, you'll find information to help you grow and harvest your own fresh vegetables, herbs, and fruits. Choose your favorite foods . . . and enjoy!

Apple

Special Features

One juicy bite of a just-picked apple is enough to convince most gardeners they would like to grow some. From the first beautiful blossoms in spring to the last luscious fruit in fall, apples are the king of Midwestern fruits.

How to Grow

Choose two or more varieties for cross-pollination. Dwarf trees are the best choice for the home landscape because they fit into a small space, put maintenance and harvesting within easy reach, and shorten the wait for the first harvest to just a couple of years. Choose a sunny site with good drainage. Avoid planting in a low area, where frost damage is more likely. Space dwarf trees about 10 feet apart. Place the tree so that the graft union (the swollen area where the tree was joined to a dwarfing rootstock) is 2 to 3 inches above the soil line. Water deeply once a week if it doesn't rain, continuing throughout the tree's first summer.

Care and Maintenance

Prune trees when dormant (see illustrated Appendix). Autumn cleanup is an important way to control disease and pest problems in trees that have begun to produce fruit. Rake up leaves and pick up any fallen fruit. In late winter, spray with dormant oil. Choose a mild, calm day when no rain or freezing temperatures are expected for the next 24 hours. If necessary, control fungus diseases with sulfur and Bordeaux; spray trees just before the blossoms open and then again after petal fall. Purchase red sticky traps for apple maggot flies, or make your own by coating bright red balls with Tanglefoot® Insect Trap Coating. Hang six in each dwarf tree.

Harvest

Apples can't be judged for ripeness on looks alone, but apple stems release easily from the tree when it's time to harvest. Another good way to judge ripeness: cut an apple open and look at the seeds. If they're brown, the apple is ripe. Apple harvest in the Midwest extends from July through October, depending on variety. The majority of apples , though, ripen in September and October.

GARDEN TIP

♦ To trap apple coddling moths and prevent wormy apples, fill a gallon-size plastic jug with 1 cup sugar, 1 cup vinegar, 1 banana peel, and water to within 2 inches of the top. Hang one trap in each tree. Replace traps during the summer if they become clogged with moths.

Recommended Varieties

'Liberty' has excellent resistance to scab and cedar apple rust, two of the most serious apple diseases. Other disease-resistant apples include 'Jonafree', 'Macfree', and 'Freedom'.

'Liberty'

Blueberry

Special Features

A blueberry plant has a lot going for it: in addition to producing delicious fruit, its white spring blossoms and scarlet or orange autumn color make it a handsome shrub for the landscape.

How to Grow

Plant blueberries in spring in a site with full sun and well-drained soil. For the best pollination and fruit set, plant at least two different varieties. Space highbush varieties 5 feet apart; plant half-high varieties 3 feet apart. If you can grow azaleas, you can grow blueberries: both plants require the same acid soil. If your soil is alkaline or neutral, dig several gallons of pre-moistened sphagnum peat moss into the soil where each plant will grow. Every two years in winter, spread about 6 ounces of powdered sulfur in a wide ring around each plant. Mulch with pine bark chips or shredded oak leaves; the decomposing mulch will help keep the soil acid. If the plants look pale and anemic when they leaf out in the spring, your blueberries are telling you that the soil is still too alkaline and needs more sulfur.

Care and Maintenance

Water when the soil is dry. Add a liquid acid fertilizer to the water, following package directions. Renew the layer of mulch whenever necessary. Prune blueberries in winter to remove dead or broken branches; also remove any stems that are more than 5 years old.

Harvest

You can't judge the ripeness of blueberries strictly by color. Berries reach their potential, both in size and in sweetness, a week or two after turning blue. When fully ripe, they'll fall easily into your hand.

GARDEN TIP

◆ Birds like blueberries as much as people do. If they take more than their share, you may have to cage your plants while the berries are ripening.

Recommended Varieties

Highbush blueberries that thrive in zones 4 to 7 include 'Blue Jay' (5 to 7 feet tall) and 'Blue Crop' (4 to 6 feet tall). Half-high varieties hardy in zones 3 to 7 are 'Northland' (3 to 4 feet tall) and 'Northblue' (30 inches tall).

'Blue Crop'

'Northblue'

Cherry

Special Features

Tart cherries provide beautiful blossoms in spring, followed by one of the earliest crops of tree-borne fruit, sometimes as early as mid-June.

How to Grow

Dwarf trees are the best choice for the home landscape since they fit into a small space, put maintenance and harvesting within easy reach, and shorten the wait for the first harvest to just a couple of years. Choose a sunny site with good drainage. Avoid planting in a low area, where frost damage is more likely. Space dwarf trees about 10 feet apart. Place the tree so that the graft union (the swollen area where the tree was joined to a dwarfing rootstock) is 2 to 3 inches above the soil line. Water deeply once a week if it doesn't rain, continuing throughout the tree's first summer.

Care and Maintenance

Prune trees when dormant (see illustrated Appendix). Autumn cleanup is an important way to control disease and pest problems in trees that have begun to produce fruit. Rake up leaves and pick up any fallen fruit. In late winter spray with dormant oil: choose a mild, calm day when no rain or freezing temperatures are expected for the next 24 hours. If necessary, control fungus diseases with sulfur and Bordeaux; spray trees just before the blossoms open and then again after petal fall.

If ripening cherries develop fuzzy gray patches, the blame goes to brown rot, a fungus disease which also spoils plum, peaches, and apricots. The fungus spreads rapidly when fruits mature in mild, moist weather. To save future crops, clean up infected fruit and dried "mummies." Prune out any dead twigs or branches with sunken lesions, where the fungus might overwinter. If desired, apply a sulfur- or copper-based fungicide every 7 to 10 days, beginning in spring when the flower buds

> ## GARDEN TIP
>
> ◆ A dwarf tart cherry is the perfect tree for a small garden. Unlike apples, pears, and sweet cherries—all of which need two varieties for cross pollination—tart cherries are self-fruiting.

begin to open. Cherry leaf spot—a fungus disease that makes the leaves drop early—is favored by a wet, mild season. Though this disease won't kill a cherry tree by itself, it weakens the tree and makes it more susceptible to other problems. Reduce cherry leaf spot by raking up and removing fallen leaves, and by spraying the foliage with wettable sulfur beginning at petal fall.

Cherry fruit flies, which look like small houseflies, are responsible for wormy cherries. You can trap many of them with sticky red ball traps like those used to catch apple maggots. For more complete control, spray with rotenone, beginning when the cherries first start to color. Continue spraying every 7 to 10 days until you no longer catch any of the flies in the sticky traps.

Harvest

Tart cherries ripen in June (sometimes early July) in most of the Midwest. Pick cherries when they're fully colored.

Recommended Varieties

Two tart cherry varieties that thrive in the Midwest are 'Montmorency', which is hardy to zone 5, and 'North Star', which is hardy to zone 4.

Grape

Special Features

Whether the grapes you grow are red, white, or blue, they'll be a hit for eating fresh or making juice and jelly. The vine they grow on is a handsome addition to the landscape, too, whether it scales a trellis or climbs the fence.

How to Grow

Plant a grapevine in spring in a site with full sun and well-drained soil. Dig a layer of compost into the soil before you plant. Water immediately after planting, then mulch.

Care and Maintenance

Spread a layer of compost and fresh mulch around the grapevine once each year. Grapes fruit only on year-old wood, so annual pruning is necessary to keep them productive (see illustrated Appendix). If grapes shrivel before they ripen, the problem is a fungus disease called black rot. It overwinters on the dried fruits, so pick off any remaining clusters and bury them in the garden or compost pile in the fall. The same winter pruning that keeps grapes productive also helps control black rot by improving air circulation. If cultural practices alone fail to control black rot, you may want to spray with a fungicide, such as Bordeaux, during the growing season.

Harvest

Some varieties are ripe in August, while others are not ready until September. Either way, grapes look ripe before they are. Wait for the stem of each cluster to turn brown and the seeds to darken; then taste a few to be sure. Cut the clusters from the vine when they're ready. A common problem with grapes is the uneven ripening of grape clusters. The most frequent cause is too heavy a crop, which means you need to prune more next winter. Hot nights can increase the problem;

GARDEN TIP

◆ Take it easy when fertilizing grapes; too much fertilizer will result in too much vine and too little fruit.

other possible causes include too little sun, herbicide drift, and lack of potassium in the soil. Occasionally ripening clusters must be protected from wasps. The wasps aren't really the culprit; they're simply attracted by grapes that have burst open, which is usually due to too much rain at ripening time. To keep wasps away, bag grape clusters with paper bags or nylon hose.

Recommended Varieties

Two varieties of table grapes that thrive in Midwest gardens are 'Mars', a blue, and 'Reliance', a deep red. Both are seedless, disease-resistant, and hardy in zones 5 to 8. They ripen in August; 'Mars' is ready first.

'Reliance'

Pear

Special Features

The tender, juicy fruit of a home-grown pear is one of the luxuries of life, and the trees are handsome enough to grow as ornamentals.

How to Grow

Choose two or more varieties for cross pollination. Dwarf trees are the best choice for the home landscape because they fit into a small space, put maintenance and harvesting within easy reach, and shorten the wait for the first harvest to just a couple of years. Choose a sunny site with good drainage. Avoid planting in a low area, where frost damage is more likely. Space dwarf trees about 10 feet apart. Place the tree so that the graft union (the swollen area where the tree was joined to a dwarfing rootstock) is 2 to 3 inches above the soil line. Water deeply once a week if it doesn't rain, continuing throughout the tree's first summer.

Care and Maintenance

Prune trees when dormant (see illustration in the Appendix). Autumn cleanup is an important way to control disease and pest problems in trees that have begun to produce fruit. Rake up leaves and pick up any fallen fruit. In late winter spray with dormant oil: choose a mild, calm day when no rain or freezing temperatures are expected for the next 24 hours. If necessary, control fungus diseases with sulfur and Bordeaux; spray trees just before the blossoms open and then again after petal fall.

Harvest

In the Midwest, pears ripen from August through October, depending on variety. Unlike most fruits, pears are best if they're picked before they are completely ripe. Wait until pears are full-sized and yellow-green, then give each one a squeeze. If the flesh gives slightly to the touch and the pear releases easily from the tree, it's ready. Store at temperatures near 70 degrees Fahrenheit; pears will soften and develop full flavor in 7 to 10 days. To keep pears longer, store them in the refrigerator and remove a few at a time to finish ripening as you need them.

Recommended Varieties

'Starking Delicious' and 'Moonglow' both offer resistance to fireblight and are hardy in zones 5 to 8.

GARDEN TIP

- If a tree branch looks as though it was burned in a fire, it is suffering from fireblight, a serious disease that causes the sudden dying of leaves and growing tips. During the winter, prune and remove the branch at least 10 inches below the visible damage.

'Moonglow'

Raspberry

Special Features

You don't need a lot of space to produce a big crop of raspberries. A few plants at the edge of the yard make a handsome hedge that will yield a plentiful crop of delicious fruit. Raspberries come in red, black, purple, and yellow; red raspberries are the most hardy and the easiest to grow.

How to Grow

Plant raspberries in full sun in well-drained soil, spacing the plants 3 to 4 feet apart. Plants spread from suckers and will quickly fill in to make a dense hedge. Spring is the best time to plant bare-root plants; container-grown raspberries can be planted any time during the growing season.

Care and Maintenance

Water in dry weather. Mulch to preserve soil moisture and control weeds. As soon as summer-bearing varieties finish producing, remove at ground level all the canes that produced fruits. Remove any canes that are diseased, damaged, or crowded, but leave healthy canes for next year's crop. Fall-bearing raspberries are pruned differently. The easiest method is to remove all canes at ground level in late winter or early spring before the new shoots emerge. This way, you sacrifice a small summer crop but get a bigger total harvest in the fall. And there's almost no chance of disease carrying over from one season to the next. Remove as many canes as necessary from either kind of raspberry patch to insure good air circulation, which helps prevent disease.

Build soil fertility by spreading a layer of compost an inch or two deep on the ground right after you cut and remove the old canes. Top the compost with a fresh layer of wood chips, shredded leaves, or other mulch.

Harvest

There should be a few berries to pick the first year after planting. You'll have many more the following year. Raspberries are easy to pick; when ripe, they pop right off the stem with very gentle pressure.

GARDEN TIP

♦ It pays to get your raspberry patch off to a healthy start by purchasing certified, virus-free plants, even if a gardening friend has plants to share. Over time, virus diseases build up in berry plantings and decrease their production. It doesn't pay to import trouble.

Recommended Varieties

Two outstanding red raspberries are 'Heritage', a fall-bearing variety, and 'Latham', a summer-fruiting type. Both are hardy in zones 4 to 8.

Related Species

Blackberries thrive in the South, but most varieties can be grown only as far north as zone 6. "Navaho", one of the best-flavored blackberries, grows on thornless bushes in zones 6 to 10. Midwest gardeners in zones 4 and 5 who want to give blackberries a try should plant 'Illini Hardy', developed at the University of Illinois and has survived temperatures to -23 degrees (Fahrenheit).

'Heritage'

Rhubarb

Special Features

Rhubarb is one of the most care-free plants you can grow. The big leaves and red stalks are so handsome that the plants could pass for ornamental shrubs or large perennials rather than productive food plants.

How to Grow

A spot with full sun and good drainage is essential. Spade some compost into the soil, then set each rhubarb plant with its crown (growing point) about 2 inches below the soil surface. Two plants produce plenty for the average family. Water and mulch after planting.

Care and Maintenance

If your plants send up seed stalks, remove them. Seed stalks that are allowed to remain will sap energy from the plant. In late fall, clean up dead leaves, then spread a 2-inch layer of compost around the plants. Top with a fresh layer of mulch. If your rhubarb begins to produce only small stalks after it has been in one place for 5 or more years, it's time to dig and divide the plants. Early spring, when the new shoots first emerge, is the best time for the job.

The curculio—a half-inch, snout-nosed weevil that punctures the stalks to lay its eggs—is the only insect pest that is apt to bother rhubarb. Damage can be trimmed away. Several different fungus diseases are common after a cold, wet spring. If your rhubarb suffers from leaf spots or collapsing stalks, remove and destroy the affected plant parts. Pull additional stalks, if necessary, to allow the plants plenty of room to "breathe."

Harvest

Give your plants a year to get established before you have a taste, then harvest sparingly. After that, you can enjoy a full harvest from spring through July, but take no more than half the stalks at one time. Harvest by pulling rather than by cutting the stalks to help avoid problems with rot. Unlike most food plants, rhubarb won't hold you to a harvest schedule. It will be there, ready to eat, when you get hungry for a rhubarb pie.

GARDEN TIP

♦ Rhubarb stalks that are exposed to a late freeze may not be safe to eat. Be cautious and discard any stalks that show signs of damage; new ones will soon grow to take their place.

Recommended Variety

'Valentine' is known for its bright red stalks. It is also blessed with resistance to disease and tends to produce fewer seed stalks than other varieties.

'Heritage'

Strawberry

Special Features

Strawberries are one of the easiest fruits to grow in your Midwest garden. You can choose from June-bearers that produce a heavy crop of fruit for two or three weeks in early summer, and newer day-neutrals that bear throughout the growing season. No matter which you choose, you won't have to wait long for a harvest of plump, juicy berries.

How to Grow

The best spot for a new strawberry patch is one that hasn't recently been part of the lawn. Grubs, which are usually more numerous in sod, can injure the roots of berry plants. Strawberries need well-drained soil where water doesn't stand. They also need sunlight for at least 6 hours a day. Avoid low-lying frost pockets, where early blossoms are most apt to be damaged. Spacing between plants is determined by which kind of strawberry you're planting: June-bearers, which spread quickly from runners, should be spaced 15 to 18 inches apart in rows that are 3 to 4 feet apart. Plant day-neutrals 6 inches apart.

Before planting, dig a 1- to 2-inch layer of compost or other organic materials into the soil. Set each plant in the ground so that the soil comes to the base of its crown (see illustrated Appendix). Fan out the roots, then cover them with soil. Gently firm the soil around each plant. Water gently but thoroughly. Immediately after planting, spread straw, shredded leaves, or other mulch on the soil around the plants to keep the soil moist, shelter the plants from wind, and control weeds. To help June-bearers put their energy into producing runners, pick off any blossoms that form in the first season. Remove the blossoms of day-neutrals for the first six weeks, then allow the plants to set fruit.

Care and Maintenance

Strawberries are shallow-rooted and can't go long

without water in dry weather. As fruit develops, be sure that straw or other mulch is tucked around the plants so that developing fruit doesn't touch the soil. When you have picked the last berry from the June-bearers each year, set the mower to cut as high as possible and mow off the whole patch. Spread a 1- to 2-inch layer of compost over the soil and wait: before long the surviving plants will generate a new and vigorous strawberry patch. If you're growing day-neutrals, replenish the soil in the fall with a fresh layer of compost, topped with additional mulch.

Harvest

To enjoy berries at their peak flavor, pick red-ripe fruit regularly. Keep disease problems to a minimum by removing any rotting berries from the patch.

Recommended Varieties

'Tristar' and 'Tribute' are the most dependable day-neutral strawberries for Midwest gardens. Some good June-bearers include 'Guardian', 'Jewel', 'Redchief', 'Sparkle', and 'Surecrop'.

Herbs

Special Features

Despite herbs' exotic reputation, most are easy to grow. All you need is a small patch of ground or a few pots in a sunny spot.

Herbs don't require coddling, and they can take all the hot, dry weather our Midwest summers can dish out. The plants don't require much fertilizer either. In fact, some gardeners claim that the least fertile spot in the garden is the best place to plant herbs; the strongest scents develop when the plants are grown on soil that isn't very rich.

Most herbs don't like "wet feet," so they thrive when planted in containers, where excess water drains away quickly. Be sure to choose pots with drainage holes. A few pots of herbs growing right outside the kitchen door make it easy to cut fresh sprigs to spice up your food. Another advantage of growing herbs in pots: at summer's end you can move the pots indoors and continue to enjoy fresh herbs. Herbs will also thrive in a raised bed or on a slope, since both spots provide the excellent drainage most kinds require.

Cilantro

Cilantro sprouts quickly when seeds are sown directly in the garden. For a continuous supply of leaves—a popular ingredient in salsas—you'll need to sow some seeds every few weeks because the leaves turn yellow when the plants begin to flower. Plants grow well in sun or partial shade.

Dill

Often called "dill weed," dill practically grows itself. Simply scratch a few seeds into the soil surface in a sunny spot and you can count on a dependable harvest of flowers, seeds, and leaves to perk up your soups and salads. Dill's one fault is that it eventually grows straggly and tends to flop over if not staked. Fortunately, the problem was solved with 'Fernleaf' dill, a 1992 All-America Selections winner. 'Fernleaf' produces compact, 18-inch-tall plants that remain green and attractive all season.

French Tarragon

Known for the anise flavor of its leaves, French tarragon is a hardy perennial that must be grown from plants, not seeds. Plant it in full sun in well-drained soil. Water in dry weather.

Mint

Both peppermint and spearmint are hardy perennials with a reputation for spreading aggressively. You can easily keep a plant within bounds, though, if you plant it in a clay pot and then sink the pot to its rim in the garden. In spring, divide each mint plant and repot it in fresh soil. The flavor of mints grown from seed is quite variable, so start with a purchased plant. Mint will thrive in sun or partial shade, but requires moist soil.

Oregano

Transplant young oregano plants to a sunny spot after the danger of frost has passed. This herb is a hardy perennial and will usually survive the Midwest winter as long as it's planted in a well-drained soil. Some plants labeled "oregano" are actually one of its mild-flavored relatives, so sniff a crushed leaf before you buy.

For peak flavor, harvest herb leaves before the plants start to bloom. If they get ahead of you, simply pinch off and discard the blooms.

Parsley

There are two types of parsley: curly parsley and the stronger-flavored flat-leaf parsley. Both are best grown as annuals. You can buy young plants in containers, or start your own from seeds. Soak the seeds in water overnight to speed up this slow-to-sprout herb. Plant parsley outside in sun or partial shade after the danger of heavy frost has passed. To harvest, cut individual stems at ground level. New stems will grow to replace those you cut.

Rosemary

A beautiful plant with dark-green, needlelike leaves, rosemary is a tender perennial. After the last spring frost, move it outside to a sunny spot. Because a plant must be brought back inside to survive the winter, rosemary is best left in its pot. Water cautiously: rosemary balks when over-watered or allowed to dry out.

To impart a wonderful flavor to grilled food, sprinkle several handfuls of damp, freshly picked herbs around the edge of the coals. Oregano, sage, and thyme are especially good for this purpose.

Sage

A must for seasoning poultry and stuffing, perennial sage has fragrant, gray-green leaves. When the danger of frost has passed, plant sage outdoors in a sunny spot. In the ground, it will live for years and eventually become a big, shrubby plant. If you grow your herbs in pots, you might prefer dwarf sage, which is only about 8 inches tall.

Summer Savory

Often called the "bean herb" because it makes a great seasoning for beans, summer savory grows rapidly from seed to an 18-inch, compact bush. The first sprigs are ready to pick about six weeks after planting. Sow some seeds every few weeks in summer for a continuous supply. A similar herb, winter savory, is a perennial that sometimes survives winter in our region. But herb purists generally prefer the flavor of the easy-to-grow annual.

Sweet Basil

A favorite for making pesto and seasoning tomato-based recipes, this annual thrives in warm weather. Plant young plants in a sunny spot after the danger of frost. Basil is also easy to grow from seed, but it needs an 8-week head start indoors. In addition to the commonly grown sweet basil, there are many other flavors, including cinnamon, lemon, and licorice flavors. You can also choose from big-leaf and dwarf varieties with green or reddish- purple leaves. Pinch off growing tips and leaves regularly to encourage the plants to make leaves, not flowers.

Thyme

There are many different kinds of thyme, some hardy and some not. All are creeping plants that require full sun and exceptionally well-drained soil. If plants start to look ratty, give them a shearing with the grass clippers.

Asparagus

Special Features

Asparagus is one of the easiest vegetables to grow, especially when you consider that one planting will likely last 20 years or more. The harvest of succulent spears is ample reward for the effort it takes to get an asparagus patch started.

How to Grow

Asparagus is usually sold bare root. Twenty to 25 plants will supply most families with plenty of fresh asparagus. The best time for planting is in early spring, as soon as the soil is dry enough for digging. Choose a spot that gets full sun and has excellent drainage. Horticulturists used to recommend digging a trench a foot deep, but most now agree that a depth of 6 inches is ample. Besides being less work the shallow trench also increases the harvest. Shovel a small mound of compost along the middle of the trench, then spread asparagus roots evenly over the compost mound (see illustrated Appendix). Allow 18 inches between plants. Water the asparagus immediately after planting.

Care and Maintenance

After the plants are up, spread a thick layer of shredded leaves, ground corn cobs or other mulch to control weeds. Replenish the mulch layer as often as necessary. Wait until late fall when the tops are completely dead to remove the foliage. Late fall is also the time to spread a layer of compost or aged manure an inch or two deep over the asparagus patch.

Harvest

Give new plants a year to grow, then begin harvesting the following year. There's no need to carry a knife to the garden to harvest; just snap 3- to 6-inch-tall spears off by hand. You'll automatically leave the tough part behind and avoid damaging any neighboring spears still underground. From a year-old patch, you can harvest for 3 weeks; harvest after that from older patches for approximately 6 weeks, then let the ferny tops grow to strengthen the roots for the next year's crop.

GARDEN TIP

◆ Fall cleanup of the asparagus patch goes a long way toward thwarting asparagus beetles, which overwinter at the base of the dead tops and under other garden trash.

Recommended Variety

'Mary Washington' is the long-time standard. Early and rust-resistant, it will give a dependable harvest for many years.

'Mary Washington'

Bean

Special Features

Fresh-picked green beans rank right up there with vine-ripe tomatoes as a superb treat. Luckily, it's easy to grow your fill. The big seeds are easy to handle and quick to sprout. You can choose between fast-to-produce bush varieties and long-lasting pole beans. Disease-resistant varieties will help you reap a successful harvest.

How to Grow

Plant bean seeds in the garden after the danger of spring frost. If you're planting a bush variety, you may want to plant another row of beans a month or two later to ensure a continuous harvest. Choose a spot where water drains away quickly and the sun shines most of the day. Go easy on fertilizer; too much nitrogen invites problems.

Care and Maintenance

Thin beans to stand about 6 inches apart. Help pole beans get started climbing on a fence, trellis, or other support, but don't handle the foliage when the leaves are wet. Bean beetles often require control in our region. You can ignore slight damage, but if bean leaves start to look like lace, it's time to dust the leaves with rotenone.

Harvest

Pick pods before the seeds inside them swell. Regular picking every few days encourages more pods to form.

Recommended Varieties

'Derby', a 1990 All-America Selections winner, is a disease-resistant bush variety that produces flavorful pods with slow-to-develop seeds. 'Blue Lake' is a highly productive pole variety.

GARDEN TIP

◆ If you have a new garden or haven't planted beans or peas recently, pick up a package of legume inoculant at the garden center. Before planting, soak bean seeds in a jar of water overnight. Then drain off the water, sprinkle in a little inoculant, and shake the jar. The good bacteria in the inoculant will help your beans grow better and produce more.

'Derby'

Broccoli

Special Features

One of the most nutritious fall vegetables, broccoli is also easy to grow. Like all members of the cabbage family, the plants make their best growth in cool weather.

How to Grow

Set plants out in spring, about a month before the last expected frost. To reduce the chance of disease, choose a spot in the garden where broccoli, cabbage, and other cole crops have not grown for the last three or four years. To grow your own transplants from seeds, give the seeds an early start indoors 6 to 8 weeks before outdoor planting time. You can also sow broccoli seeds directly in the ground, but an early indoor start will help the plants mature before the weather is hot. Dig the planting holes 18 to 24 inches apart and add compost and garden fertilizer to each hole. Set the plants at the same depth they were growing in their pots. Firm the soil around each transplant and water gently. To protect the plants from cutworms, put collars around their stems; recycled paper cups work well.

Care and Maintenance

Water in dry weather, and mulch to retain soil moisture. To grow a satisfactory crop you must control cabbage worms (the larvae of white butterflies). Most gardeners resort to spraying their plants, a job that must be repeated once a week. Use Thuricide® or another product that contains *Bacillus thuringiensis*. Known simply as *"Bt,"* it will kill the worms without killing anything else, such as the bird that eats a dying worm. If weekly spraying does not appeal to you, or if your schedule won't allow it, then simply

FOOD GARDEN: VEGETABLES

cover the plants with cheese-
cloth or one of the lightweight
floating row covers sold in garden centers.

Harvest

Harvest when heads are fully
developed but before any yellow flowers open. Use a knife
to cut the central head at a
sharp slant so that water will
drain off. Continue harvesting
side shoots throughout the
season. Scratch a little more
slow-release fertilizer into the

> ## GARDEN TIP
>
> ◆ If broccoli or cauliflower
> produces buttons rather
> than full-sized heads,
> blame it on stress, such as
> too little water or plants
> left too long in their packs.
> Broccoli will still produce
> many tasty side-shoots,
> and cauliflower sometimes
> grows a small central head
> in the fall.

ground around the plants in midsummer to give them a boost. In
extremely hot weather, quality is likely to be poor and the flowers
may open too quickly, but keep removing the side shoots. As soon
as cooler weather returns, the quality will improve.

Recommended Varieties

'Premium Crop', winner of a 1975 All-America Selections award,
and 'Packman' are outstanding varieties that produce large heads
followed by many good-sized side shoots. 'Small Miracle' grows
only about a foot tall and is perfect for small gardens and containers. The main head and side shoots are slightly smaller than
other varieties, but they're just as delicious.

Related Species

Cabbage, cauliflower, kohlrabi, brussels sprouts, and kale all
belong to the same family and share the same problems. Like
broccoli, they should be rotated to a different spot of the garden
each year. All require control of cabbage worms to produce a successful crop. In the Midwest, cauliflower and Brussels sprouts are
best grown as fall crops. Plants set out by midsummer mature in
cool fall weather. Brussels sprouts need a fall frost in order to grow
sweet and firm.

Carrot

Special Features

The soil in many Midwest gardens may not allow you to grow long, pointed carrots like the ones in the grocery store. But by choosing the right variety, anyone can grow sweet, crunchy carrots. If you have heavy clay soil, plant a variety with short, blocky roots. Nantes types produce some of the sweetest carrots you've ever tasted.

How to Grow

Plant carrot seed in spring about a month before the last expected frost. Dig compost into the soil before planting. Avoid fresh manure or a fertilizer with high nitrogen, which may cause forked or hairy carrots. After you scatter the seeds and cover them lightly, firm the soil with the back of the hoe or rake to keep the seeds in close contact with the soil. Firming also makes the seeds less likely to wash away in a hard rain. Thin plants to stand 2 inches apart. If you have trouble getting a good stand of carrots up and growing, try sowing a few radish seeds along with the carrot seeds. Radishes come up quickly and will break the soil crust for the carrots. In 30 days the radishes will be ready to harvest, making way for the still-growing carrots.

Care and Maintenance

Water carrots in dry weather to help prevent hairy roots. (Other causes of hairy roots include too much nitrogen, aster yellows disease, herbicide residue, and heavy, clayish soil.) Tuck mulch around the plants to protect the tops of the maturing roots from sunburn. Pull and dispose of any carrot with a yellow, stunted top that is growing in a tight, bushy bunch. The culprit is a disease called aster yellows, which is spread to healthy carrots by leafhoppers. Rotating your carrots to a different spot each year and fall cleanup will help combat the "worms" that sometimes attack carrots: wire-worms, weevils, and root maggots.

Harvest

Check days to maturity on your seed packet and dig carrots when the time arrives.

GARDEN TIPS

♦ Carrots need a little time to accumulate sugar, which is why the last carrots from the row tend to taste a lot better than the early thinnings.

♦ Plant carrots again in midsummer. Late carrots that mature during fall's warm, sunny days and cool nights are apt to be the sweetest of all.

Recommended Species

'Ingot' is a Nantes-type carrot that matures in 68 days. Its cylindrical roots are crisp and sweet. 'Little Finger' develops sweetness and a bright orange color early, so it's ideal if you'd like to harvest 3-inch baby carrots. 'Thumbelina', a 1992 All-America Selections winner, is an extra-sweet carrot the size and shape of a golf ball. This variety is ideal for growing in containers or in clay soil and is ready for harvest in 60 days.

'Thumbelina'

Corn

Special Features

Fresh-picked sweet corn has always been one of summer's greatest pleasures. Today's gardener has more choices than ever before, from the old standards to the new supersweet hybrids.

How to Grow

Plant sweet corn after the danger of spring frost. If you're planting one of the extra-sweet varieties, wait a bit longer; these seeds tend to rot if planted in cold ground. Plant corn seeds in groups, or "hills," spaced 2 1/2 feet apart in each direction rather than in a couple of long rows. This close planting helps pollinate the ears and produce full rows of kernels. Prepare each hill by spading in some slow-release vegetable fertilizer and a shovelful or two of compost. Start six seeds to a hill, with 2 inches between seeds. Thin to the three best plants after the seedlings are up and growing.

Care and Maintenance

Water in dry weather, and mulch to conserve soil moisture. Watering and mulching are particularly important when the silks first appear. If rain-softened soil and strong winds topple the corn, rescue the plants by straightening the stalks, then firming the soil around them with your foot. You can keep worms out of the ears by putting 5 or 6 drops of mineral oil on the corn silks just as they begin to brown. But since damage is usually confined to the end of the ear, it's easier to simply chop off and discard the tip, including the worm and the damaged kernels. Ugly gray or black growths on corn are a fungus called smut. Take a sack to the garden and prune the growths directly into the sack for disposal. This will prevent them from bursting and spreading the disease.

Harvest

When the silks are brown and dried and the ears are firm and fat, it's time to enjoy the feast. Depending on how hot the weather is, corn is usually ready 2 to 3 weeks after silks begin to form. Some gardeners like to use the thumbnail rule as a final test: Puncture a kernel with your thumbnail; if the corn is ready, a milky juice will squirt out. But the old thumbnail test doesn't apply to some of today's extra-sweet varieties, which have juice that is clear, not milky.

> ## GARDEN TIP
>
> ◆ To keep raccoons from raiding your corn patch, plant vining crops such as melons, cucumbers, or squash around its perimeter. By the time the ears begin to ripen and the raccoons are tempted, the vines will have grown into a jungle that looks too tricky to cross.

Recommended Varieties

For a long-lasting harvest, plant both an early and late variety. A good pair: 'Early Xtra Sweet', a 1971 All-America Selection award winner, and 'Silver King', an improved version of the ever-popular 'Silver Queen'.

'Silver Queen'

Cucumber

Special Features

You won't have to wait very long to harvest fresh cucumbers. Most varieties begin producing 50 to 60 days after you plant the seeds, and some cucumber varieties are ready even sooner.

How to Grow

Cucumber plants resent transplanting, so it's best to grow them from seeds. Wait until the soil is thoroughly warm and the chance of frost has passed. You may also want to make a second planting later in the season; any time through mid-July will give the vines plenty of time to produce before fall frost. Add a slow-release vegetable fertilizer to the soil before planting. Also add compost to the soil before you plant to help retain the moisture the vines need. Plant a "hill," or group, of four seeds together in a 12-inch circle. If you want to grow cucumbers in a pot, use a 12-inch container that's at least a foot deep; this will be big enough to grow four bush-type cucumber vines.

Care and Maintenance

Cucumber vines require lots of moisture, so be sure to water the ground deeply in dry weather. Provide a trellis or other support for the vines to climb; you'll be rewarded with fruits that are straight, not curled.

The biggest bugaboo cucumbers face in the Midwest is bacterial wilt, a disease spread by cucumber beetles. Stressed plants are more likely to attract the beetles, so keep the soil moist. If the beetles appear (they're yellow and about the size of ladybugs), spray or dust the plants with rotenone.

Harvest

Pick cucumbers as soon as they're big enough to suit you. If they get fat and yellow, toss them in the compost pile and try again. The more frequently you pick, the more the vines will produce.

> ## GARDEN TIP
>
> ◆ If the plants don't get enough water in hot, dry weather, the cucumbers may be bitter. Most of the bitterness is concentrated in the stem end, so slice it off before you eat.

Recommended Varieties

'Bush Pickle' is small enough to grow in a pot and produces plenty of 3- to 4-inch picklers. 'Fanfare', winner of a 1994 All-America Selections award, is a disease-resistant compact variety that produces full-size slicers.

'Bush Pickle'

Eggplant

Special Features

Purple flowers and velvety leaves make eggplant one of the prettiest plants in the vegetable garden. The fruits come in many colors, shapes, and sizes. They may be purple, black, white, or pink; shaped like pears, eggs, or cylinders; and vary in size from 2-inch miniatures to 10-inch giants.

How to Grow

Set out plants in a sunny spot after the danger of spring frost. If you grow eggplants from seeds, plant them indoors about 8 weeks before the last expected spring frost. Keep them in a warm spot until they sprout. Space plants in the garden 18 to 24 inches apart. To reduce the possibility of disease, choose a spot where you haven't recently grown eggplant or its relatives (tomatoes, peppers, and potatoes). Add a shovelful of compost and a light sprinkling of slow-release vegetable fertilizer to each planting hole. Put a cardboard collar or other barrier around the stem to protect each plant from cutworms. Cover the soil with mulch to conserve soil moisture.

Care and Maintenance

Water if the weather is dry. If plants are loaded with fruit, you may need to add a stake for support. Leaves riddled with small holes are a sure sign of flea beetles, tiny insects that jump like fleas when disturbed. Damaged leaves dry up and fall off, affecting the plant's health as well as its beauty. Sometimes control is as simple as hosing off the leaves in the sunlight. If this isn't enough, try spraying plants with insecticidal soap or dusting the leaves with rotenone in the morning while they are still wet with dew. You can also keep flea beetles off your plants with a floating row cover, available at garden centers.

Harvest

Just as soon as each eggplant looks glossy, press your finger against its skin. If you see only a very slight depression, cut the fruit from the plant with scissors. Don't wait too long to harvest; an over-mature eggplant is seedy and bitter. The more you harvest, the more the plants will produce.

Recommended Varieties

'Dusky' produces glossy-purple, pear-shaped fruits 56 days after transplanting. 'Imperial Black Beauty' has dark-purple oval fruits and is ready to harvest 80 to 85 days after transplanting.

Lettuce

Special Features

No salad bar can compare with a big bowl of fresh, home-grown greens. Dozens of different lettuces—many of them difficult or impossible to find in the grocery store—offer gardeners an exciting array of flavors, textures, and colors. You don't need a formal vegetable garden to grow your own salads: you can plant lettuces in containers or tuck them into flower beds. Unlike most vegetables, lettuce will thrive in partial shade as well as in full sun.

How to Grow

Lettuce grows best in cool weather, so plant it in early spring as soon as the soil can be worked. Plant a second crop a month later, followed by a third in August that will mature during cool fall weather. A 1-inch layer of compost dug into the soil will furnish all the nutrients lettuce needs. A little slow-release vegetable fertilizer will also do the trick. Leaf and butterhead lettuce seeds can be sown directly in the garden. Mix the seeds of dark-seeded varieties with a little sand to help you get a thin scattering of seeds and get the seed evenly covered with soil. Plant head and romaine varieties indoors about 4 weeks before outdoor planting time so they'll have time to mature before hot weather arrives.

Care and Maintenance

Water as needed to keep the soil evenly moist. When the seedlings are about 2 inches tall, thin the plants to leave 5 inches between leaf lettuce varieties, and 10 inches between butterheads. Mulch to conserve soil moisture. Mulch also eliminates the need to hoe, and thus helps protect the shallow roots from possible damage.

Harvest

Harvest leaf lettuce whenever the leaves are big enough to suit you. Pick off leaves individually, or shear off the plants an inch or two above the ground; they'll soon sprout a new crop of fresh leaves. Once the plants "bolt" (send up seed stalks), the leaves will taste bitter. This is the time to pull the plants up and toss them in the compost. Wait to harvest butterhead, romaine, and head lettuce varieties until they develop their heads, so you can enjoy their crunchy, light-colored interiors. Harvest these lettuces by cutting them off at ground level.

> ## GARDEN TIP
>
> ◆ You can grow an assortment of salad greens without buying a lot of seed packets. "Mesclun" is a mixture of many different kinds that comes in a single packet. Make small successive sowings every couple of weeks for a continuous supply of fresh, young leaves.

Recommended Varieties

The lime-green color of 'Black Seeded Simpson' has been a fixture in Midwest gardens for years. Now there's a new strain of this dependable leaf lettuce that's even better: 'Simpson Elite' is slower to "bolt" in hot weather. Both Simpsons are ready to harvest in 40 to 42 days. 'Buttercrunch', a 1963 All-America Selections winner, has earned a reputation as the classic butterhead lettuce, with a delicious buttery flavor and crunchy semi-heads. It's ready for harvest 55 days after sowing the seed. Growing head lettuce in the Midwest is a challenge: at about the same time the heads mature, the hot weather often makes them rot. But 'Mini-Green' succeeds where others fail, producing perfect tennis-ball-size heads in 75 days.

Melon: Cantaloupe and Watermelon

Special Features

Hot, sunny days are perfect for ripening melons. The more the sun shines, the sweeter the melons taste.

How to Grow

To get melons off to a fast start, plant seeds indoors in pots 3 weeks before the last expected frost. The roots resent disturbance, so plant three seeds per pot. When the weather is warm and settled, slide the soil ball out of the pot without disturbing the roots and plant all three seedlings as a group. You can also sow melon seeds directly in the garden, provided you grow a variety that will mature before September. Prepare planting holes 4 feet apart. Add a slow-release vegetable fertilizer to the holes before planting. Also add compost to the soil before you plant to help retain the moisture vines will need.

Care and Maintenance

Melon vines need lots of water, so water deeply in dry weather, and mulch to conserve soil moisture. Cucumber beetles and the bacterial wilt disease they spread are the biggest threats to melons in our area. Watch for yellow beetles about the size of ladybugs; if they show up, dust the plants with rotenone. To protect young plants from beetles, cover them with a floating row cover (available at garden centers). But remove the cover as soon as plants begin to bloom so that bees can pollinate the blossoms.

Harvest

Harvesting juicy melons is a gardener's delight; knowing when to harvest is sometimes a gardener's dilemma. As harvest time draws near, keep a close eye on the melon patch. Easiest to spot is a ripe cantaloupe, which turns from green to yellowish-tan as it ripens. A ripe cantaloupe will slip right off the vine into your waiting hands when you pull it gently. Ripe watermelons have a dull look with a yellowish underside. The tendrils closest to the melon should be dark and shriveled, and the stem should be dark and crisp. Some Midwest gardeners pride themselves on being able to judge the ripeness by thumping watermelons: a dull thud means it's ready for picking. Once in a while, even a ripe melon is a disappointment. Melons have poor flavor if the weather is cloudy or rainy when the melon is ripening, if the plant is diseased, or if the plant is growing in poor soil.

GARDEN TIP

◆ Before you cut into a cantaloupe, or muskmelon, push a fingernail into a "seam" on the melon's side. If your nail goes in easily without a crunch, the melon is ready. If not, give it another day or two on the kitchen counter before cutting it open.

Recommended Varieties

'Burpee Hybrid' cantaloupes ripen in about 85 days and have an outstanding sweet flavor and thick orange flesh. 'Crimson Sweet' watermelons ripen in 85 days, producing 20- to 25-pound melons with dark red flesh and a high sugar content. For a small "icebox"-type melon, try 'Sugar Baby', which produces 12-pound melons.

Onion

Special Features

Whether you want a juicy, sweet onion or a pungent bulb that will keep all winter, there are varieties that can deliver. You can start with seeds, sets, or plants, depending on what's most important to you. Planting small bulbs called "sets" is the easiest way to grow onions, but sweet varieties are not available as sets. Purchased transplants give a two-month head start but can be tricky to get established. Seeds are the most economical option and offer the greatest choice of varieties, but they require more work in the form of weeding and thinning.

How to Grow

The secret to growing big, sweet onions is early planting and plenty of fertilizer. The plants require a ready supply of nitrogen in order to grow big tops as early as possible: the larger the tops before the bulbs start to form, the bigger the onions will be. Plant onion seeds, sets, or plants as soon as the snow has melted and the soil is dry enough to work. Don't worry about the cold: onions are hardy to 15 degrees Fahrenheit and aren't hurt even if the tops yellow. Space plants and sets 4 inches apart. If you are growing onions from seeds, thin the seedlings to 4 inches apart.

Care and Maintenance

Water in dry weather and mulch to conserve soil moisture. Soil moisture is particularly important once the bulbs start to form: the sweetest onions have the most water content. Lack of water will stress the plants and may cause them to send up seed stalks.

FOOD GARDEN: VEGETABLES

Thrips may cause streaking, wilting, and browning in the leaves; spray plants with insecticidal soap to control an infestation.

Harvest

Harvest bulbs for fresh eating whenever the bulbs are big enough to suit you. If growing bulbs to store, wait until the tops die down naturally, then pull up the plants. Lay them in a single layer in a dry, shady place for several weeks, or hang small bunches in a dry shed or garage to cure.

GARDEN TIPS

♦ A raised bed is perfect for growing onions. The soil dries out more quickly, allowing earlier planting, and the onions get the good drainage they need to prevent the bulbs from rotting.

♦ Any onion that produces a seed stalk won't be a "keeper," whether you remove the stalk or not.

Sort out split or damaged bulbs to use right away. Cut the tops off the rest to within an inch of the bulbs, and store the cured onions in a mesh bag. To keep one rotting onion from destroying the whole batch, you can tie each one individually into an old pair of panty hose with a little space left between each bulb. Hang the bags in the basement, attic, or other place where they will stay cool (above freezing) and dry.

Recommended Varieties

'Mr. Society' onions grow into medium-large, sweet, yellow bulbs. 'Candy' produces sweet jumbo bulbs with white flesh. It is a better keeper than most other sweet varieties.

Pea

Special Features

Only a gardener can enjoy peas at their best. Once they're picked, both traditional garden peas and the newer sugar snaps lose their sweetness rapidly. For a super taste treat, pick peas shortly before you serve them. Better yet, eat them raw, right in the garden.

How to Grow

Because the plants thrive in cool weather, early planting is the secret to a bumper crop of peas. Plant garden peas as soon as the snow melts and the soil is dry enough to work. Wait a little longer, until a month before the last expected frost, to plant sugar snap peas; their high sugar content makes the seeds more apt to rot in cool soil. If you have rich garden soil, you don't need to add additional fertilizer to grow peas. Soak the seeds in a jar of water for a short time, then drain off the water and sprinkle a little powdered legume inoculant on the peas. Shake the jar, then plant the seeds. The beneficial bacteria in the inoculant will help your peas grow better and produce more.

Care and Maintenance

Provide stakes, branches, or other supports for the vines to climb. Water in dry weather, but try not to get water on the foliage. Mulch to conserve soil moisture and to keep the roots cool. Don't worry when the vines start to yellow and wither; it's natural for these cool-season plants to stop producing and die once warm weather arrives.

Harvest

Keep a close watch on garden peas: they have a way of getting too big and starchy when your back is turned. Garden peas are at their best when tiny and sweet, so pick the pods just as soon as they're plump. Sugar snap varieties—which are delicious to eat, pod and all—are at their best as fat, 3-inch pods.

GARDEN TIP

* If you're baffled about whether your garden peas are big enough to harvest, just face the sun as you pick: you'll have "x-ray" vision right through the pods.

Recommended Varieties

'Wando' garden peas produce a prolific crop ready to pick in just over two months. Plants stand up well to both hot and cold weather. 'Maestro' can be harvested slightly earlier and is known for its resistance to powdery mildew and other diseases. 'Sugar Snap', which made its debut in 1979 as an All-America Selections award winner, quickly became a favorite with gardeners, who love the sweet, edible pods. The vines grow 6 feet tall. 'Cascadia' is an earlier, shorter snap pea, with built-in resistance to disease.

'Sugar Snap'

Pepper

Special Features

With their bright green, glossy leaves and bushy shape, pepper plants are pretty enough to grow in the flower garden. They also perform to perfection in large pots. You can choose from varieties in a rainbow of colors, with flavors ranging from mild to fiery hot, and shapes from small and round to long and skinny.

How to Grow

Peppers are as easy to grow as tomatoes, but they require less space. After all danger of spring frost, set out plants in a sunny spot protected from wind. If you grow peppers from seeds, plant them indoors about 8 weeks before the last expected spring frost. Keep them in a warm spot until they sprout.

Space plants in the garden 12 to 18 inches apart. To reduce the possibility of disease, choose a spot where you have not recently grown tomatoes or peppers. Add a shovelful of compost and a light sprinkling of slow-release vegetable fertilizer to each planting hole. Place a cardboard collar or other barrier around the stem to protect each plant from cutworms. Mulch plants to conserve soil moisture and help prevent blossom-end rot.

Care and Maintenance

Peppers are drought-resistant but produce best if watered in dry weather. Some kinds of peppers grow large enough to need a small cage or other support when they're bearing a heavy load of fruit.

Harvest

Harvest peppers by cutting, not pulling, in order to avoid breaking a branch. You can harvest them before they're fully grown if you wish, but peppers allowed to mature on the plant will be both more colorful and more nutritious.

Recommended Varieties

'Jingle Bells' is first to fruit, with peppers ready only 60 days after transplanting. This compact plant is perfect for growing in containers and is a dependable producer regardless of weather. The little peppers are quick to ripen to red, with loads of both green and red peppers on the plant at once. For a bell-shaped stuffer, try disease-resistant 'Bell Boy'. The first peppers are usually ready to pick 70 days after transplanting. Habañero peppers are the hottest of the hot. If you prefer your hot peppers on the mild side, try 'Garden Salsa'.

GARDEN TIPS

◆ If your pepper plants don't have any peppers, blame the weather. The blossoms often drop off if it's too cold, too hot, or too windy. Small-fruited varieties are less apt to be affected than those with big, blocky fruits.

◆ Weather is also to blame if hot peppers aren't hot; the fruits need hot, dry weather to develop their full spiciness.

Potato

Special Features

If you've never tasted a fresh-dug, home-grown potato, you can't imagine how moist and flavorful a potato can be. With the many different varieties of seed potatoes available today, growing your own spuds can be a real adventure. In addition to old standbys like white 'Kennebec' and red 'Pontiac', you can also grow yellow-fleshed potatoes that look buttery without adding a single teaspoon of fat.

How to Grow

Plant potatoes in spring at about the same time when dandelions bloom. A week or two before planting, spread the tubers out in a single layer in a spot out of direct sunlight to sprout at room temperature. The day before planting, cut large tubers into pieces about the size of a hen's egg. Each piece should have two or three "eyes." Plant the pieces 12 to 15 inches apart and 6 inches deep. Add a slow-release vegetable fertilizer.

The best time to solve one particularly bothersome potato problem—a disease called scab—is before you plant. If your home-grown potatoes are usually covered with brown, corky patches, choose a scab-resistant variety, such as 'Norland'. To help control scab, don't spread any lime, wood ashes, or fresh manure in the patch. Planting the potatoes in a different part of the garden each year helps, too.

Care and Maintenance

Mulch to conserve soil moisture. The mulch also protects tubers developing near the surface from exposure to light, which can turn them green. Colorado potato beetles are a common pest in the Midwest potato patch. If your garden is small, pick off the fat red grubs and hard-shelled, striped adults. Smash any clusters of orange-yellow eggs you find on the underside of potato leaves. If your garden is large, spray M-One®, *Bacillus thuringiensis* var. *san diego*. It won't harm anything but the beetles.

Harvest

You can harvest new potatoes any time after the plants have flowered. Dig alternate plants in the row, leaving more room for the others to mature. If you planted your seed potatoes under a layer of thick straw mulch rather than soil, you can reach under the mulch and pick new potatoes without disturbing the plant. As they mature, potato plants die down. Dig as many as you want to eat fresh, but temporarily store the rest in the ground. Be sure to dig them up and bring them indoors before frost, though.

Recommended Varieties

'Kennebec', the favorite white tuber grown in this region, is resistant to late blight. 'Red Pontiac' is one of the best keepers. 'Yukon Gold', also a good keeper, is not quite as productive as the other two, but its superb flavor makes it a winner.

GARDEN TIP

◆ If space is limited, you can grow a bumper crop of potatoes in a vertical cage. Plant seed pieces 4 inches deep and 6 to 8 inches apart in a 2-foot-wide circle. Set a cage made out of poultry netting over the planting. As the plants grow, gradually add compost or soil inside the cage. Potatoes form between the seed pieces and the surface of the soil, so harvest is easy: Just remove the cage and sift through the loose soil for your spuds.

Squash and Pumpkin

Special Features

With a steady harvest of summer squash during the growing season and winter squash that can be stored "as is" the rest of the year, a gardener always has the makings of a tasty meal. Pumpkin—a close relative that grows like squash—makes tasty pies, though many gardeners seem more interested in growing either giant jack-o'-lanterns or tiny pumpkins for autumn decorations.

How to Grow

After the last spring frost, prepare a planting "hill" by dumping a bucketful of compost on a spot about 18 inches in diameter and turning the soil with a garden fork. Space hills for zucchini and other bush squash 3 feet apart; hills for full-sized winter squash and pumpkins should be 5 feet apart. Add a little slow-release fertilizer, then plant six or seven seeds in each prepared area.

Care and Maintenance

When the seedlings are up and growing, thin to three or four of the strongest plants. Water in dry weather, and mulch to conserve soil moisture. You may be able to thwart vine borers if you dust the base of plants once a week with rotenone from the time the vines start to "run" until mid-August. But if a vine suddenly wilts, you can be pretty sure there are vine borers tunneling inside the stem. Look for a pile of sawdust-like stuff near the base of the stem where a worm entered, and use a syringe to shoot some Thuricide® or other product containing *Bacillus thuringiensis* into the hole. Mound soil over the injured stem. Squash bugs, another serious pest of squash and pumpkins, require constant diligence: Lay a small board at the base of each plant. Lift the board in the morning and destroy any of the large, dark-colored adults you find. Scrape any copperish-colored egg masses from the under-side of the leaves. If the eggs have already hatched, dust the leaves with rotenone.

Harvest

Cut zucchini or other summer squash from the vine when they're no bigger than 8 inches long. Harvest winter squash and pumpkins when fall frost threatens, leaving stems an inch or two long. Winter squash and pumpkins will keep for months if stored on a shelf in a cool, dry place.

GARDEN TIP

◆ When squash bugs are a problem, here's a trick to help the next year's crop: After harvest, clean up most of the vines, but leave a couple of immature squash or pumpkins on the ground. Check in a few days; chances are you'll find dozens of squash bugs congregated beneath each immature fruit. Squash the bugs or knock them into a pail of hot water.

Recommended Varieties

Two of the best zucchini varieties for Midwest gardens are All-America Selections winners: 'Black Beauty', a 1957 winner, is a glossy dark green. 'Gold Rush Hybrid', a 1980 winner, produces bright golden-orange zucchinis. To save space in small gardens, plant 'Spacemiser'. 'Eight Ball', 1999 All-America Selections award winner, is a round variety. Harvest 2- or 3-inch babies, or let them grow big enough to hollow out to make serving 'bowls." For winter squash, try 'Early Butternut Hybrid'. It grows on space-saving vines and matures in only 76 days. Like other butternuts, it resists damage from vine borers. For the biggest pumpkins, plant 'Atlantic Giant'. For the smallest, try 'Jack Be Little'.

Tomato

Special Features

If a gardener grows only one kind of vegetable, chances are it will be a tomato. The reason is simple: You just can't beat a home-grown, vine-ripe tomato for flavor. Of course, not all tomatoes taste the same. Some people prefer the big, juicy beefsteaks, while others love sweet cherry tomatoes, or solid paste tomatoes, or heirloom varieties. Not all tomatoes are red, either: there are also orange, pink, purple, white, and yellow varieties. If the tomato that tastes best to you also happens to be packed with resistance to disease, you're in luck. It's a lot easier to grow a variety that stays healthy than it is to cure a plant that's infected with disease.

How to Plant

Plant tomatoes in a different spot in the garden each year on a 4-year rotation schedule, if possible. If your sunny garden space is too limited and you've had trouble growing healthy tomatoes in the past, plant your tomatoes in large pots filled with fresh soil. Standard-size varieties will thrive in a container that's 18 inches deep; small varieties will grow in 8-inch pots. A selection of young plants is available at garden centers in spring, or you can grow your own from seed started indoors about 6 weeks before the last expected frost. Dig several shovelfuls of compost into the planting hole; research studies have shown that compost helps plants resist disease. Add a slow-release fertilizer that is highest in phosphorus. Plant standard varieties a minimum of 3 feet apart after the danger of spring frost has passed. Cage or stake the plants, or put them near a fence so you can tie the plants to the fence for support.

Care and Maintenance

Cover the ground around each plant with damp newspaper sections, topped with a 2- or 3-inch layer of shredded leaves,

GARDEN TIP

◆ Watch out for walnut trees. A tomato planted within the reach of the tree's root is likely to succumb to walnut wilt before it produces even one ripe fruit.

grass clippings, or other mulch. This thick blanket will reduce the need for watering and weeding. It will also help prevent the spread of fungus diseases from soil to leaves, as well as problems with cracking, splitting, and blossom-end rot of the fruits. In dry weather, water the soil deeply without getting the foliage wet. Don't bother with pinching off tomato suckers that develop between branches: research shows that pruned plants are more apt to produce cracked, split, or sunburned plants. If leaves get spots, then yellow and die, clean out all the dead foliage; this not only makes the plants look better but lets in more air. Add a fresh layer of mulch. If the problem is severe, you may want to spray the plants once a week with a fungicide such as Bordeaux.

Harvest

For the best flavor, pick tomatoes when they're fully colored. If you pick them sooner, spread tomatoes out on a counter out of direct sunlight to finish ripening.

Recommended Varieties

'Celebrity', winner of a 1984 All-America Selections award, is one of the most popular in Midwest gardens. The medium-sized fruits ripen 70 days after transplanting. 'Early Girl' produces a dependable harvest of slightly smaller fruits beginning at least two weeks earlier.

Ground Covers

Ground covers solve many landscape problems. Unlike the lawn, they don't need mowing every week. Some will grow where grass won't, such as in poor soil or in the dry shade under trees. Others work well to control erosion and eliminate mowing on steep slopes. Many kinds spread into dense mats that discourage weeds.

Ground covers are beautiful, too. Many have colorful flowers, while others have showy foliage, sometimes with silver, white, or yellow markings. The plants also serve to blend the whole landscape together, especially when a single variety is planted in a large mass.

What makes a plant a ground cover? Often, we refer to low-growing creepers, like periwinkle and bugleweed, as ground covers; but any vigorous, spreading plant under two feet tall can qualify. Hostas, daylilies, and many other plants described in the perennial chapter are just as much at home when used to cover a large, troublesome spot in the yard as they are in a smaller flower bed.

If you want to grow a ground cover in the dense shade under a tree where nothing much grows, you need only scratch the surface lightly with a hoe before you plant. But if you're replacing part of the lawn with a ground cover, you must begin by killing the grass. One way to do the job is with a non-selective herbicide containing glyphosate, such as Roundup, but be careful not to spray it on the leaves of plants you want to keep.

Another way to prepare for planting is to blanket the ground with black plastic, sections of newspaper, or any cover that will exclude all light. When the grass no longer shows any trace of green, the soil will be easy to till. To prepare a weed-free planting area, till the soil shallowly, then repeat in a week or two; or you can leave the dead grass in place and dig the holes for your plants in the sod. That works especially well if you are planting on a slope, where tilled soil might wash away in a heavy rain.

How far apart should the planting holes be? It depends: How vigorously does your chosen variety spread? How big are the containers in which the plants are growing? How fast do you want complete coverage? How much can you afford to spend? As a general rule, ground covers growing in 4-inch pots should be planted 12 to 18 inches apart. Fast-spreading plants in large containers can be planted two to four feet apart.

As soon as you finish planting, water the plants, then spread shredded bark or other weed-free mulch two inches deep between the plants to help control weeds. It takes most ground covers two or three years to completely cover the ground, but it's worth the wait.

No matter what kind of landscape problem you have, chances are one of the hardy plants described in this chapter can help you solve it. Whether your site is wet or dry, in dense shade or full sun, you're sure to find a ground cover that is up to the challenge.

Barrenwort

Epimedium × rubrum

OTHER COMMON NAMES:
Red Barrenwort, Bishop's Hat

ZONES: 4 to 8

BLOOM TIME: April and May

BLOOM COLOR: Red

LIGHT REQUIREMENT:
Full to partial shade

HEIGHT × WIDTH: 8 to 12 inches × 12 to 18 inches

Special Features

In spring, dainty red flowers that look like tiny columbine blossoms hover just above handsome clumps of heart-shaped leaves. The red-tinged spring foliage turns to dark green in summer, then to bronze in autumn, with color often persisting through December or even beyond. Barrenwort makes an ideal ground cover to plant beneath trees because the plants thrive in dense shade and, once established, can compete successfully with tree roots for nutrients and water.

How to Grow

Plant container-grown specimens any time during the growing season in fertile, well-drained soil. Space individual plants 12 inches apart.

Care and Maintenance

Despite barrenwort's reputation for surviving in dry soil, the plants grow and look their best if grown in moist soil. Water is especially important until the plants are well established. Spread shredded bark or other mulch to preserve soil moisture and

control weeds. Because barrenwort spreads slowly, the
plants rarely require division.
If you have older, crowded
clumps or want extra plants to
increase the area covered, you
can dig and divide plants in
spring or fall.

Related Hybrids

There are many wonderful
kinds of barrenwort available,
all beautiful and well-behaved.

> ## GARDEN TIPS
>
> ◆ In early spring, clip the
> foliage back to the ground
> so you can enjoy the soon-
> to-emerge fresh leaves and
> attractive flowers.
>
> ◆ For a beautiful woodland
> garden, try combining
> barrenwort with ferns.

'Sulphureum' (a variety of bicolor barrenwort, *E. × versicolor*) is an
excellent yellow-flowered variety. Try white-blooming 'Niveum'
or lilac-pink 'Roseum', both varieties of *E. × youngianum.*

'Sulphureum'

'Niveum'

Bethlehem Sage

Pulmonaria saccharata

OTHER COMMON NAME: Lungwort

ZONES: 3 to 7

BLOOM TIME: April and May

BLOOM COLOR: Blue, pink, or white

LIGHT REQUIREMENT: Full to partial shade

HEIGHT × WIDTH: 9 to 15 inches × 18 to 24 inches

Special Features

Neat mounds of speckled leaves make an attractive ground cover all season. The clusters of bell-shaped flowers in spring are a bonus.

How to Grow

You can plant container-grown Bethlehem sage any time during the growing season. Plant in moist soil that is rich in organic materials such as decaying leaves or compost. Space plants about a foot apart.

Care and Maintenance

Keep the soil moist until the plants are well established. Continue to water in dry weather to help the plants stay lush and green and to decrease their susceptibility to mildew and leaf scorch. Control slugs with baited traps, or deter them with a barrier of copper strips or coarse sand sprinkled on the ground around the plants. If clumps of established plants become crowded, dig and divide them in late spring after blooms fade, or in fall.

Recommended Varieties

A collector's dream, Bethlehem sage comes in many different forms with interesting variations in both leaves and flowers. A favorite of many gardeners is 'Mrs. Moon', which has pink buds that open to bright-blue flowers, highlighting the silver-spotted leaves. 'Roy Davidson' has blue flowers and long, narrow, speckled leaves. For white flowers with silver-spotted leaves, plant 'Sissinghurst White'.

GARDEN TIP

◆ If leaves are diseased or damaged by midsummer, prune them off at ground level. Top-dress with an inch or two of compost and keep the soil moist. In a couple of weeks, new leaves will replace the old.

'Roy Davidson'

'Mrs. Moon'

'Sissinghurst White'

Bugleweed

Ajuga reptans

ZONES: 3 to 9

BLOOM TIME: May to June

BLOOM COLOR: Blue; sometimes white or purple

LIGHT REQUIREMENT: Full sun to partial shade

HEIGHT × WIDTH: 4 to 8 inches × 24 inches or more

Special Features

Bugleweed is a vigorous spreader that quickly carpets the ground and successfully competes with weeds. Bees love the attractive 4- to 6-inch flower spikes. The foliage is attractive year-round.

How to Grow

Bugleweed tolerates all types of soil as long as it is well drained. A location protected from the wind works best; otherwise, the plants may dry out and die during winter if there is no snow cover. Space plants a foot or more apart, depending on how fast you want them to completely cover the ground. Plant any time during the growing season.

Care and Maintenance

Water plants regularly until they are well established. Mulch to conserve soil moisture. After that, this tough plant can take care of itself. Diseases and pests are seldom a problem. Cut back runners as necessary to keep the plants from spreading out of bounds. If the plants become too crowded or you want new plants to move to another area, you can dig and divide them any time during the growing season.

Recommended Varieties

The foliage of the species is deep green, but many varieties produce leaves of other colors. For bronze foliage, one of the best varieties is 'Bronze Beauty'. It has deep-blue flower spikes. 'Catlin's Giant' has huge, 8-inch-long, purple-bronze leaves. The leaves of 'Burgundy Glow' are a multicolored mix of pink, green, and white.

GARDEN TIPS

♦ Given half a chance, bugleweed will spread quickly into the lawn, so plant it where you can easily contain it.

♦ You can make a large area of bugleweed look better in a jiffy by using the mower to cut off faded blossoms.

'Burgundy Glow'

'Bronze Beauty'

'Catlin's Giant'

Creeping Juniper

Juniperus horizontalis

ZONES: 2 to 9

LIGHT REQUIREMENT:
Full sun

HEIGHT × WIDTH: 8 to
24 inches × 4 to 8 feet

Special Features

This attractive evergreen ground cover is a tough plant for diffi-cult sites and will thrive in hot, dry, windblown locations. Its trailing branches eventually form a dense mat, making creeping juniper an excellent ground cover for slopes. The green or blue-green foliage often takes on a purple tinge in the fall.

How to Grow

As long as it is well drained, creeping junipers tolerate any kind of soil, from heavy clay to the sandy, rocky soil that is their native habitat. Plant container-grown specimens any time during the growing season, spacing the plants at least four feet apart. Check for circling roots and untangle any you find before planting.

Care and Maintenance

Prune whenever creeping junipers threaten to outgrow their space. You can cut junipers back as much as you wish, provided you cut back to green foliage. Twig blight, a fungus disease that kills branch tips, may occur. If it does, prune and remove infected tips during dry weather. Avoid getting foliage wet when you water surrounding areas. If further control is necessary, apply a fungicide every 7 to 10 days throughout the growing season.

Recommended Varieties

There are dozens of creeping juniper selections. 'Blue Rug' (also called 'Wiltonii') has silvery-blue foliage and is one of the most popular.

Related Species

In the past, pfitzer juniper (*J. chinensis* 'Pfitzeriana') has been widely planted around foundations. Though these plants often grows 5 to 10 feet tall or more, annual pruning will keep them from blocking your view out the windows. Like other junipers, pfitzer branches can be pruned anywhere, as long as you never cut back further than the last green shoot.

GARDEN TIPS

◆ If you have an automatic sprinkler system, be sure the water doesn't fall on junipers. Overwatering these drought-tolerant plants encourages fungus diseases and root rot.

◆ For a plant that grows like creeping juniper but thrives in the shade, substitute Russian cypress (*Microbiota decussata*).

'Blue Rug'

Pfitzer Juniper

Creeping Phlox

Phlox subulata

OTHER COMMON NAME:
Moss Pink

ZONES: 3 to 8

BLOOM TIME: Mid- to late spring

BLOOM COLOR: Blue, pink, reddish-purple, or white

LIGHT REQUIREMENT: Full sun

HEIGHT × WIDTH: 3 to 6 inches × 24 inches

Special Features

Mounds of flowers cover low mats of evergreen, needle-like foliage in spring. Creeping phlox is ideal for the rock garden or retaining wall, or along the garden path.

How to Grow

Creeping phlox tolerates poor, gravelly soil, but a well-drained spot is a must. Space plants 1 to 2 feet apart, depending on the size of the container they were growing in.

Care and Maintenance

Water with an overhead sprinkler in dry weather to maintain soil moisture and help control spider mites. When the plants become crowded or their centers start to die out (often in three or four years), divide them after their blooms fade. Maintain fertility by adding compost or a slow-release organic fertilizer after you dig and divide the plants. Avoid quick-acting fertilizer, which often does more harm than good.

Recommended Varieties

There are many wonderful varieties available, such as 'Millstream Jupiter', 'Emerald Cushion Pink', and 'White Delight'. Many gardeners select creeping phlox by flower color, buying in spring when the plants are in bloom.

GARDEN TIP

◆ Mow or shear creeping phlox right after the blooms fade to make the plants look neater.

Related Species

Broadleaf creeping phlox (*Phlox stolonifera*) makes a superb ground cover for a shady spot. As its common name suggests, the small leaves are broad rather than needle-like. The plants, however, form a dense, low mat similar to that of the sun-loving species. 'Sherwood Purple' and 'Bruce's White' are two outstanding varieties.

'Sherwood Purple'

'Bruce's White'

Periwinkle

Vinca minor

OTHER COMMON NAME:
Creeping Myrtle

ZONES: 4 to 9

BLOOM TIME: Spring and sporadically throughout the season

BLOOM COLOR: Blue; sometimes white or purple

LIGHT REQUIREMENT: Sun or shade

HEIGHT × WIDTH: 4 to 6 inches × spreading

Special Features

This plant's evergreen foliage makes a thick, attractive carpet. Periwinkle is ideal for use on steep slopes or under shrubs and trees.

How to Grow

Plant in well-drained soil any time during the growing season. You'll get more blooms if you choose a spot in full sun, though the plants thrive in shade, too. To protect tips of plants from winter dieback, plant in a spot that is sheltered from winter winds. Space small starter plants 12 to 18 inches apart; place large clumps 2 to 4 feet apart. Water until plants are well established.

Care and Maintenance

No maintenance is necessary, but if you want to make a patch of periwinkle look neater, you can mow the plants in early spring with the mower blade set as high as possible. Periwinkle is drought tolerant, though the plants will flower more if you water in dry weather. To lessen the chance of disease, water early in the day so that leaves dry before sundown.

Recommended Varieties

'Bowles Variety' is an outstanding variety with large, bright-blue flowers that bloom over an extended period. The plants are somewhat slower to spread, which is an advantage in smaller areas where the species might be considered invasive. 'Sterling Silver' has violet blossoms and beautiful white-edged leaves. 'Atropurpurea' has lovely deep-purple flowers.

GARDEN TIPS

◆ Don't worry about fertilizing periwinkle. Excess nitrogen only encourages the plants to rot at the soil line.

◆ Underplant periwinkle with short varieties of daffodils, tulips, and other hardy bulbs for a spectacular spring show. After the flowering bulbs fade, the ground cover will help conceal the bulbs' foliage as it yellows and dies.

Related Species

Big-leafed periwinkle (*V. major*) is less hardy, with long-term winter survival only through zone 6. 'Variegata' is nevertheless a popular choice for containers and hanging baskets in colder areas. It has white-blotched leaves.

'Bowles Variety'

'Variegata'

Spotted Dead Nettle

Lamium maculatum

OTHER COMMON NAME:
Silver Nettle

ZONES: 3 to 8

BLOOM TIME: May to
August

BLOOM COLOR: Pink or
white

LIGHT REQUIREMENT:
Partial to full shade

HEIGHT × WIDTH: 6 to
12 inches × 12 to 24 inches

Special Features

The fragrant, silver-mottled foliage of spotted dead nettle lights up a shady nook. The whorls of flowers are an attractive bonus. Plants grow vigorously but in slowly-spreading clumps and are never invasive.

How to Grow

Plant container-grown specimens any time during the growing season. Space plants 10 inches or more apart, depending on the size you purchase. Spotted dead nettle grows best in moist soil, but it is tolerant of dry shade once established.

Care and Maintenance

Water until well established and during dry weather. Spotted dead nettle is usually free of trouble, but the foliage may scorch in sun or be infected with leaf spot or other fungus disease. Plants may also become floppy in hot weather. If your plants begin to look ratty by midsummer, simply shear them back to fresh leaves. Dig transplants or thin spotted dead nettle in either spring or fall. If you want to prevent reseeding, remove dying flowers before they set seed.

Recommended Varieties

'White Nancy' is favored for its beautiful silvery leaves and the outstanding white flowers that bloom spring through summer. 'Beacon Silver' is a popular pink-flowered variety.

GARDEN TIP

◆ Spotted dead nettle is also a beautiful trailing plant for hanging baskets and other containers. Once you have an established patch, use it as a source for spring transplants.

Related Genus

Yellow archangel (*Lamiastrum galeobdolon*), sometimes called false lamium, is similar to spotted dead nettle except for its yellow blossoms. The species is a fast-growing spreader suitable only for large areas, but 'Herman's Pride'—as well-behaved as it is beautiful—grows in slow-spreading clumps of attractive variegated silver-and-green leaves.

'Beacon Silver'

'Herman's Pride'

Sweet Woodruff

Galium odoratum

OTHER COMMON NAME:
Bedstraw

ZONES: 4 to 7

BLOOM TIME: Mid- to late spring

BLOOM COLOR: White

LIGHT REQUIREMENT:
Partial to full shade

HEIGHT × WIDTH: 5 to 8 inches × 18 inches or more

Special Features

Sweet woodruff's dainty white flowers contrast beautifully with its whorls of bright-green leaves. It is a delightful ground cover for a woodland garden. The dried leaves are often described as smelling like new-mown hay or vanilla. They are delightful in sachets or potpourris, and can also be used to flavor drinks or fruit salads.

How to Grow

Plant in moist but well-drained soil that has been enriched with shredded leaves, compost, or other organic materials. In zone 4, plant sweet woodruff in a spot that is protected from winter winds. Space plants about a foot apart. You can plant container-grown specimens any time spring through fall, though early planting allows more time for the plants to become well established before winter.

Care and Maintenance

Water when necessary to keep the soil moist, particularly if you want to encourage sweet woodruff to spread as fast as possible.

Pests and diseases are seldom a problem. If you live in zone 4, add a light layer of shredded leaves for winter protection. Divide in spring or fall if plants are crowded or if you want to get new plants for another area. Rake out dead tops in spring if they are unsightly.

GARDEN TIPS

◆ Sweet woodruff makes a lovely ground cover in the deep shade beneath trees. It thrives under evergreens and, unlike many other plants, it is immune to the toxins produced by the black walnut tree.

Wintercreeper

Euonymus fortunei

ZONES: (4)5 to 8

LIGHT REQUIREMENT:
Sun or shade

HEIGHT × WIDTH: 8 to
36 inches × spreading

Special Features

Wintercreeper is a vigorous, evergreen ground cover that also makes a fine vine, clinging to a trellis or other support by its clusters of aerial roots. Mature branches show off in fall with persistent reddish fruit.

How to Grow

Plant this adaptable ground cover anywhere except in soggy soil. Amend heavy clay with organic materials before planting. Space slow-growing dwarf varieties 10 to 24 inches apart, depending on the size of the container they are growing in. Space others 1 to 3 feet apart. You can plant container-grown plants any time during the growing season, though early planting allows more time for the plants to become established. To encourage faster spreading, use wire to pin runners to the ground where you want them to grow.

Care and Maintenance

Water to keep soil moist until plants are established. Prune as necessary to keep wintercreeper in bounds. Check plants periodically for scale insects; control when necessary with a horticultural oil spray applied in late spring and again in midsummer. Prune out and destroy any branches with large, irregular growths, a sign of crown gall disease.

Recommended Varieties

There are many different varieties available, variable in both size and color. One of the most popular is 'Coloratus', the purple-leaf wintercreeper, which turns from deep green to plum-purple in fall and winter. For a small, delicate dwarf, plant 'Minimus' or 'Kewensis'. Variegated varieties, though often not quite as cold hardy, have colorful foliage marked with cream, gold, or white.

GARDEN TIPS

- In dry weather, provide occasional deep waterings to keep the plants looking their best.

- For the best fall color, plant in full sun.

'Coloratus'

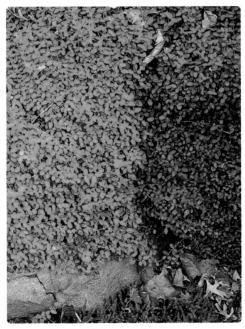

'Kewensis'

Ornamental Grasses

Ornamental grasses are appealing for many reasons. Their graceful forms are beautiful, especially when backlit by sunlight. Their swaying flower plumes and rustling leaves add movement and sound to the garden. They come in sizes to fit any spot, with heights ranging from tiny tufted grasses or low mounds less than a foot tall to giants up to ten feet tall. The flowers of many kinds of grasses are beautiful in fresh or dried arrangements, and the autumn colors are often spectacular.

During the winter, ornamental grasses are indispensable. Their gold and tan leaves and attractive seedheads often remain erect throughout our long, cold winters, adding their subtle beauty when we need it most.

Ornamental grasses are a brown-thumber's delight. Many are tough perennials that will thrive for years with little attention. Others are easy-to-grow annuals. Once established, most are drought tolerant. They thrive in lean soils, requiring little or no fertilizer. Pests and diseases are seldom a problem; even deer usually pass over ornamental grasses. Most can go for years without dividing. The only recommended routine care is easily done in early spring: Cut the plants close to the ground before new growth begins.

Removing the old foliage, a job once performed by prairie fires, is done more for appearance than out of necessity. The plants simply look better when they don't have dried brown leaves mixed with fresh green ones. The cleanup also helps grasses start growing earlier than they would otherwise. If your grasses are small varieties, you can do the job quickly with pruning shears or grass clippers. If your grasses are growing in thick clumps, use a weed whip or power hedge trimmer. If your grasses are naturalized in a wildflower meadow, just mow over the whole patch.

There are two ways to plant ornamental grasses. Many kinds, especially native prairie grasses such as little bluestem, Indian grass, and switch grass, are easy to grow from seeds planted on bare soil. That's the best planting method for a large area. You can also buy container-grown plants. In fact, if you want to grow some of the named varieties recommended in this chapter, you will have to start with container plants. That's the only way to be sure you'll get each variety's special attributes.

Some people miss the pleasure of growing ornamental grasses because they fear the plants might quickly spread out of control. It's true that a few such as ribbon grass (*Phalaris arundinacea*) and blue lyme grass (*Elymus arenarius*) are invasive; these are best planted in containers or on a slope, where their aggressive nature is needed to control erosion. But the vast majority of ornamental grasses grow in slowly expanding clumps, just like most other perennials.

Blue Fescue
Festuca glauca

ZONES: 4 to 8

BLOOM TIME: June

BLOOM COLOR: Gold

LIGHT REQUIREMENT:
Full sun, light shade

HEIGHT × WIDTH: 6 to
10 inches × 8 to 12 inches

Special Features

The low tufts of narrow blue-green blades contrast beautifully with the colors of just about any other plant. Blue fescue's small size makes it an ideal candidate for the rock garden and it retains some color throughout the winter. Planted along the sidewalk or street, its salt tolerance helps the grass survive runoff from de-icers.

How to Grow

Well-drained soil is a must for blue fescue's survival. Poor or average soil is a better choice than one that is rich and moist, and a sandy soil is preferred over clay. If your soil is heavy clay, lighten it before planting by digging in a 2-inch layer of compost or other organic materials. To develop the best color, blue fescue needs sunlight, but the plants have a difficult time coping with summer's heat in the Midwest. The best site will offer morning sun and then light afternoon shade to protect these cool-loving plants from the sun's heat in the hottest part of the day. Plant in spring so the plants will have a chance to become established before summer's heat arrives. Space the plants about 8 inches apart.

Care and Maintenance

Water in dry weather until plants are established. Mulch to control weeds and retain soil moisture. Cut plants back close to the ground in early spring. Unlike most ornamental grasses, blue fescue tends to be short-lived—but you can prolong its life if you dig and divide the plants every two or three years.

Recommended Varieties

'Elijah Blue' is one of the best blue fescues. It has beautiful silver-blue leaves that stand up to summer's heat without browning. If you want to grow blue fescue just for its leaves, plant 'Solling', a variety that bears no flowers.

GARDEN TIPS

◆ Some gardeners love blue fescue's nodding flowers, while others think they look ratty. If you prefer a neat, formal look, cut off the flowers as they form. You'll prevent unwanted seedlings and probably prolong the plant's life as well.

◆ Blue fescue's drought tolerance and small size make it an ideal ornamental grass for planting in a container.

'Elijah Blue'

Feather Reed Grass

Calamagrostis × acutiflora

ZONES: 4 to 8

BLOOM TIME: June through winter

BLOOM COLOR: Reddish-bronze, turning to beige

LIGHT REQUIREMENT: Full sun

HEIGHT × WIDTH: 60 to 80 inches × 30 inches

Special Features

One of the longest-blooming grasses, this vase-shaped plant makes a beautiful vertical accent in the garden. The graceful feathery plumes gradually take on the color and appearance of wheat. The plumes are excellent for dried bouquets (if you can bear to part with their beauty in the garden). Feather reed grass sails through summer's heat. It's a winter asset, too, often remaining upright throughout the season and even rebounding after being bent to the ground by a heavy snow.

How to Grow

Space plants 2 feet apart in ordinary soil or in soil that is moist and well drained. You can plant container-grown plants at any time, but planting in spring or early summer will allow them to become established in time for a good fall showing.

Care and Maintenance

Water until the plants are well established, and during dry weather even after they are established. Cut plants to the ground in early spring before new growth begins. When clumps become crowded, divide in early spring as soon as new shoots appear. A fungus disease called rust sometimes develops in wet years, but it is usually not severe enough to require any control.

Recommended Varieties

'Karl Foerster' is an outstanding choice for Midwest gardens. 'Overdam' is variegated, with leaves edged with cream or white.

GARDEN TIPS

◆ If you have clay soil, feather reed grass is an excellent choice for your garden; it's one of the few ornamental grasses that thrives in a wet, heavy soil.

◆ Put one plant in a tub or other large container. Although it probably won't survive the winter above ground, you can enjoy its long-season performance from June to March.

'Karl Foerster'

'Overdam'

Fountain Grass

Pennisetum alopecuroides

OTHER COMMON NAMES:
Perennial Fountain Grass,
Chinese Pennisetum

ZONES: 5 to 9

BLOOM TIME: August to
October

BLOOM COLOR: Pink,
turning to reddish-brown

LIGHT REQUIREMENT:
Full sun

HEIGHT × WIDTH:
36 inches × 36 inches

Special Features

The graceful fountain shape that gives this grass its name makes
a lovely garden accent. Fuzzy bottlebrush flowers add to the show.
In autumn, the foliage turns golden.

How to Grow

Choose a site with moist but well-drained soil, and enrich the soil
with compost or other organic materials before you plant. Space
plants 3 feet apart.

Care and Maintenance

Water in dry weather. Deadhead when flowers shatter in late fall
or early winter, but allow the foliage to remain for winter interest.
For winter protection, mulch the plants after the ground freezes.
Cut the leaves to the ground in early spring. If the clumps become
crowded or die out in the center, divide the plants when new
growth begins.

Recommended Varieties

'Hameln' is an excellent compact variety that grows about 2 feet tall and wide. For a still smaller version of fountain grass, try 'Little Bunny', which grows only about a foot tall.

Other Species

Purple fountain grass (*Pennisetum setaceum* 'Rubrum') is a popular annual, beautiful in large containers or in flower beds. Its reddish-purple plumes accent its burgundy foliage.

GARDEN TIPS

◆ Fountain grass may reseed if conditions are favorable. To prevent reseeding, deadhead before the plumes shatter.

◆ Fountain grass is not tolerant of heavy, wet soil. If your soil is clay, it's especially important to improve it by adding organic materials such as shredded leaves or compost.

'Hameln'

'Rubrum'

Indian Grass

Sorghastrum nutans

ZONES: 4 to 9

BLOOM TIME: August to late fall

BLOOM COLOR: Golden-brown, turning to burnt orange

LIGHT REQUIREMENT: Full sun

HEIGHT × WIDTH: 48 to 70 inches × 30 inches

Special Features

One of our region's beautiful native prairie grasses, Indian grass has blue-green leaves that turn to orange or yellow in autumn. The silky seedheads are lovely and long-lasting in the garden or in dried arrangements. Indian grass makes a tall, attractive accent plant.

How to Grow

Choose a site with well-drained soil. Dig compost or other organic materials into the soil before planting to retain moisture. Set the plants 2 feet apart in spring or summer, or sow seeds in May through August.

Care and Maintenance

Water in dry weather. Cut the plants to the ground before growth begins in spring. If the centers of the clumps die out, dig the plants when spring growth begins; discard the centers and replant the healthy shoots.

Recommended Variety

'Sioux Blue' boasts metallic-blue foliage in stiff, upright clumps.

GARDEN TIP

◆ To create your own beautiful mini-prairie, allow Indian grass to naturalize with native wildflowers. The grass will slowly spread by self-seeding.

'Sioux Blue'

Japanese Silver Grass

Miscanthus sinensis

OTHER COMMON NAMES:
Eulalia Grass, Chinese Silver Grass

ZONES: 5 to 9; some to zone 4

BLOOM TIME: Late summer to winter

BLOOM COLOR: Pink or silver

LIGHT REQUIREMENT: Full sun

HEIGHT × WIDTH: 36 to 96 inches × 24 to 60 inches

Special Features

The most popular of the ornamental grasses, Japanese silver grass is loved for its gracefully arching leaves and large pink or silver plumes. Its seedheads are a favorite for drying. Use a single plant as an accent or multiple plants for a living screen. You can count on the beauty of most varieties to last through the winter.

How to Grow

Plant in any well-drained soil in spring or summer. A rule of thumb: Space plants as far apart as their mature height (4 or 5 feet for most varieties). Allowing each plant plenty of room helps control the rust which sometimes develops on crowded plants in wet seasons.

Care and Maintenance

Keep the soil moist until the plants are established, and continue to water during droughts. Cut back nearly to ground level in early spring before new growth begins. If the center of a clump dies out, dig and divide the plant in spring when new growth begins. If the variety you chose is marginally hardy in your area, apply a 2- or 3-inch layer of mulch for winter protection after the ground freezes.

Recommended Varieties

Gardeners in zones 5 or 6 can choose from many beautiful kinds of Japanese silver grass in a variety of colors and sizes. Maiden grass ('Gracillimus') is a favorite with its narrow leaves and copper flowers. Porcupine grass ('Strictus') has yellow bands on green leaves. Unlike zebra grass ('Zebrinus'), another variety with yellow horizontal stripes, porcupine grass remains erect without staking. If your garden is in zone 4, you can count on two cold-hardy varieties to survive the winter: 'Silberfeder' (or 'Silver Feather') has large silver-white flowers that grow to a height of 6 to 8 feet; 'Purpurascens', also known as flame grass, is a compact 4 feet with silvery plumes. The leaves' reddish tint in summer gives way to a beautiful orange-red color in fall.

GARDEN TIPS

◆ A large clump of Japanese silver grass can be a chore to divide. To make the job easier, divide plants every four years. If necessary, use a saw or ax for the task.

◆ Don't accidentally use silver pampus grass (*M. sacchariflorus*). Unlike Japanese silver grass, this invasive member of the family spreads by hard-to-control rhizomes.

'Purpurascens'

Little Bluestem

Andropogon scoparius

ZONES: 3 to 9

BLOOM TIME: Late summer to fall

BLOOM COLOR: Bluish-white

LIGHT REQUIREMENT: Full sun

HEIGHT × WIDTH: 24 to 48 inches × 36 to 40 inches

Special Features

A native of the Midwest prairie, little bluestem has gently arching leaves that are often a mixture of greens and blue-greens. In fall the foliage turns russet-red, and the attractive color persists through the winter.

How to Grow

Little bluestem is an especially good choice for sandy soils, though it grows well in any well-drained soil. Space plants 3 feet apart, or sow seeds May through August in a well-prepared seedbed.

Care and Maintenance

Cut plants to near ground level in early spring before new growth begins. Dig and divide plants after new growth begins in spring if the centers are dying out. This grass tends to be floppy when it's flowering. To fix the problem, simply pull out the seedheads.

Recommended Variety

If you're looking for outstanding red color that will last from fall through winter, try 'Blaze'.

Switch Grass

Panicum virgatum

ZONES: 3 to 9

BLOOM TIME: Late summer to fall

BLOOM COLOR: Pink, purple, or red, turning yellow, then beige

LIGHT REQUIREMENT: Full sun

HEIGHT × WIDTH: 36 to 72 inches × 36 inches

Special Features

A native prairie grass with fine-textured deep-green or blue-green leaves, switch grass turns burgundy, gold, or orange-bronze in autumn. The large airy spikes of flowers in fall are excellent for cutting and drying. Later in the season, count on the beige leaves to add their subtle beauty to the winter landscape.

How to Grow

The plants grow well in any well-drained soil, but they prefer sandy soil to clay. Space plants 3 feet apart or sow seeds May to August. Avoid planting in either a rich soil or in too much shade, as both conditions make the grass more likely to flop.

Care and Maintenance

Switch grass plants are drought tolerant, but they'll grow taller if you water them in dry weather. Cut the foliage to near ground level in early spring before new growth begins. Divide crowded clumps in spring after new growth begins.

Recommended Variety

'Heavy Metal' has sturdy metallic-blue leaves that have an attractive yellow fall color.

Perennials

From the first Lenten rose blossom in March to the last fading monkshood flower in fall, a garden filled with perennials is constantly changing. Long before the weather is warm enough to plant annuals, early perennials are already blooming . . . and as one flower fades, another takes its place.

This constant change makes the perennial garden both interesting and challenging. Because most perennials bloom for only a few weeks, the challenge is to fine-tune your plantings over the years, working toward a parade of continuous blooms. But there is a short cut: include a few super-performers which bloom all summer, such as 'Moonbeam' coreopsis or 'Butterfly Blue' scabiosa, and even if you are a beginner you can have season-long color. Include as well some plants with terrific foliage that looks good all season, whether the plants are blooming or not. Ferns, hostas, and peonies, for example, all have attractive foliage.

A successful perennial garden begins by matching perennials to your site. If your garden bed is hot and sunny, for example, choose drought-tolerant perennials such as Russian sage and 'Autumn Joy' sedum. If your garden is a poorly drained area where water sometimes stands, select perennials that can stand wet "feet," such as Siberian iris. If you garden in shade, plant shade-lovers like astilbe and bleeding heart. In this chapter you will find all the information you need to help you place your perennials in a site where they will thrive.

The most attractive gardens include perennials with a variety of heights, with low creepers next to the path and tall perennials at the back of the border. Planting each kind of perennial in a group or "drift" of three or five plants often produces the most pleasing effect.

As pleasurable as perennials are, they don't deserve their reputation for being low- (or no-) maintenance. While it's true you can save work and money by not having to start from scratch every spring, perennials do have to be divided occasionally. If the plants have extensive root systems, as do daylilies, this routine maintenance is no small task (see illustrated Appendix).

How often is division necessary? It depends on the perennial. Some, such as peonies, can be left alone for years. Others, like chrysanthemums, do best when divided every spring. In general, perennials require division every three to five years.

Today's gardeners can choose from a huge palette of perennials, and there are many more available every year. The following pages describe some of the best for the Midwest. Be sure to also consider planting some of the region's tough and beautiful native perennials, described in the wildflower chapter. There's always a new plant waiting to be discovered. That's what makes perennial gardening so exciting!

Anise Hyssop

Agastache foeniculum

ZONES: 5 to 9

BLOOM TIME: July to September

BLOOM COLOR: Blue-violet

LIGHT REQUIREMENT: Full sun or partial shade

HEIGHT × WIDTH: 30 to 36 inches × 18 inches

Special Features

Bold, 5-inch flower spikes attract hummingbirds, butterflies, and honeybees. The blossoms are easy to dry. Erect plants have a strong vertical effect. The soft foliage, which smells like licorice or anise, is a favorite for tea or seasoning.

How to Grow

Plant container-grown specimens at any time spring through early fall, spacing plants 18 inches apart. You can also grow anise hyssop from seeds planted in spring. Plant in average garden soil that is moist but well drained. Plants bloom best in full sun but also tolerate partial shade.

Care and Maintenance

Remove spent blossoms to improve appearance. Plants self-seed readily, but unwanted seedlings are easy to pull. Pests and diseases are seldom a problem and require no control. If plants become crowded, dig and divide in spring or fall.

Recommended Varieties

Recommended varieties include 'Firebird', which has coppery-orange blossoms, and 'Tutti Frutti', with raspberry-pink flowers. 'Fragrant Delight' has stiff spikes of pale blue flowers. 'Snow Spike' grows wider and bushier, with white blossoms.

Related Species

Hummingbird mint (*A. cana*), stands 3 feet tall and has fragrant dark-pink flowers. Giant hummingbird mint (*A. barberi*) grows 5 feet tall and has lavender-pink flower spikes.

GARDEN TIPS

◆ Anise hyssop makes a great container plant.

◆ If you're a zone 4 gardener, you can still enjoy anise hyssop in your garden. The mother plants may succumb to winter's cold, but volunteer seedlings will replace them.

Hummingbird Mint

Astilbe

Astilbe × arendsii hybrids

OTHER COMMON NAME:
False Spirea

ZONES: 4 to 9

BLOOM TIME: June and July

BLOOM COLOR: Lavender, pink, red, or white

LIGHT REQUIREMENT: Shade or partial shade

HEIGHT × WIDTH: 24 to 48 inches × 15 to 30 inches

Special Features

Feathery plumes, outstanding for cut-flower bouquets or for dried flowers, light up the summer shade garden. The ferny foliage, a rich green with tints of bronze or purple in some varieties, enhances the garden even when the plants aren't blooming.

How to Grow

Plant container-grown specimens spring through early fall. Space plants 15 to 30 inches apart, depending on the mature size of the hybrid you select. Plants bloom best with filtered sun but otherwise thrive in full shade. Fertile, humusy, moist soil is best during the growing season, but it must be well drained to insure winter survival. Dig compost or other organic materials into the soil before planting.

Care and Maintenance

To prevent browning of leaves, water in dry weather and mulch to conserve soil moisture. When growth begins each spring, apply a general-purpose fertilizer and add a fresh layer of organic mulch.

Astilbes are heavy feeders; for peak performance, apply a liquid fertilizer once a month during the growing season.

Remove spent flowers if desired to improve appearance. Divide every three to five years in spring or fall. If you notice the white or gray dust of mildew on the foliage, thin plants to improve air circulation, and clean up dead foliage in fall. You can also spray plants with wettable sulfur or other fungicide when you first notice the problem; repeat the spray one week later. Insects are seldom a problem in this region.

GARDEN TIPS

◆ To add subtle beauty to the winter landscape, allow the dried flower spikes to remain standing in the garden.

◆ Dwarf Chinese astilbe (*A. chinensis* var. *pumila*) makes a great ground cover. The plants creep by means of underground stems and grow only 8 to 10 inches tall, with lavender-pink flowers in late summer. The plants are also more tolerant of dry soil than are other astilbes.

Recommended Varieties

'Bridal Veil' has elegant, lacy-white flower spikes in June that bloom against a backdrop of attractive bright-green foliage. 'Fanal' features red flowers in June and July, and dark reddish-green foliage.

Related Species

'Sprite' (*A. simplicifolia*), named the 1994 Perennial Plant of the Year by the Perennial Plant Association, grows 12 inches tall and has pale-pink flower spikes.

Balloon Flower

Platycodon grandiflorus

ZONES: 3 to 9

BLOOM TIME: Early to midsummer

BLOOM COLOR: Blue

LIGHT REQUIREMENT: Full sun or partial shade

HEIGHT × WIDTH: 24 inches × 24 inches

Special Features

Buds that look like miniature balloons are a favorite with children and grownups alike. The buds open to attractive bell-shaped flowers that are excellent for cutting. In fall, the foliage turns an attractive golden color.

How to Grow

Plant container-grown specimens spring through fall, spacing them 18 inches apart. Balloon flower thrives in well-drained soil of average fertility.

Care and Maintenance

Snip off dead flowers to improve appearance and promote continued flowering. To control flopping, you can stake plants, or cut them back by one half in late spring. Plants seldom require division and are best left undisturbed, since the long taproots make division difficult. If you attempt it, do it in spring. Balloon flower is seldom bothered by pests or diseases; no controls are necessary.

Recommended Varieties

'Mariesii', a compact variety that grows only about 15 inches tall, never requires staking. 'Sentimental Blue' is a true dwarf. Only 8 inches tall, it is ideal for growing in containers. If you'd rather have a white-flowering variety, try 'Albus', which has large, pure-white blossoms on 2-foot plants.

'Mariesii'

'Albus'

Beebalm

Monarda didyma

OTHER COMMON NAMES:
Bergamot, Oswego Tea

ZONES: 3 to 7

BLOOM TIME: Summer

BLOOM COLOR: Scarlet-red, pink, purple, or white

LIGHT REQUIREMENT:
Full sun or partial shade

HEIGHT × WIDTH: 24 to 48 inches × 24 to 36 inches

Special Features

Beebalm's attractive flowers attract hummingbirds, butterflies, and bees. One of the showiest of summer flowers, its blossoms are good for cutting. Leaves and stems smell like mint.

How to Grow

Plants require rich, moist soil. Dig compost or other organic materials into the soil before planting to help retain soil moisture. Plant 24 inches apart any time during the growing season, or sow seeds in spring.

Care and Maintenance

Water in dry weather, and mulch to conserve soil moisture. Snip off spent blooms to promote continued flowering. Thin out crowded shoots to increase air circulation and to help control mildew and leaf spot. If plants become infected, cut them back to the ground after flowering—clean new leaves will soon emerge. Divide clumps every two years in spring. Clean up foliage after frost to help control disease.

Recommended Varieties

Mildew-resistant varieties help to eliminate beebalm's chief affliction. An excellent choice for Midwest gardens is 'Marshall's Delight', which has pink flowers. 'Petite Delight', a new dwarf variety, grows only 15 to 18 inches tall, and has rosy-pink blossoms and good resistance to disease.

GARDEN TIP

◆ Beebalm spreads by rhizomes, so it's ideal for naturalizing. It can also be grown in a limited space because extra shoots are easy to pull out.

Related Species

Wild bergamot (*M. fistulosa*) is a prairie native with lavender-pink flowers. A white form (*M. fistulosa* f. *albescens*) demonstrated good resistance to mildew in trials at the Chicago Botanic Garden.

'Petite Delight'

'Marshall's Delight'

Bleeding Heart

Dicentra spectabilis

ZONES: 3 to 8

BLOOM TIME: Spring

BLOOM COLOR: Pink

LIGHT REQUIREMENT: Partial shade

HEIGHT × WIDTH: 30 to 36 inches × 36 inches

Special Features

Heart-shaped flowers dangle from the arching stems of this old-fashioned favorite. They are unsurpassed for their unique beauty and are excellent for cutting. The bright-green, fine-textured foliage is also quite appealing.

How to Grow

Bleeding heart makes an outstanding accent specimen in the woodland garden. Plant in spring in moist, well-drained soil enriched with compost or other organic materials.

Care and Maintenance

Water in dry weather to delay summer dieback. Cut stems to the ground when they yellow. Division is not necessary and is difficult because the roots are somewhat brittle. If you attempt it, divide roots after plants have entered their summer dormancy. Be sure each piece retains both a growth bud, or "eye," and a root. There are often a few volunteer seedlings you can dig and replant for extra plants.

Recommended Variety

Although the plants are not quite as vigorous, 'Alba' offers gardeners a pure-white bleeding heart.

Related Species

Two other related species (*D. eximia* and *D. formosa*) have the advantage of foliage that lasts throughout the season.

GARDEN TIP

♦ Surround plants with hostas, ferns, or other woodland plants. These companions will fill the gap left when old-fashioned bleeding heart collapses in the heat of our Midwest summers.

The flowering period is also longer, with some varieties blooming intermittently until early fall. It's a trade-off: the flower-form isn't as exquisite at that of the old-fashioned bleeding heart (*D. spectabilis*). An outstanding variety is 'Luxuriant' (*D. formosa*), which has cherry-red flowers throughout the season on one-foot-tall plants.

'Luxuriant'

Cheddar Pinks

Dianthus gratianopolitanus

OTHER COMMON NAME:
Clove Pinks

ZONES: 3 to 8

BLOOM TIME: May to July

BLOOM COLOR: Pink

LIGHT REQUIREMENT:
Full sun

HEIGHT × WIDTH: 4 to
12 inches × 18 to 24 inches

Special Features

Lacy and cheerful, the 1-inch daisylike flowers of cheddar pinks show off in early summer. Clumps of blue-green, grasslike foliage make a great foil for the flowers, as well as an attractive addition to the garden throughout the season. The blossoms of this old-fashioned favorite are good for cutting and possess a delicious, clovelike fragrance.

How to Grow

Plant in well-drained soil. Cheddar pinks thrive in the neutral to alkaline soils that are typical of much of the Midwest. Space plants 6 to 18 inches apart, depending on the variety you select. Cheddar pinks are also easy to grow from seeds, but the plants will be variable.

Care and Maintenance

Division is seldom required to keep plants vigorous. If needed, divide in spring, when new growth begins. Clean up dead leaves in spring. If leaf spot develops, apply a fungicide.

Recommended Varieties

'Bath's Pink', one of the best garden performers, has soft-pink flowers and grows about 10 inches tall. 'Tiny Rubies', a bright rose-pink, grows only about 4 inches tall. Silver-white spots and edges decorate the rose-red petals of foot-tall 'Spotty'.

Related Species

'Little Boy Blue' (*D.* × *all-woodii*) has white blossoms with pink centers, highlighted by beautiful silver-blue foliage. Many varieties of maiden pinks (*D. deltoides*) are also superb perennials for Midwest gardens. Try 'Arctic Fire', white with a red center, or 'Zing Rose', a 6-inch creeper with cerise-scarlet flowers.

GARDEN TIP

♦ After flowering, encourage new growth and spiff up your pinks in a wink by shearing off old flowers. Removing flowers before they have a chance to set seed will also prevent the variations of colors and sizes common with volunteer plants.

'Spotty'

'Arctic Fire'

'Bath's Pink'

Chrysanthemum

Chrysanthemum hybrids

OTHER COMMON NAME:
Garden Mum

ZONES: Variable, some to zone 4

BLOOM TIME: Autumn

BLOOM COLOR: Every color except blue

LIGHT REQUIREMENT:
Full sun

HEIGHT × WIDTH: 12 to 30 inches × 12 to 30 inches

Special Features

Chrysanthemems' endless variety of flower forms and colors dresses up the autumn garden.

How to Grow

Plant any time throughout the growing season, spacing plants 18 to 24 inches apart. If you want your mums to survive the winter, choose a site with well-drained soil.

Care and Maintenance

Water and mulch to keep soil moist, and apply a water-soluble or liquid fertilizer once a month throughout the summer. If you're growing a tall variety, stake plants. Better yet, limit the height by pinching off stem tips several times between late spring and the Fourth of July (see illustrated Appendix). If aphids or spider mites attack, apply insecticidal soap. After fall frost, cut plants back to 6 or 8 inches. Mulch after the ground freezes. Divide plants every year in spring, discarding their woody centers.

Recommended Varieties

There are many wonderful chrysanthemums available, but their winter hardiness is quite variable. If it's important to you to have mums that behave as true perennials, choose a super-hardy variety like yellow-blooming 'Mary Stoker'; or try 'Clara Curtis', which covers itself with yellow-centered, pink, daisy-like flowers. Both are hardy through zone 4. 'Clara Curtis' is unusual for a mum: it spreads by rhizomes and often blooms from midsummer to frost.

GARDEN TIP

♦ Chrysanthemums require full sun, but that doesn't mean you can't enjoy these fall beauties in a shade garden. Once flower buds are set, mums can be planted anywhere you want them, sun or shade. Buy at the garden center in autumn, or set out young plants in the spring in your own sunny garden. Chrysanthemums transplant easily, even when in full bloom.

'Mary Stoker'

'Clara Curtis'

Columbine

Aquilegia hybrids

ZONES: 2 to 9

BLOOM TIME: May to June

BLOOM COLOR: Blue, lavender, pink, red, white, or yellow; often bicolored

LIGHT REQUIREMENT: Partial shade

HEIGHT × WIDTH: 6 to 36 inches × 6 to 24 inches

Special Features

Unique spurred flowers are a favorite for cutting. Hummingbirds love the blossoms, too. Airy-appearing plants make fine partners for other garden perennials.

How to Grow

Plant in moist, well-drained soil, spacing most varieties 12 to 18 inches apart, or sow seeds in spring. Either way, you can expect blooms the second spring. In the Midwest, plants do best with afternoon shade.

Care and Maintenance

Mulch to conserve soil moisture. If you're growing one of the tall varieties, you may need to stake the plants when they are blooming. After blooms fade, cut flowering stalks to the ground. If you want to prevent volunteer seedlings with their varying colors and sizes, remove dying flowers before they drop seed. Division is not necessary because plants are normally short-lived. If leaf miners make wavy tracks through the leaves, simply pick off and destroy the affected leaves. If mildew occurs, thin out plants to improve air circulation.

Recommended Varieties

If you want to attract hummingbirds, you can't beat red varieties such as 'Crimson Star'. The Music Hybrids ('Musik') offer an exciting mix of colors and compact plants.

GARDEN TIP

◆ Although columbines are short-lived, these handsome perennials will naturalize in the woodland garden if you allow them to self-seed.

Related Species

The red-and-yellow native species (*A. canadensis*) is also great for attracting hummingbirds. 'Mini-Star' (*A. flabellata*), which stands only 6 inches tall and has bright blue flowers, is an excellent choice for the rock garden.

'Music Box'

Coral Bells

Heuchera hybrids

OTHER COMMON NAME:
Alumroot

ZONES: 3 to 9

BLOOM TIME: Late spring to late summer, depending on variety

BLOOM COLOR: Coral, cream, pink, red, salmon, scarlet, or white

LIGHT REQUIREMENT: Full sun or partial shade

HEIGHT × WIDTH: 12 to 24 inches × 12 to 24 inches

Special Features

Dainty bell-shaped flowers float on wiry stems above low, mounded foliage. Some varieties are grown not for their flowers but for their colorful foliage that may be ruffled or deeply lobed, with contrasting marbling or veins. The blossoms attract hummingbirds and make long-lasting cut flowers.

How to Grow

Plant in moist but well-drained soil that is enriched with compost or other organic materials. Space plants 12 to 24 inches apart, depending on variety. Container-grown plants are best set out in spring or early summer so they'll have a chance to become well established by winter.

Care and Maintenance

Remove spent flowers to prolong the bloom season. Pick off faded top leaves in late summer—you'll find a new layer of colorful leaves below. Remove dead leaves in spring. Every three or four years in spring, divide plants and discard the woody centers of each clump.

Recommended Varieties

'Bressingham Hybrids' bloom in a pleasing mix of pink, rose, dark red, and white, and have attractive green foliage.

'Splendens' is a popular bright scarlet-red choice. 'Firefly' has a light fragrance and pretty vermilion-red flowers. 'Palace Purple', named Plant of the Year in 1991 by the Perennial Plant Association, has small white flowers but is grown primarily for its colorful foot-tall mounds of reddish-purple foliage. 'Montrose Ruby', which also has white flowers, is noted for its pretty deep-purple leaves with silver marbling. Pink-flowered 'Snow Angel', introduced by Bluebird Nursery in Clarkson, Nebraska, features foot-tall mounds of light-green leaves mottled with creamy white.

'Palace Purple'

'Snow Angel'

Cranesbill

Geranium sanguineum

OTHER COMMON NAMES:
Hardy Geranium, Bloody
Cranesbill

ZONES: 3 to 9

BLOOM TIME: May and
June; sporadically in cool
weather until fall

BLOOM COLOR: Magenta

LIGHT REQUIREMENT:
Partial shade

HEIGHT × WIDTH: 10 to
15 inches × 15 to 24 inches

Special Features

These neat mounded plants with cup-shaped flowers and red autumn foliage are good candidates for the front of the border. They also make a great ground cover.

How to Grow

Space plants 15 inches apart in well-drained soil. The longest blooming period occurs when plants are shaded from the hot afternoon sun, but cranesbill also thrives in full sun as long as the soil isn't allowed to dry out.

Care and Maintenance

Mulch to control weeds and conserve soil moisture. Plants are tough and low-maintenance: division is seldom needed, and pests and diseases are rarely a problem.

Recommended Varieties

'Album' is an outstanding pure-white variety, and var. *striatum* is soft pink with crimson veins.

Related Species and Hybrids

'Johnson's Blue', a hybrid of the lilac and meadow cranesbills, is exceptionally long- flowering, with 2-inch blue-violet flowers. The bigroot cranesbill (*G. macrorrhizum*) makes a beautiful and undemanding foot-tall ground cover. Try 'Ingwersen's Variety', which has beautiful soft rose-pink flowers.

GARDEN TIP

◆ After flowers fade and plants start to look ratty, shear off old growth to expose clean, fresh foliage.

'Album'

'Johnson's Blue'

Daylily

Hemerocallis hybrids

ZONES: 3 to 9

BLOOM TIME: Varies, but peaks in July

BLOOM COLOR: Every color except blue

LIGHT REQUIREMENT: Full sun or partial shade

HEIGHT × WIDTH: 12 to 48 inches × 18 to 36 inches

Special Features

Trumpet-shaped blossoms and straplike leaves are handsome additions to the garden. Choose from hundreds of varieties, plain or ruffled, large or small; some are striped or bicolored.

How to Grow

Plant any time during the growing season, spacing most varieties 18 to 24 inches apart. Choose a spot with well-drained soil and dig a layer of compost or other organic materials into the soil before planting.

Care and Maintenance

Once established, daylilies are drought-resistant and long-lived, requiring little maintenance. You can make the plants look better, however, by snapping off dead flowers and removing yellowed flower stalks. In late summer, don't be surprised if you see many of the leaves turning yellow; this is normal, but you can spiff up your daylily patch by pulling yellowed leaves from the plants. If soil moisture is adequate, fresh new leaves will soon take their place.

When the number of blooms begins to decline (after three to five years), it's time to divide daylilies (see illustrated Appendix). An ideal time for the job is when the weather cools down after bloom time, though daylilies can survive division any time during the growing season.

GARDEN TIPS

♦ Plant red and purple varieties where they'll receive afternoon shade to protect the dark colors from fading.

♦ If you choose a repeat bloomer, you can help your plants bloom more by removing dead flowers before seedpods develop.

Recommended Varieties

There are so many beautiful daylilies to choose from that it's difficult to single out a few for special recognition. 'Hyperion', an old-fashioned yellow variety that is one of the most fragrant, is still a favorite. Its plants are large and vigorous, often growing at least three feet tall. If you want your daylilies to bloom for more than just a few weeks, however, try some of the rebloomers. 'Stella de Oro', with golden-yellow flowers, is one of the best and often blooms from spring to fall frost. Other popular rebloomers are lemon-yellow 'Happy Returns' and bright-red 'Pardon Me'.

'Stella de Oro'   'Pardon Me'

Ferns

Plant container-grown ferns throughout the growing season in dappled shade. Enrich soil with compost, shredded leaves, or other organic materials. Most ferns prefer moist soil, though some can take "wet feet" and others require well-drained soil. Mulch to conserve soil moisture. Water in dry weather.

Christmas Fern *Polystichum acrostichoides*

ZONES: 3 to 8

HEIGHT × WIDTH:
24 inches × 24 inches

The leathery evergreen fronds are great as holiday greenery. Plant in well-drained acid or neutral soil. Established plants tolerate dry soil.

Japanese Painted Fern *Athyrium nipponicum* 'Pictum'

ZONES: 4 to 8

HEIGHT × WIDTH:
12 to 20 inches × 20 inches

Fronds are "painted" in beautiful muted colors and have silver markings. Stems and veins are wine-red. For best color, plant in bright, filtered light. This fern requires moist, well-drained soil.

Leatherwood Fern

Dryopteris marginalis

ZONES: 4 to 8

HEIGHT × WIDTH: 36 to 24 inches × 36 inches

This fern has the deep-green fronds you're likely to see in florists' bouquets. Plants are erect with only a gentle arch. Plant in a spot protected from both sun and drying winds, and keep the soil moist.

Maidenhair Fern

Adiantum pedatum

ZONES: 3 to 8

HEIGHT × WIDTH: 18 inches × 24 inches

Graceful fan-shaped fronds are delicate and lacy, and they make pretty fillers in bouquets. Shiny black stems and golden fall color add to the plant's appeal. Plant in neutral to alkaline soil.

Foxglove

Digitalis grandiflora

ZONES: 4 to 8

BLOOM TIME: June and July

BLOOM COLOR: Creamy yellow

LIGHT REQUIREMENT: Partial shade

HEIGHT × WIDTH: 24 to 36 inches × 18 inches

Special Features

Charming bell-shaped blossoms droop from the tall spikes of this old-fashioned favorite. Foxgloves make a wonderful vertical accent in the garden and are also excellent cut flowers.

How to Grow

Plant container-grown plants any time during the growing season in evenly-moist, well-drained soil that has been enriched with compost or other organic materials. Space plants 24 inches apart. You can also grow foxglove from seed scattered on the soil surface after the last spring frost.

Care and Maintenance

Water and mulch to keep the soil moist. Removing dead flowers may promote new secondary bloom stalks. If necessary, trap slugs with bait. Other pests or diseases are seldom a problem. Divide plants in spring or fall if they become crowded after five or more years.

Recommended Varieties

'Carillon' is a yellow dwarf that grows only 12 to 15 inches tall.

Related Species

Common foxglove (*D. purpurea*) is a biennial that produces colorful flowers of pink, purple, red, white, and yellow. Strawberry foxglove (*D.* × *mertonensis*) is a rose-pink hybrid that is hardy in zones 5 to 9.

GARDEN TIPS

- For a steady supply of volunteer plants, let some of your plants go to seed in the garden.

- Some kinds of foxglove are short-lived, but you can count on *D. grandiflora* to survive winter in your Midwest garden.

Common Foxglove

Garden Phlox

Phlox paniculata

OTHER COMMON NAMES:
Summer Phlox, Perennial
Phlox, Border Phlox

ZONES: 3 to 9

BLOOM TIME: July to
September

BLOOM COLOR: Pink,
purple, red, or white, often
with contrasting centers

LIGHT REQUIREMENT:
Full sun or partial shade

HEIGHT × WIDTH: 24 to
40 inches × 20 to 30 inches

Special Features

Showy flower clusters are enormous, often growing 5 to 10 inches
wide. They are excellent for cutting and also possess outstanding
fragrance.

How to Grow

Space plants 24 inches apart in rich soil. Plant container-grown
specimens any time during the growing season.

Care and Maintenance

Water as necessary to keep soil evenly moist. Remove spent blossoms to promote continued blooming. Stake if needed to keep
plants upright. Dig and divide plants every three years in spring
or fall.

Mildew, a common problem in the Midwest, causes yellowing and death of leaves, and sometimes kills the entire plant. Thin
clumps to three to five shoots per plant to provide good air circu-

lation. Avoid overhead sprinkling. Choose disease-resistant varieties. Clean up and destroy plant debris in fall. If growing a disease-prone variety, spray once a week with fungicide.

Recommended Varieties

There are dozens of beautiful varieties of garden phlox. Where mildew is a problem, it pays to select disease-resistant varieties such as 'David', which has pure-white blossoms supported by extra-strong stems that seldom need staking. 'Eva Cullum' is also disease-resistant. It has lavender-pink flowers and red centers.

GARDEN TIPS

- Remove volunteer phlox seedlings. They seldom produce desirable plants and often crowd out the originals.

- If you have a tall, spindly variety that requires staking, cut back plants by about one half in late May or early June. Flowering will be slightly delayed but the plants will grow shorter and stockier.

Related Species

All varieties of meadow phlox (*P. maculata*) have built-in resistance to mildew. Flower clusters are slightly smaller and more cone-shaped than those of garden phlox. Their bloom time (June through August) is somewhat earlier. Some outstanding varieties of meadow phlox are 'Alpha' (rose pink), 'Delta' (white with pink eyes), 'Miss Lingard' (white), and 'Rosalinde' (dark pink).

Timber phlox (*P. divaricata*) is a shade-loving native wildflower. Also called wild blue phlox, woodland phlox, or wild sweet William, the foot-tall plants bloom in May. 'London Grove' (a compact blue bloomer) and 'Fuller's White' are two lovely named varieties.

Iris

Iris hybrids

OTHER COMMON NAME:
Bearded Iris

ZONES: 4 to 9

BLOOM TIME: Late spring

BLOOM COLOR: Every color of the rainbow, often with contrasting "beards"

LIGHT REQUIREMENT: Full sun

HEIGHT × WIDTH: 6 to 48 inches × 24 inches

Special Features

Showy flowers with fuzzy "beards" make lovely cut flowers and possess a delicious fragrance. Swordlike leaves add handsome structure to the perennial garden.

How to Grow

Choose a spot with well-drained, fertile soil. Plant container-grown irises any time, or plant bareroot rhizomes in July or August, when they are available. Space 12 to 15 inches apart and cover rhizomes with an inch of soil.

Care and Maintenance

To control borers and leaf spot, remove all leaves in early spring before new growth begins. Apply a slow-release fertilizer that is high in phosphorus. Remove flower stalks after blooms fade. During the summer, remove dead or spotted portions of leaves as soon as you notice them. Divide plants every three or four years (when the number of blooms declines) in July or August (see illustrated appendix.

Recommended Varieties

There are hundreds of beautiful bearded irises. The best way to choose is to pick your favorites when the plants are blooming.

Related Species

For low-maintenance irises,

> ### GARDEN TIP
>
> ◆ When planting an iris, place the end of the rhizome with the newest leaves pointing in the direction you want the plant to grow.

try the Siberians (*I. siberica*), elegant relatives of bearded irises. Their blooms open a bit later, usually in June, and the foliage stays lush and green all summer, unscathed by the leaf-spot diseases that may affect bearded iris. These plants grow well in moist soil and can tolerate "wet feet." Some favorite Siberian irises are deep-blue 'Caesar's Brother' and white 'Snow Queen'.

'Caesar's Brother'

'Snow White'

Japanese Anemone

Anemone × hybrida

OTHER COMMON NAME:
Windflower

ZONES: 5 to 8

BLOOM TIME: Late summer and fall

BLOOM COLOR: Pink or white

LIGHT REQUIREMENT:
Partial shade

HEIGHT × WIDTH: 24 to 36 inches × 24 to 36 inches

Special Features

Graceful flowers with a silky sheen nod above the lush maplelike leaves. The blooms are excellent for cutting, and the foliage is a garden asset all season long.

How to Grow

Plant in spring in fertile, moist soil which has ample organic matter and excellent drainage. Plants do best in a site with afternoon shade. Space plants 18 to 24 inches apart.

Care and Maintenance

Water and mulch to keep the soil moist. Expect little or no problem from pests or diseases. After the soil freezes, add winter protection with a covering of evergreen boughs or other loose mulch. Plants are often slow to emerge in spring, so be sure to mark their location. Division is seldom necessary; if you attempt it, divide plants in spring.

Recommended Varieties

Two of the most dependable varieties for zone 5 gardens are pink 'September Charm' and white 'Honorine Jobert'.

Related Species

Zone 4 gardeners can count on pink 'Robustissima' (*A. tomentosa*) to survive the winter.

'Robustissima'

'Honorine Jobert'

Lady's Mantle

Alchemilla mollis

ZONES: 3 to 8

BLOOM TIME: May and June

BLOOM COLOR: Chartreuse

LIGHT REQUIREMENT: Partial shade

HEIGHT × WIDTH: 12 to 15 inches × 24 inches

Special Features

The small, frothy flowers—good for cutting and for drying—are lovely, but this plant's main asset is its foliage. Morning dew sparkles like jewels on the scalloped, fan-shaped leaves. Plants are spreading and make an attractive ground cover.

How to Grow

Plant in moist but well-drained soil of average fertility. Space plants 10 inches apart.

Care and Maintenance

Water in dry weather. Hitting the leaves with a forceful spray of water will help deter spider mites. Division is seldom necessary. If plants become invasive, remove spent flowers before seeds drop.

Related Species

Mountain lady's mantle (*A. alpina*) is a dwarf version that has silvery 6-inch-tall foliage.

GARDEN TIP

◆ If plants become ragged-looking in midsummer, shear back to within several inches of the ground.

Lenten Rose

Helleborus orientalis

ZONES: 4 to 9

BLOOM TIME: March to May

BLOOM COLOR: White or dusky rose

LIGHT REQUIREMENT: Full to partial shade

HEIGHT × WIDTH: 15 to 18 inches × 15 to 24 inches

Special Features

The 2-inch nodding flowers appear in March, just when you need a breath of spring. Blooms become tinged with green as they age and are good for cutting. The dark-green foliage is semi-evergreen.

How to Grow

Plant in spring in a protected spot in rich, moist, well-drained soil. Space plants 2 feet apart.

Care and Maintenance

Water and mulch to preserve soil moisture. Prune off winter-damaged leaves in early spring. Remove any diseased foliage that develops when the summer weather turns hot and humid. Division is not recommended.

GARDEN TIPS

◆ Lenten rose is slow to establish, but it is also long-lived and dependable.

◆ For a spectacular late-winter show, plant Lenten rose with crocuses and other early-spring bulbs.

Monkshood

Aconitum carmichaelii

OTHER COMMON NAMES:
Wolfbane, Helmet Flower,
Azure Monkshood

ZONES: 3 to 7

BLOOM TIME: September
to October

BLOOM COLOR: Deep blue

LIGHT REQUIREMENT:
Partial shade

HEIGHT × WIDTH: 36 to
48 inches × 24 inches

Special Features

These plants get their name from their late-blooming flowers that
are shaped like tiny helmets or hoods. Their blue color contrasts
beautifully with the yellows of autumn. Monkshood is a wonderful perennial for the back of the border and offers old-fashioned
flowers that are long-lasting in bouquets.

How to Grow

Plant in rich soil where plants will not be forced to compete with
tree roots. Space plants 18 to 24 inches apart.

Care and Maintenance

Mulch to keep soil moist but avoid overwatering. Fertilize in
spring with slow-release fertilizer that is high in both phosphorus
and potassium. Stake tall, floppy varieties. Divide in spring or fall
if plants become crowded.

Recommended Varieties

'Arendsii' has strong stems that seldom need staking.

Related Species

The English monkshood (*A. napellus*) blooms earlier: its dark blue-violet flowers open in mid- to late summer.

GARDEN TIP

* All parts of this plant are poisonous, so avoid planting monkshood near areas where small children play.

'Arendsii'

English Monkshood

Peony

Paeonia hybrids

ZONES: 3 to 8

BLOOM TIME: May to June

BLOOM COLOR: Coral, pink, red, or white

LIGHT REQUIREMENT: Full sun to partial shade

HEIGHT × WIDTH: 36 inches × 36 inches

Special Features

Fragrant old-fashioned favorites, peonies are beloved both in the garden and in bouquets. Flowers come in an intriguing variety of forms and colors. Autumn foliage may be tinged with red or purple. The bushy plants combine well with other perennials, or you can use a single peony as a small shrub.

How to Grow

As long as the soil is well drained, peonies are long-lived and dependable. You can find many peonies still thriving on long-abandoned homesteads throughout the Midwest. Because a peony occupies its space for a long time, it's important to enrich the soil before you plant. Dig several bucketsful of compost or other organic material into a 3-foot-square area.

Plant in September, placing the root so that the pink buds, or "eyes," on the top of the root are 1 to 2 inches below the soil surface. Allow 36 inches between peonies.

Care and Maintenance

To help support the heavy blossoms, add a three-legged wire ring or other support in spring when new peony shoots are about one foot tall (see illustrated Appendix). To help prevent disease problems, cut to the ground and remove all the foliage after fall frost. Add a fresh layer of shredded bark or other mulch. This autumn cleanup is usually all it takes to control diseases, but if you still have problems with leaf spots or blighted buds, you can spray the plants with a fungicide in spring as soon as the shoots appear. The American Peony Society recommends repeating the spray two weeks later and again when buds appear ready to open. If an old, established peony is declining, dig and divide the roots in the fall. Replant in rich soil in full sun.

GARDEN TIPS

♦ An old gardener's tale says you need ants to "open" peony buds. Not so. Ants are seen on the buds simply because they like the sweet honeydew.

♦ When peony shoots are 6 to 8 inches tall, you can lay a 2-foot-square piece of welded-wire fencing material with 2-by-4-inch openings over the plant. As the shoots push up through the openings, the wire holds the stems upright (see illustrated Appendix).

Related Species

If you'd like something a little different, plant the fernleaf peony (*P. tenuifolia*). Red blossoms cover the dainty 20-inch clumps of soft, delicate foliage.

Fernleaf Peony

PERENNIALS

Perennial Salvia

Salvia nemorosa (superba)

OTHER COMMON NAME:
Sage

ZONES: 4 to 9

BLOOM TIME: Summer

BLOOM COLOR: Blue-violet

LIGHT REQUIREMENT:
Full sun

HEIGHT × WIDTH: 18 to 24 inches × 18 to 24 inches

Special Features

Salvia's attractive flower spikes and fragrant foliage are a delight in the garden for many weeks. These dependable plants easily shrug off the heat of the Midwest summer.

How to Grow

Space plants 18 to 24 inches apart, depending on the variety. Plant in well-drained soil; good drainage is the key to long-term survival. Be sure soil is not too rich or plants will be weak and floppy.

Care and Maintenance

Remove dead flowers to encourage blooming. If plants fall apart with open centers in summer, cut them back to attractive growth. Plants are drought-tolerant but bloom best if watered in dry weather. Insects and diseases are rarely a problem. Divide in spring if crowded.

Recommended Varieties

'May Night', named Perennial Plant of the Year in 1997 by the Perennial Plant Association, is a gardener's favorite. It has indigo-violet flowers on compact, 18-inch-tall plants. 'East Friesland', has dark-violet flowers.

Pincushion Flower

Scabiosa columbaria

ZONES: 3 to 9

BLOOM TIME: May to October

BLOOM COLOR: Lavender-blue, pink

LIGHT REQUIREMENT: Full sun, very light shade

HEIGHT × WIDTH: 12 to 20 inches × 12 inches

Special Features

A magnet for butterflies, pincushion flowers are one of the longest-blooming perennials in Midwest gardens. Low mounds of gray-green leaves topped by long-stemmed, graceful blossoms make an inviting border for a path.

How to Grow

Plant in well-drained soil, spacing plants 12 inches apart. You can plant container-grown specimens any time during the growing season.

Care and Maintenance

Water in dry weather, and mulch to conserve soil moisture. Remove dead flowers to improve the plants' appearance and encourage more blooms. Remove dead leaves before new spring growth begins. Division is not necessary unless the clumps show signs of declining.

Recommended Varieties

Two excellent choices are 'Pink Mist', which has pink flowers on 20-inch plants, and 'Butterfly Blue', a 12-inch-tall variety with lavender-blue flowers.

Plantain Lily

Hosta species, hybrids

ZONES: 3 to 9

BLOOM TIME: Variable, often in midsummer

BLOOM COLOR: Lavender, purple, or white

LIGHT REQUIREMENT: Shade, partial shade

HEIGHT × WIDTH: 3 to 48 inches × 3 to 60 inches

Special Features

A favorite for woodland gardens, hostas offer endless variations of showy foliage. You can choose varieties with green, yellow or blue leaves that are smooth or puckered, plain or variegated. The lily-like blossoms are sometimes fragrant, depending on variety.

How to Grow

Hostas grow in any good garden soil but are at their best when the soil is moist, well drained, and rich in organic matter. The dappled shade beneath high branches is ideal: it gives hostas the protection they need from the hot sun, and enough light to bloom well. Plant container-grown hostas any time during the growing season. Space according to the mature spread of the varieties you choose.

Care and Maintenance

Water when the weather is dry, particularly during hostas' first season. Provide a protective winter mulch for young plants after the ground freezes in fall. Apply a slow-release fertilizer in spring. Use baited traps to protect hosta leaves from damage by slugs and snails, or deter these pests with a barrier of copper strips or coarse sand sprinkled on the ground around the plants. Remove dead flower stalks to improve appearance. Pick off any dead or marred leaves in mid-summer. If clumps become crowded, divide plants in spring when new shoots emerge.

If the outer leaves wilt and yellow, inspect the center of the plant for obvious white fungal growth. That growth is a sure sign of crown rot, and—at this time—there is no cure. Remove the plant and the surrounding soil, and disinfect your tools in a 10-percent bleach solution.

GARDEN TIPS

◆ If your hosta leaves look scorched, the plants need more shade.

◆ 'Blue Angel' and other hostas with blue leaves require shade to remain true blue. Gold-leafed hybrids such as 'August Moon' respond to sunlight by glowing brighter.

Recommended Varieties and Species

With hundreds of different kinds of hostas available, it's easy to match their colors and sizes to your landscape needs. Two popular choices are 'Great Expectations', which is green with cream centers and white flowers, and 'Patriot', a lavender-flowered variety with dark-green leaves bordered with white. If you want loads of fragrant white flowers, plant the August lily (*H. plantaginea*) or one of its offspring.

'Great Expectations'

'Patriot'

Russian Sage

Perovskia atriplicifolia

ZONES: 4 to 9

BLOOM TIME: July to September

BLOOM COLOR: Violet-blue

LIGHT REQUIREMENT: Full sun

HEIGHT × WIDTH: 36 inches × 36 inches

Special Features

Airy and aromatic, the silvery foliage of Russian sage is covered with small flowers from mid to late summer. The care-free, bushy plants make a beautiful foil for other garden perennials.

How to Grow

Space plants 3 feet apart in well-drained soil. Plant container-grown plants any time during the growing season.

Care and Maintenance

Plants thrive in the heat of the Midwest summer and tolerate drought with ease. No controls are needed for pests or diseases, which are rarely a problem. Plants continue flowering without the removal of spent blossoms. Stake plants if necessary to keep them upright. Division is seldom necessary.

Recommended Variety

'Longin' grows to 48 inches and has less sprawl than the species.

GARDEN TIP

♦ Avoid rich soil and shade, which make Russian sage less able to stand on its own.

♦ Cut Russian sage back to the ground in early spring, even if above-ground growth survives the winter. A sturdier, more vigorous plant will result.

'Longin'

Shasta Daisy

Leucanthemum × superbum

ZONES: 5 to 9, some varieties to zone 4

BLOOM TIME: June and July, sporadically to frost

BLOOM COLOR: White with yellow centers

LIGHT REQUIREMENT: Full sun

HEIGHT × WIDTH: 12 to 24 inches × 18 to 24 inches

Special Features

The classic daisy, shastas are prized as cut flowers. In the garden, they form attractive clumps of dark-green foliage that is covered with prolific flowers for most of the summer.

How to Grow

Plant in spring in moist but well-drained soil that has been enriched with compost or other organic materials. Space plants 12 to 24 inches apart, depending on variety. Shasta daisies can also be grown from seeds.

Care and Maintenance

Water in dry weather, and mulch to conserve moisture. Apply a slow-release fertilizer in spring. Remove spent flowers to promote more blooms and improve appearance. After the ground freezes, apply shredded leaves, evergreen boughs, or other loose mulch for winter protection. Tall varieties may require support. Divide every two years in spring.

Recommended Varieties

If you live in zone 4, plant super-hardy 'Alaska'. 'Snow Lady', an All-America Selections winner in 1988, is a compact dwarf that grows only 10 to 12 inches, though there's nothing small about its 2½-inch-wide flowers. This variety is a good choice if you want to start shastas from seeds.

GARDEN TIPS

♦ Pinch stems back in late spring to force tall varieties to grow more compact and less floppy.

♦ Shasta daisies are often short-lived, but their versatility and beauty make it worth the trouble to replace them when necessary.

'Snow Lady'

'Alaska'

Speedwell

Veronica spicata

ZONES: 3 to 7

BLOOM TIME: June to August

BLOOM COLOR: Blue, pink, or white

LIGHT REQUIREMENT: Full sun

HEIGHT × WIDTH: 12 to 36 inches × 16 to 24 inches

Special Features

These easy-care plants are long-lived, and the colorful spikes make beautiful, long-lasting cut flowers.

How to Grow

Transplant container-grown plants any time during the growing season. Space plants 12 to 24 inches apart, depending on variety. Plant in average, well-drained soil.

Care and Maintenance

Cut plants back to side buds after flowers fade. Divide every four to five years in spring. Stake taller varieties that tend to flop. After blooms fade, shear back to fresh new leaves at base. Pests and diseases are seldom a problem.

Recommended Varieties

'Sunny Border Blue', named Perennial Plant of the Year by the Perennial Plant Association in 1992, grows into a sturdy 2-foot-tall plant. One of the longest-blooming varieties, it is often covered with navy-blue flowers from June through September. For rose-red flowers on a compact 14-inch plant, try 'Red Fox', another heavy-flowering variety.

'Red Fox'

GARDEN TIPS

♦ To force taller varieties to become more compact and sturdy, pinch off several inches from each growing tip in late spring.

♦ To grow sturdy plants, avoid planting speedwell in overly rich soil.

'Sunny Border Blue'

Stonecrop

Sedum spectabile

OTHER COMMON NAMES:
Live Forever, Showy
Stonecrop

ZONES: 3 to 9

BLOOM TIME: August to
frost

BLOOM COLOR: Pink, red,
or white

LIGHT REQUIREMENT:
Full sun or light shade

HEIGHT × WIDTH: 18 to
24 inches × 18 to 24 inches

Special Features

Stonecrop's beautiful flat-topped flowers are a highlight of the late-season perennial border, and they attract butterflies.

How to Grow

Transplant container-grown specimens any time during the growing season. Space plants 12 to 18 inches apart, depending on the size of the variety you choose. Plant in well-drained soil.

Care and Maintenance

Established plants are drought-tolerant and long-lived, requiring little care. Avoid excessive fertilizer, which makes plants grow weak and floppy. Divide in spring when clumps become crowded. Diseases and pests are seldom a problem.

Recommended Varieties

'Autumn Joy' ('Herbstfreude'), a well-known hybrid, has rose-pink flowers which gradually turn a beautiful bronze in fall. The 18-

inch-tall plants have blue-green foliage. Another favorite hybrid is 'Frosty Morn', which grows a foot tall and has green leaves with white borders. Its buds are pink and the flowers are pink or white, depending on the temperature. 'Vera Jameson' has dusky-pink flowers that beautifully complement the purple, foot-tall foliage. 'Ruby Glow' ('Robustum') is noted for its deep-pink fall flowers which top the 10-inch-tall blue-green plants.

GARDEN TIPS

- To keep tall varieties from flopping, cut plants back by half in late spring.

- When you clean up your perennial border at the end of the season, allow 'Autumn Joy' to remain. The dried flowers often remain intact and attractive until spring.

Related Species

Sedums include many outstanding varieties of low creepers that can be used for ground cover. Some popular choices are 'Dragon's Blood' (*S. spurium*), which has crimson flowers and red leaves in fall, and the yellow-flowered 'Weihenstephaner Gold' (*S. floriferum*). 'Variegatum' (*S. kamtschaticum*) is especially striking, with white markings on dark-green leaves.

'Vera Jameson'

'Autumn Joy'

'Frosty Morn'

Threadleaf Coreopsis

Coreopsis verticillata

OTHER COMMON NAME: Tickseed

ZONES: 3 to 9

BLOOM TIME: June to October

BLOOM COLOR: Yellow

LIGHT REQUIREMENT: Full sun

HEIGHT × WIDTH: 18 to 24 inches × 18 inches

Special Features

Bright daisylike flowers contrast beautifully with ferny foliage and provide summer-long color. The plants are long-lived and easy to grow.

How to Grow

Plant in average garden soil any time during the growing season. Space plants 18 inches apart.

Care and Maintenance

Shear to remove dead flowers after the first flush of bloom. A thorough fall cleanup is usually all that is necessary to eliminate problems with leaf spot diseases. Other diseases and pests are seldom a problem. Dig and divide in spring if plants become crowded and flowering declines.

Recommended Varieties

'Moonbeam' well deserves the Perennial Plant of the Year award bestowed on it by the Perennial Plant Association in 1993. The lemon yellow flowers bloom nonstop on attractive 18-inch-tall plants. 'Zagreb' has bright yellow flowers on somewhat more compact plants.

Related Species

Another species, *C. rosea*, has pink flowers.

GARDEN TIP

♦ Once they're established, these plants can be virtually ignored. They are drought tolerant and seldom need watering. Avoid excessive fertilizer—it just makes the plants sprawl.

'Moonbeam'

'Rosea'

Yarrow

Achillea millefolium

ZONES: 3 to 10

BLOOM TIME: June to August

BLOOM COLOR: Pink, red, or white

LIGHT REQUIREMENT: Full sun

HEIGHT × WIDTH: 24 to 36 inches × 18 to 24 inches

Special Features

The broad flower heads are wonderful for cutting or drying, and they complement the aromatic, ferny foliage. These easy-to-grow plants are tough and dependable.

How to Grow

Plant any time throughout the growing season in ordinary, well-drained soil. Space the plants 18 to 24 inches apart. You can also grow yarrow from seeds, but expect the colors and sizes of plants to vary.

Care and Maintenance

Cut off dead flowers to improve appearance and prevent reseeding. If mildew or stem rot is a problem, simply cut the affected stalks to the ground—new shoots will soon appear. Some varieties may require staking. Dig and divide plants in spring every two or three years.

Recommended Varieties

'Appleblossom' is a hybrid that is adored for its lilac-pink flowers. 'Paprika' produces ruby-red blossoms. 'Terra Cotta' flowers are bright peach and gradually turn the color of clay pots. 'Summer Pastels', winner of an All-America Selections award in 1990, offers a delightful mix of pastel colors. If you want to grow yarrow from seed, this variety is a dependable choice. 'Moonshine' is a hybrid with brilliant yellow flowers and silvery foliage.

GARDEN TIP

◆ Top-dressing plants once a year with compost will supply ample nutrients. Plants grow lanky and may spread aggressively in overly rich soil.

Related Species

'The Pearl' (*A. ptarmica*) has double white flowers and long, narrow leaves. It is more tolerant of shade than are most yarrows.

'The Pearl'

'Moonshine'

'Appleblossom'

Shrubs

Shrubs offer a gardener all the beauty of perennials without as much effort. Your reward for planting a single shrub is likely to be dozens—or even hundreds—of flowers, season after season. And your shrub, unlike most perennials, will maintain its vigor without any need for periodic digging and dividing.

But shrubs are more than beautiful; they're also real workhorses in the garden. They make a great framework, providing structure that remains throughout the winter when perennials have disappeared. You can use shrubs for a privacy screen or hedge, to direct foot traffic, or to hide the compost pile from view. Shrubs also make lovely backdrops for annuals or perennials, and create special niches for flowers that need protection from sun or wind.

By planting a variety of shrubs it's easy to create a garden that's beautiful in all seasons. In addition to the well-loved spring bloomers like lilac and forsythia, you can choose summer-flowering shrubs such as althea and summersweet. Some shrubs, including arrowwood viburnum and burning bush, dress for autumn in beautiful colors. Shrubs such as winterberry and barberry have small, inconspicuous flowers but produce colorful, long-lasting berries to brighten the winter garden and provide food for birds. Evergreen shrubs like arborvitae and yew provide year-round color that's especially welcome in the winter.

Shrubs come in sizes to fit every landscape need, from foot-tall selections of Japanese spirea to 15-foot witchhazels. When choosing a shrub, be sure to learn the shrub's mature size. If you allow enough room, you'll save a lot of work with pruning shears later on. Spacing plants properly helps prevent fungus diseases, too.

You can eliminate many pest and disease problems by matching each shrub to the site it prefers. Lilac and butterfly bush, for example, demand well-drained soil, while winterberry and summersweet thrive in wet soil. Hydrangea and yew perform just fine in shade, but shrub rose and potentilla need sun.

Shrubs are sold in three forms: bare root, balled and burlapped, and in containers. You can find tips for planting in the appendix.

Providing the nutrients most shrubs need isn't difficult. Just add a slow-release complete fertilizer (such as one marked 10-10-10) in early spring; or, if you prefer, nourish your plants by spreading a 2-inch layer of compost on the ground around them once a year. A few shrubs have special needs. Fertilizing instructions for these are noted in the following pages. Add a layer of mulch, such as shredded bark or leaves; the mulch will provide additional nutrients as it slowly decomposes and will also help preserve soil moisture and control weeds. Annual pruning keeps shrubs in peak form (see illustrated Appendix).

The plant portraits that follow include 22 favorite shrubs for Midwest gardens, along with dozens of recommended varieties.

Althea

Hibiscus syriacus

OTHER COMMON NAME:
Rose-of-Sharon

ZONES: 5 to 9

BLOOM TIME: Midsummer
to fall

BLOOM COLOR: Pink,
purple, red, or white

LIGHT REQUIREMENT:
Full sun to partial shade

HEIGHT × WIDTH: 8 to
10 feet × 6 to 8 feet

Special Features

Valued for their end-of-season color, these tall, upright shrubs
make a beautiful hedge or screen. Depending on the variety you
choose, the showy flowers may be singles or doubles with overlapping petals, measuring two to four or more inches across.
Unless you choose a sterile variety, your shrub will have ornamental seedpods for winter garden interest or dried bouquets.

How to Grow

Althea adapts to almost any soil as long as it is well drained. If the
shrub is borderline hardy in your area, choose a protected spot
and mulch for winter protection. Plant container-grown shrubs in
spring or summer so they will be well established before winter.

Care and Maintenance

Water regularly during althea's first season and thereafter in dry
weather. Apply a general-purpose fertilizer in spring. Prune in
early spring as needed to control size, increase branching, and
remove dead or damaged branches. If desired, you can prune the

shrub to grow as a small tree. Don't worry that spring pruning or a late freeze will reduce the number of blossoms, because althea flowers on the current season's growth. Remove dead flowers to improve the shrub's appearance and promote continued blooming. Deadheading will also prevent the formation of seedpods: good if you don't want volunteer seedlings, but

GARDEN TIPS

◆ Don't skip spring pruning or you'll end up with a tall, skinny shrub with all its flowers at the top.

◆ Give your althea time before you declare it dead in spring. This shrub is notoriously late to leaf out.

bad if you'd like the decorative pods for winter interest. In the Midwest, althea suffers from few pests or diseases. Aphids may occasionally build up in large enough numbers to distort the blossoms and the young leaves. These insects may excrete a sticky honeydew which encourages the growth of black sooty fungus. To prevent damage, control aphids with an insecticidal soap spray.

Recommended Varieties

There are four outstanding varieties that produce few, if any, volunteer seedlings: 'Diana', an early bloomer with pure-white blossoms that stay open all night; 'Helene', also white but with dark red in the centers that radiates out along the veins; 'Minerva', lavender with a pink eye; and 'Aphrodite', dark pink with red centers. Other favorites are 'Blushing Bride', with double, carnation-like flowers that emerge pink, then change to white; and 'Blue Bird', considered the best violet-blue variety.

Related Species

Hardy hibiscus, or rose mallow (*H. moscheutos*) is a showy perennial, not a shrub. Favorite hybrid varieties for the Midwest include pink 'Lady Baltimore' and red 'Lord Baltimore'. Chinese hibiscus (*H. rosa-sinensis*) is the evergreen shrub you've probably seen if you've traveled to a tropical climate. In the Midwest, it is a favorite for growing in outdoor containers in summer, but it needs an indoor spot near a sunny window to survive the winter.

Arborvitae

Thuja occidentalis

OTHER COMMON NAMES:
White Cedar, Eastern
Arborvitae

ZONES: 3 to 7

LIGHT REQUIREMENT:
Full sun

HEIGHT × WIDTH: 2 to
30 feet × 2 to 10 feet,
depending on variety

Special Features

With its pyramidal shape and evergreen needles, arborvitae makes an attractive hedge in all seasons. Though something of a cliché for foundation plantings, the shrubs are valuable for adding winter interest in the garden.

How to Grow

Plant in moist, well-drained soil in a spot protected from wind. Plant container-grown specimens throughout the growing season; plant balled-and-burlapped shrubs in spring or fall.

Care and Maintenance

Water in dry weather, and mulch to conserve soil moisture. To protect branch tips from drying out, be sure to water plants deeply before the ground freezes in autumn if it doesn't rain. If there is a mid-winter thaw, water again. Prune when arborvitae is actively growing in spring. You can shear as much as you want without harm, as long as you avoid cutting beyond green growth into the brown interior.

In hot, dry weather, use a forceful spray of water from the garden hose to dislodge spider mites; or control mites with insecticidal soap. If bagworms attack, handpick the brown, 2-inch bags from the branches any time between late summer and early spring. Spray "Bt" (*Bacillus thuringiensis*) in June about the time the Japanese tree lilacs bloom to control the caterpillars before they move into their bags.

Recommended Varieties

By choosing the right variety, you can avoid the disappointment of planting an arborvitae

> ## GARDEN TIP
>
> ◆ Don't be alarmed if you notice needles browning and falling in the autumn. It's normal for an arborvitae to shed two-year-old needles at this time.
>
> ◆ If deer frequently damage plants in your yard, you might prefer to substitute a juniper or dwarf spruce for arborvitae.

that turns an ugly yellow-brown during cold weather. 'Techny', selected in Illinois, is a popular, dark-green variety that grows slowly, eventually maturing at a height of 10 to 15 feet with a five-foot spread. Two other varieties that grow to about the same height and remain attractive in winter are 'Emerald', with bright, emerald-green needles, and 'Brandon', with a soft-green color. 'Nigra', sometimes called "dark green arborvitae," matures at 20 to 30 feet. 'Holmstrup' is a more compact arborvitae which grows only 6 to 8 feet tall.

'Techny'

'Brandon'

'Nigra'

Arrowwood Viburnum

Viburnum dentatum

ZONES: 3 to 8

BLOOM TIME: June

BLOOM COLOR: White

LIGHT REQUIREMENT: Sun or partial shade

HEIGHT × WIDTH: 6 to 12 feet × 6 to 12 feet

Special Features

Creamy-white summer flowers are followed by blue-black berries in autumn. The berries last only until they're discovered by hungry birds. Fall color—variably red, purple, or yellow—is often spectacular.

How to Grow

Plant in well-drained soil any time during the growing season. Water regularly until plants are well established.

Care and Maintenance

Water deeply once a week in dry weather. Mulch with shredded bark or other coarse mulch. Little pruning is needed other than removing dead or damaged branches and controlling unwanted suckers at the base. When mature shrubs become overgrown, renewal pruning (see Appendix) will solve the problem. Pests and diseases seldom require control.

Recommended Varieties

Three varieties from the Chicagoland Grows plant introduction program have proved themselves in the Midwest. Autumn Jazz®, as you might guess from the name, offers sensational fall color in a kaleidoscope of yellow, orange, red, and burgundy, while Northern

GARDEN TIP

♦ Bouquets don't have to come from a flower garden. Viburnum blossoms are perfect for cutting. Many are shaped like umbrellas, others like balls. They come in cream, pink, or white and are often deliciously fragrant.

Burgundy® is a rich blend of wine-red and burgundy in fall. The leaves of Chicago Lustre® don't change color in autumn, but the variety is exceptional for its glossy, dark-green summer foliage and ornamental clusters of blue-black berries.

Related Species

Viburnums are one of the most beautiful and trouble-free groups of shrubs. They include dozens of species and hundreds of varieties in sizes to fit any garden or landscape.

A few Midwest favorites are Koreanspice (*V. carlesii*) and its hybrids, Judd viburnum (*V. × juddii*) and burkwood viburnum (*V. × burkwoodii*), which are some of the most fragrant choices. American cranberry bush (*V. trilobum*) offers long-season color with white spring flowers followed by bright-red berries that usually last well into winter (if not discovered by a flock of hungry waxwings first). The handsome, maplelike leaves turn deep red in autumn. European cranberry bush (*V. opulus*) is similar in fruit and bloom, but it often doesn't show significant fall color. It tends to be more prone to aphid attacks, too. 'Roseum', a variety of *V. opulus* known as the "snowball viburnum," blooms with 3-inch, white balls in spring. 'Mariesii' doublefile viburnum (*V. plicatum* var. *tomentosum*) has an interesting horizontal branching pattern, white flowers, bright red fruit, and purple-red fall foliage.

Azalea

Rhododendron hybrids

ZONES: 4 to 8

BLOOM TIME: May to June

BLOOM COLOR: Orange, pink, purple, red, white, or yellow

LIGHT REQUIREMENT: Partial shade

HEIGHT × WIDTH: 2 to 6 feet × 2 to 6 feet

Special Features

The many large clusters of funnel-shaped blossoms make azalea one of our most colorful spring-blooming shrubs. Some varieties are fragrant, and a few grow only two feet tall and wide, making them an easy fit for small spaces.

How to Grow

Azaleas bloom and grow best with morning sun and afternoon shade. Plant on the north or east side of the house or in a grouping of other shrubs and trees where they will be protected from wind. Azaleas require a moist, acid soil that is well drained. Before you plant, amend the soil by adding 50 percent pre-moistened peat moss in a planting area about 2 feet deep and 4 feet wide. You can plant container-grown azaleas in spring or summer.

Care and Maintenance

Water as necessary in dry weather to keep the soil moist. Spread a coarse mulch, such as shredded bark, and add more as needed to maintain a covering about 2 inches deep. Pruning is seldom needed, but if you must, do it immediately after flowering. To maintain soil acidity, scatter 6 ounces of sulfur evenly on the ground in a 4-foot circle around each plant every two years in winter, then top with more mulch. Or apply an acid fertilizer once or twice during the growing season.

Dispose of spotted or fallen leaves to help control leaf-spot diseases, which are caused by fungi. If tips of some branches wilt and die, prune out and destroy the affected branches. The following spring, spray the plant with Bordeaux solution after flowers fade. Repeat twice more at 2-week intervals. To control scale insects (flat, scaly bumps on branches or the undersides of leaves), spray dormant oil in early spring before new growth begins. Pale, stippled leaves and very fine webbing in hot, dry weather indicate spider mites; control them with a forceful spray of water from the garden hose every few days.

GARDEN TIPS

♦ If the edges of the older leaves are browning, your fertilizer may be to blame. Water heavily to wash excessive salts away, and temper future applications of fertilizer.

♦ Yellowing leaves may indicate that it's time to apply soil sulfur or take other steps to acidify the soil.

Recommended Varieties

If you live in USDA zones 5 or 6, you can choose from hundreds of different azaleas. Zone 4 gardeners can enjoy azaleas in their gardens, too, thanks to the Northern Lights series, which was developed at the Minnesota Landscape Arboretum. The shrubs there deliver a dependable show despite winter temperatures of 30 degrees below zero. 'Rosy Lights', 'Golden Lights', 'White Lights', and 'Spicy Lights' (tangerine) have fragrant flowers. 'Northern Hi-Lights' is creamy white with yellow highlights and has mildew-resistant foliage that turns red in the fall.

Burning Bush

Euonymus alatus

OTHER COMMON NAME: Winged Euonymus

ZONES: 4 to 8

FRUIT TIME: Fall

FRUIT COLOR: Red, with exposed red-orange seeds

LIGHT REQUIREMENT: Sun or shade

HEIGHT × WIDTH: 6 to 15 feet × 6 to 15 feet

Special Features

Burning bush's flaming fall color is one of the brightest reds in the landscape. The corky "wings" of the stems add interest. The red-orange seeds, exposed when the fruits split open, are ornamental, too, although they may be overlooked when the shrub is wearing its red coat. Burning bush is ideal for use as either a hedge or an accent plant.

How to Grow

For the best fall color, plant in full sun. Burning bush adapts to any soil, providing it is well drained. This shrub is easy to transplant and can be planted any time during the growing season.

Care and Maintenance

Water in dry weather. Plants tolerate any amount of pruning and can be trimmed to a smaller size, if desired. Pruning also encourages new, strong growth for the best autumn color. Early spring is the best time for pruning. Burning bush seldom suffers problems from pests or diseases.

Recommended Variety

Dwarf burning bush (*E. alatus* 'Compactus'), which grows 6 to 8 feet tall, may be the best choice for small properties. Its fall color is just as spectacular, but the winged branches are not as prominent.

Related Species

Eastern wahoo (*E. atropurpureus*), a Midwest native, grows as a small understory tree in woodlands. After its reddish-purple leaves drop in autumn, the attractive, bright-scarlet seeds remain to add winter interest.

GARDEN TIP

♦ There's no need to worry about scale insects with burning bush. Although they often attack other kinds of euonymus, including the eastern wahoo, these pests don't go for burning bush.

Eastern Wahoo

Butterfly-Bush

Buddleia davidii

OTHER COMMON NAME:
Summer Lilac

ZONES: 5 to 9

BLOOM TIME: July to frost

BLOOM COLOR: Lilac,
pink, purple, red, or white

LIGHT REQUIREMENT:
Full sun

HEIGHT × WIDTH: 3 to
8 feet × 3 to 8 feet

Special Features

The graceful, arching spikes of fragrant flowers are a magnet for butterflies. In all but the warmest parts of the Midwest, butterfly-bush behaves more like a perennial than a shrub, with the top dying down to the ground during the winter. But it doesn't matter: Even in the South, butterfly-bush performs best if cut almost to the ground in spring, allowing vigorous new shoots to sprout from the base.

How to Grow

Plant in well-drained soil, setting out the plants in spring or early summer so they will be well-established before winter. Butterfly-bush is also easy to grow from seed, but the flower color and shrub size won't necessarily be the same as that of the parent plants.

Care and Maintenance

Water in dry weather. Cut spent flowers for best appearance and to promote continued blooming. Cut plants back to near the ground when new shoots appear in spring. Insects are seldom a problem. Occasionally, spider mites may attack in hot, dry weather, but they're easy to control with a forceful spray of water from the garden hose.

Recommended Varieties

Two favorite pink varieties are 'Pink Delight', with pure pink blossoms, and 'Summer Beauty', with rosy-pink flowers and silver leaves. 'Black Knight' is a hardy, deep-purple variety, with flowers that appear almost black. Other favorites are 'Royal Red', the most popular red variety, and 'Petite Plum', reddish-purple with an orange eye.

GARDEN TIP

◆ If you have trouble getting butterfly-bush through the winter, be sure to choose a site with well-drained soil in full sun. Allow the bush to stand intact until new growth begins in spring. Don't be too quick to declare your plant dead; new shoots are often slow to show.

'Royal Red'

'Petite Plum'

'Pink Delight'

Cotoneaster

Cotoneaster divaricatus

OTHER COMMON NAME:
Spreading Cotoneaster

ZONES: 4 to 7

FRUIT TIME: Fall

FRUIT COLOR: Red

LIGHT REQUIREMENT:
Sun

HEIGHT × WIDTH: 5 to
6 feet × 6 to 8 feet

Special Features

The wide, spreading form of cotoneaster makes it ideal for a low hedge or accent plant in an informal setting. The pink flowers in late spring are small and often hidden by the glossy, green leaves, but you can't miss the combination of red fruits and reddish-purple leaves in autumn. The berries are a favorite with cedar waxwings and other birds, too.

How to Grow

Plant container-grown specimens any time during the growing season; plant balled-and-burlapped shrubs in spring. Cotoneaster tolerates any soil as long as it is well drained. Space plants 5 to 6 feet apart.

Care and Maintenance

Cotoneasters are drought tolerant and generally require little care. If you've allowed the plants enough room to grow, little pruning is needed except to remove damaged branches. You can thin shrubs in late winter by removing a few of the oldest stems at ground level. Mulch to control weeds. Cotoneaster is susceptible to a bacterial disease called fireblight. If young branches look like they've been burned by fire, prune in winter by cutting the branches a foot below visible damage. Destroy the infected wood. If you see deformed berries and blisters on the undersides of leaves, pearleaf blister mites are probably to blame. Apply a dormant oil spray in early spring before new growth begins.

Related Species

Cranberry cotoneaster (*C. apiculatus*) grows 3 feet tall and up to twice as wide. Its pink spring flowers are followed by bright-red fruit and reddish-purple leaves in fall. If you garden in zone 5, three additional species make fine groundcovers: Creeping cotoneaster (*C. adpressus*) grows 12 to 18 inches tall, rooting wherever its branches touch the soil. Berries turn bright red in late summer. Bearberry cotoneaster (*C. dammeri*) has evergreen foliage that grows 12 to 18 inches tall. It boasts white flowers in spring and bright-red fruit in late summer. Rock spray cotoneaster (*C. horizontalis*) grows 2 to 3 feet tall, spreading horizontally to a width of 6 to 8 feet. Reddish-purple leaves and bright red fruit make a fine display in autumn.

Bearberry Cotoneaster

Cranberry Cotoneaster

Forsythia

Forsythia hybrids

ZONES: (4) 5 to 8

BLOOM TIME: March or April

BLOOM COLOR: Yellow

LIGHT REQUIREMENT: Sun or light shade

HEIGHT × WIDTH: 2 to 10 feet × 2 to 10 feet

Special Features

The early yellow flowers are a welcome and familiar harbinger of spring. Attractive, dark-green foliage often turns reddish-purple in fall. This quick-growing shrub is lovely when used as an accent plant, and it also makes a fine hedge.

How to Grow

Plant with daffodils and other spring-flowering bulbs, allowing room for forsythia to retain its natural and graceful shape. If growing as a hedge, allow 6 feet between most varieties. Forsythia is easy to establish in any kind of soil and can be planted any time during the growing season. Best flowering occurs in full sun.

Care and Maintenance

Remove one-third of the oldest stems at the base every year in late winter or in spring. If you want to do any other pruning, wait until after blooms fade. Pests and diseases are seldom serious enough to require control; simply remove diseased branches.

Recommended Varieties

In northern areas, forsythia often blooms only near the base, where the buds were protected from cold by snow; but the hardy flower buds of 'Meadowlark' put on a dependable show even after the temperature dips to 35 degrees below zero. 'Broxensis', a dwarf variety that grows only 1 to 2 feet tall with a spread of 2 to 3 feet, is a favorite for planting in flower gardens.

GARDEN TIPS

♦ When forsythia blooms, it's time to apply pre-emergent herbicide to control crabgrass.

♦ For an early taste of spring, cut branches of forsythia in mid-winter and put them in a vase of water. The flowers will soon burst into bloom. For a longer lasting show, keep the vase out of direct sun and change the water every day.

'Meadowlark'

Fragrant Sumac

Rhus aromatica

ZONES: 4 to 9

BLOOM TIME: April

BLOOM COLOR: Yellow

LIGHT REQUIREMENT:
Sun or partial shade

HEIGHT × WIDTH: 2 to
6 feet × 6 to 8 feet

Special Features

Glossy green foliage—fragrant when crushed—turns scarlet or yellow-orange in autumn. These low, spreading shrubs root wherever the stems touch soil, making them an ideal groundcover for slopes.

How to Grow

Select a site with well-drained soil of poor-to-average fertility. Plant any time during the growing season, allowing 6 feet between plants.

Care and Maintenance

Remove any broken branches and cut back outer branches as needed to keep the plants within bounds. Otherwise, little care is needed. Once established, fragrant sumac tolerates drought. Pests and disease seldom require control.

Recommended Variety

'Gro-Low' grows only 2 feet tall, with scarlet to orange fall color.

Related Species

'Laciniata' cutleaf smooth sumac (*R. glabra*) grows about 8 feet tall, with bright-red leaves and persistent scarlet fruit in fall.

'Lacinata'

'Gro-Low'

Honeysuckle

Lonicera tatarica

OTHER COMMON NAME
Tatarian Honeysuckle

ZONES: 3 to 8

BLOOM TIME: May

BLOOM COLOR: Pink, red, or white

LIGHT REQUIREMENT: Sun or partial shade

HEIGHT × WIDTH: 6 to 10 feet × 6 to 10 feet

Special Features

A profuse display of fragrant spring flowers is followed by bright-red summer berries that are loved by birds. The shrubs grow fast, making them ideal for use as hedges or screens.

How to Grow

Plant in full sun for the biggest display of flowers. Honeysuckle is tough and undemanding, and it thrives in any soil with good drainage. You can plant it any time during the growing season.

Care and Maintenance

Established plants tolerate dry soil and need little care. Practice renewal pruning (see Appendix). In recent years, distorted shoots called "witches' brooms" have ruined the beauty of many of these old-fashioned favorites. Damage is caused by the imported Russian aphid. Remove and destroy witches' brooms whenever you see them, cutting a foot below visible damage. Resistant varieties (see recommendations below) may escape damage.

Recommended Varieties

'Arnold's Red', which has the darkest-red flowers of any honeysuckle, is somewhat resistant to Russian aphids. Two varieties demonstrating even more resistance to the aphids are 'Freedom', which has white, pink-tinged flowers, and 'Honeyrose', a rosy-red variety.

Related Species

'Emerald Mound' honeysuckle (*L. xylosteum*) grows only 2 to 3 feet tall, with yellow-white flowers and dark-red berries.

GARDEN TIPS

♦ If a honeysuckle is straggly and overgrown, perform radical surgery: Cut the shrub to near the ground and fertilize. In several years you'll have a beautiful, vigorous specimen.

♦ Take a winter walk in the garden to inspect your honeysuckle shrubs. Any witches' brooms you find and remove now will eliminate overwintering aphid eggs before they have a chance to hatch.

'Honeyrose'

'Emerald Mound'

Hydrangea

Hydrangea species

ZONES: 3 to 9, depending on species

BLOOM TIME: Midsummer to fall

BLOOM COLOR: Blue, pink, or white

LIGHT REQUIREMENT: Partial shade

HEIGHT × WIDTH: 3 to 10 feet × 3 to 10 feet

Special Features

Popular in Victorian times for their large, showy flowers, hydrangeas are once again becoming favorites. They stage their show in late summer when few other shrubs are in bloom, making the flowers especially welcome. Varying flower forms include round globes, flat "lacecaps," and fat cones. All are excellent for fresh or dried bouquets.

How to Grow

Plant in a spot that is protected from winter wind and hot afternoon sun. Ideally, the soil should be moist, fertile, and well-drained. Hydrangeas perform best in acid soil.

Care and Maintenance

Water as often as necessary to keep the soil moist. Mulch to preserve moisture and to protect the shallow roots from temperature extremes. If you're growing a variety that is borderline hardy for your area, apply 5 to 6 inches of a coarse winter mulch after the ground freezes in fall. Removing a few of the oldest stems in late winter (see renewal pruning in Appendix) will help most kinds of mature hydrangeas look their best. Panicle and smooth hydrangeas, however, bloom on new wood and perform better if cut back by half in spring.

Recommended Species

Panicle hydrangea (*H. paniculata*) is hardy to zone 3. The most cold-hardy of all hydrangeas, it has white, cone-shaped flowers that change to pinkish-bronze as they age. You can stretch the season of bloom if you plant two varieties: 'Grandiflora', also known as PeeGee hydrangea, blooms in July or August. Flowers of 'Tardiva', the late panicle hydrangea, often don't open until September. The white, billowing flowers of another cold-hardy species, smooth hydrangea (*H. arborescens*), bloom in midsummer several weeks before PeeGee. 'Annabelle' is one of the best varieties.

Bigleaf hydrangeas (*H. macrophylla*) are adored for their colorful globe-shaped or lacecap blossoms, but only gardeners in zone 6 and protected areas of zone 5 are lucky enough to get blooms. Favorite varieties include 'Nikko Blue', 'Forever Pink', and the red 'Glowing Embers'. Allow faded flowers to remain over winter to help protect new buds from cold temperatures. After the last spring frost, cut the flowers and remove any dead leaves. Oakleaf hydrangeas (*H. quercifolia*) also have tender flower buds that are apt to be killed by cold if planted north of zone 6. The attractive leaves, however, turn red or purple in the fall and are reason enough for many gardeners in zone 5 to plant this shrub.

GARDEN TIPS

- To dry hydrangea flowers, cut blossoms and remove all the leaves. Stand the stems in a container and add one inch of water. Allow the stems to absorb all the water and remain in the container for several weeks. When dry, the petals will be papery thin and tawny beige.

- If the blossoms of your blue-flowered varieties are pink, acidify the soil by adding sulfur or aluminum sulfate according to package instructions.

Japanese Barberry
Berberis thunbergii

ZONES: 4 to 8

FRUIT TIME: October to winter

FRUIT COLOR: Bright red

LIGHT REQUIREMENT: Full sun

HEIGHT × WIDTH: 2 to 5 feet × 2 to 5 feet

Special Features

The flowers of barberry aren't showy but the berries, which persist until birds eat them in winter, are eye-catching. You can choose from varieties with green, red, or gold leaves. The autumn foliage of green varieties often turns orange, red, or yellow. The stems are thorny, making barberry a useful barrier plant. Deer usually shun barberry, too.

How to Grow

Barberry is a great plant for hot, dry locations and is a good choice for planting under the eaves on the west side of the house. Plant in any type of well-drained soil. This shrub is easy to transplant and can be planted any time during the growing season. If growing barberry as a hedge, set dwarf varieties 18 inches apart, and full-sized ones 3 feet apart. Barberries can be sheared to any shape, but they rarely need pruning if allowed to grow naturally.

Care and Maintenance

Barberries tolerate poor, dry soil, so plants need little in the way of water or fertilizer. Pests and diseases are seldom a problem.

Recommended Varieties

'Crimson Pygmy', a dwarf that grows only 18 to 24 inches tall, has reddish-purple foliage and is one of the most popular. 'Bonanza Gold' and 'Gold Nugget' are pint-size shrubs with golden leaves. Both are resistant to sunburn, a frequent problem for gold-leaf varieties grown in hot sun. 'Kobold' is prized for its lustrous, dark-green leaves.

GARDEN TIPS

◆ If your barberries become straggly, you can renew them by pruning to within a few inches of the ground in early spring.

◆ Keep barberries out of the path of the automatic sprinkler system. The regular watering used for lawns is death to these drought-tolerant shrubs.

Related Species

Korean barberry (*B. koreana*) has showy yellow flowers and bright-red berries. It is hardy in zones 3 to 7 and grows 4 to 6 feet tall.

'Kobold'

'Gold Nugget'

Japanese Spirea

Spiraea japonica

ZONES: 4 to 8

BLOOM TIME: Summer

BLOOM COLOR: Carmine, pink, or rose

LIGHT REQUIREMENT: Sun or partial shade

HEIGHT × WIDTH: 12 inches to 4 feet × 2 to 4 feet

Special Features

Say "spirea" and many people think first of tall shrubs bearing white blossoms in May. Japanese spireas, though, are compact shrubs that fit easily into small gardens. Their flowers come mostly in shades of pink, and many varieties have colorful foliage, too. Use these spireas in shrub borders or foundation plantings. Some dainty spireas are also great for planting in the perennial garden or using as a groundcover.

How to Grow

Spireas adapt to almost any soil, sun or shade. If you plant them in full sun, however, you'll be rewarded with more blooms and more colorful foliage. Plant any time during the growing season. Japanese spirea and other types that bloom in summer flower on new wood. You can cut this type of spirea back by half or more in early spring without hurting the plant or sacrificing any blooms.

Care and Maintenance

Japanese spireas are extremely easy, low-maintenance shrubs. Removing spent flowers—although not necessary—will encourage continued flowering and make the plant look neater.

Recommended Varieties

Daphne spirea (var. *alpina*) is the tiniest spirea. It spreads into a dense, foot-tall mat that is covered with light-pink flowers. It makes a beautiful groundcover. 'Magic Carpet' grows 18 to 24 inches tall, with red-tipped foliage and deep-pink flowers. 'Little Princess' and 'Goldmound' mature at about 2 feet tall and have pink flowers, but the foliage of 'Little Princess' turns from soft-green to red in autumn, while 'Goldmound' has gold foliage throughout the season.

> ## GARDEN TIP
>
> ◆ Spring bloomers like Vanhoutte spirea flower on the previous season's wood. Renewal pruning (see Appendix) in late winter is usually all that is needed. This allows the shrub to retain its graceful, natural shape. If you need to shorten any branches, however, wait until after the blooms fade.

Related Hybrids and Species

Vanhoutte spirea (*S.* × *vanhouttei*) is the beloved old-fashioned spirea that still graces many Midwest yards with its fountainlike sprays of white flowers every May. If you don't have room for a shrub that spreads up to 8 feet tall, try 'Snowmound' (*S. nipponica*). It looks a lot like Vanhoutte but grows only half as big. The bumald hybrids (*S.* × *bumalda*) include spireas that grow only 2 to 3 feet tall; many have colorful foliage as well as summer flowers. 'Goldflame' starts out with red-and-orange leaves that change to yellow, and finally to yellow-green by the time the pink flowers open. Its fall foliage is burnt-orange. 'Crispa' has pink flowers and slightly twisted, burgundy-red leaves. The flowers of 'Coccinea' are crimson.

Lilac

Syringa vulgaris

ZONES: 3 to 7

BLOOM TIME: May

BLOOM COLOR: Lilac, magenta, pink, purple, or white

LIGHT REQUIREMENT: Sun

HEIGHT × WIDTH: 8 to 15 feet × 6 to 15 feet

Special Features

If you grew up in the Midwest, one whiff of a lilac in bloom will likely transport you back to your childhood. This old-fashioned favorite with its showy flower clusters is still one of the most popular of all flowering shrubs in this region.

How to Grow

The keys to growing lilacs successfully are sunlight and well-drained soil. Plant bare-root lilacs in spring; plant container-grown shrubs any time during the spring or summer. To help prevent problems with mildew, allow plenty of room between plants, up to 15 feet for large varieties.

Care and Maintenance

Water in dry weather the first several years after planting. After that, lilac can tolerate drought. Control scale insects by applying a dormant oil spray in spring before new leaves appear. For best appearance and better air circulation, remove spent flowers. Practice renewal pruning (see Appendix). If further pruning is necessary, do it immediately after flowering. Control suckers to keep plants from crowding out neighboring plants. Seriously overgrown lilacs can be rejuvenated by cutting all the branches to within one foot of the ground.

Recommended Varieties

There are hundreds of different varities of lilacs to choose from. Some of the most popular varities include purple 'Ludwig Spaeth', pink 'Katherine Havemeyer', white 'Ellen Willmott', magenta 'Charles Joly', and blue 'President Lincoln'. 'Sensation' is an outstanding bicolored lilac whose flowers are purple edged in white.

GARDEN TIPS

♦ The easiest way to control unwanted shoots from suckering varieties is with the lawn mower or string trimmer. Be careful not to nick the trunks: Borers are attracted to injured bark.

♦ As long as your lilac is growing in full sun, don't worry if it doesn't bloom right away. Lilacs often need a couple of years to get used to their new surroundings.

Related Species

'Palibin', often called dwarf Korean lilac (*S. meyeri*), grows only 4 to 5 feet tall. Reddish-purple buds open to fragrant, pale lilac flowers. 'Miss Kim' (*S. patula*) grows 5 to 6 feet tall and blooms a few weeks later, after most lilacs have finished blooming. This variety delivers another show in autumn, when the foliage turns a pretty burgundy-red. Japanese tree lilac (*Syringa reticulata*) is a beautiful small tree that blooms in June. 'Ivory Silk', one of the best, produces numerous white flowers.

'Sensation'

'Miss Kim'

Potentilla

Potentilla fruticosa

OTHER COMMON NAME:
Bush Cinquefoil

ZONES: 2 to 6

BLOOM TIME: June to frost

BLOOM COLOR: Pink, red, white, or yellow

LIGHT REQUIREMENT:
Sun or partial shade

HEIGHT × WIDTH: 2 to 4 feet × 2 to 4 feet

Special Features

Tough and easy to grow, these compact plants are also one of the longest blooming of all shrubs, with a profusion of 1-inch flowers for most of the growing season. Tuck them into your perennial garden or shrub border in groups of three or more for a long-lasting splash of color.

How to Grow

Plant potentillas in full sun to promote heavier flowering. Choose a site with well-drained soil. You can plant container-grown potentillas any time during the growing season.

Care and Maintenance

To reduce twiggy growth and the tendency of potentillas to flop open in their centers, cut plants back by one-half in late winter. Fungus diseases are rarely serious enough to require any control.

Recommended Varieties

There are a number of strong, yellow-flowered varieties that thrive in the Midwest. The bright yellow flowers of 'Coronation

Triumph' are some of the first to open. 'Goldfinger' produces extra-large, golden-yellow blossoms on a more compact, 3-foot-tall bush. 'Jackmanii' has deep yellow flowers on somewhat taller bushes. The flowers of 'Primrose Beauty' are pale yellow, highlighting the silver-gray foliage. 'McKay's White' is a strong performer in Midwest gardens; its flowers are creamy white. For a potentilla with clear-pink blossoms, try 'Pink Beauty'.

GARDEN TIP

◆ Although potentillas flower best in full sun, pink or red varieties show off better if planted where they'll get a little shade in the afternoon. Both colors are prone to fading if the light is too bright.

'Pink Beauty'

'McKay's White'

'Primrose Beauty'

Privet

Ligustrum amurense

OTHER COMMON NAME:
Amur Privet

ZONES: 4 to 7

BLOOM TIME: June

BLOOM COLOR: White

LIGHT REQUIREMENT:
Sun or partial shade

HEIGHT × WIDTH:
12 feet × 9 to 12 feet

Special Features

This fast-growing shrub makes a fine hedge. The small flowers aren't showy, but they're fragrant and attract butterflies. Birds eat the small berries that follow.

How to Grow

Privets are adaptable and easy to grow. They tolerate both poor soil and drought. They won't tolerate wet soil, though, so be sure to plant them in a well-drained site. If growing as a hedge, space plants 3 feet apart. You can plant privet any time the ground isn't frozen.

Care and Maintenance

Prune a privet hedge so that the bottom is slightly wider than the top. This insures that upper branches won't shade the lower ones, resulting in loss of leaves at the bottom. If you don't care about the flowers, you can prune any time winter through summer, cutting as much as you like. Otherwise, delay pruning until after the flowers fade. Sunken areas, called cankers, can girdle and kill a stem. If you see any, remove the branch by pruning below the affected area.

Related Species

Many privet hedges in the Midwest are planted with European privet (*L. vulgare*), which is of a similar size but more prone to develop blight or cankers. Because little pruning is required, 'Lodense' is particularly popular. It's compact and dense, ideal if you'd like to maintain a low hedge 3 to 4 feet tall without much pruning. Variegated forms of European privet are also available. The regal privet (*L. obtusifolium* var. *regelianum*) is a dense, compact species that grows 5 to 6 feet tall. Golden privet (*L. × vicaryi*) is hardy in zones 5 to 8 and retains golden-yellow leaves all season if it's grown in full sun.

GARDEN TIP

◆ Don't let an automatic sprinkler system tempt you to water privets too often. Root rot, canker, and blight diseases are more apt to attack shrubs that are stressed by being grown in wet soil.

Regal Privet

'Lodense'

Golden Privet

SHRUBS

Shrub Rose

Rosa hybrids

ZONES: 2 to 9, variable

BLOOM TIME: June or everblooming, variable by variety

BLOOM COLOR: Pink, red, white, or yellow

LIGHT REQUIREMENT: Sun

HEIGHT × WIDTH: 2 to 6 feet × 2 to 6 feet

Special Features

Everyone knows and loves roses, but not everyone is willing to go to the lengths necessary to grow hybrid teas. That's why shrub roses are becoming so popular. Hardy and disease-resistant, they produce fragrant and beautiful blossoms with little care.

How to Grow

Most shrub roses are grown on their own roots and should be planted at the same depth they were growing before moving to your garden. Any grafted variety, however, should be planted with the swollen knob of the graft union placed 2 inches below the soil surface for winter protection. (See Appendix for planting details.) Plant bareroot roses in early spring; plant container-grown roses any time during the spring or summer. Space plants 3 to 6 feet apart depending on the size of the variety, allowing space for good air circulation.

Care and Maintenance

Water an inch a week in dry weather, being careful to water the soil, not the foliage. In spring, apply a slow-release fertilizer recommended for roses and spread a fresh layer of shredded bark or other mulch. Prune roses when the leaf buds begin to swell in spring, removing weak, damaged, and crisscrossed canes. When pruning roses that bloom all summer, shorten remaining canes at the same time. When pruning roses that bloom only in June, wait until after blooms fade for additional pruning.

Rose leaves are prone to blackspot and mildew during humid summer weather. The easiest way to prevent these

GARDEN TIPS

◆ Keep fungicides off rugosa roses. The foliage of these roses are hurt, not helped, by spraying.

◆ What if your favorite rosebush suddenly sends up long, lanky shoots with little or no flowers? Chances are your rose was produced by grafting and the desirable top portion has died. That means it's time to buy a replacement.

fungal diseases is to plant disease-resistant varieties. Removing fallen leaves and spreading a fresh layer of mulch around plants helps control both diseases. If you're growing a disease-prone rose, you'll need to spray or dust plants with a fungicide. Some organic gardeners control spider mites and other small pests as well as fungus diseases by dusting plants once a week with sulfur.

Recommended Varieties

Rugosa roses are a group of tough, dependable shrubs. All have disease-resistant, crinkly, deep-green leaves. Most flower all summer before producing colorful fruits, called hips, in fall. Light-pink 'Frau Dagmar Hastrup' and white 'Alboplena' are two of the many outstanding rugosas. The Explorer series, developed at the Ottawa Experiment Station in Canada, includes some of the hardiest and most disease-resistant roses available. Pink-blooming 'David Thompson' and white-flowered 'Henry Hudson' are two outstanding rugosa roses in the series. 'William Baffin' has pink blooms and is an unusually hardy climber, with canes that survive in zone 4 without any winter protection.

Summersweet

Clethra alnifolia

OTHER COMMON NAME:
Sweet Pepperbush

ZONES: 4 to 9

BLOOM TIME: July and August

BLOOM COLOR: White or pink

LIGHT REQUIREMENT:
Sun or shade

HEIGHT × WIDTH: 3 to 8 feet × 4 to 6 feet

Special Features

Spicy-sweet flower spikes are a special delight in the summer garden when few other shrubs are blooming. In fall, the glossy, deep-green leaves turn a lovely yellow-orange. This adaptable shrub will grow almost anywhere, but it is especially valued for its ability to thrive in shade and wet soil.

How to Grow

Summersweet grows best in a moist, acid soil. Add compost, shredded leaves, or other organic matter to the soil before you plant. A spot protected from the hot afternoon sun is best. You can plant a container-grown summersweet any time during the growing season.

Care and Maintenance

Water in dry weather, and mulch to preserve soil moisture. Plants are seldom bothered by pests or diseases. Spider mites may attack in hot, dry weather, but washing off the foliage with water from the garden hose is usually all it takes to prevent these tiny insects from damaging the foliage. Summersweet can go for years without requiring much in the way of pruning. If you want to prune, early spring before new growth begins is the best time for the job.

Recommended Varieties

'Hummingbird' is a compact variety and a favorite white-

GARDEN TIP

♦ Summersweet spreads slowly from suckers. If an established plant threatens to crowd its neighbors, just pull out some of the extra shoots, or dig up the volunteers and plant them in another part of the garden.

bloomer in Midwest gardens. The pink buds of 'Rosea' open to pale-pink flowers that gradually fade to white, while the deep-pink flowers of 'Ruby Spice' hold their color without fading.

'Hummingbird'

'Rosea'

'Ruby Spice'

Weigela
Weigela florida

OTHER COMMON NAME:
Cardinal Shrub

ZONES: 4 to 8

BLOOM TIME: Late spring; sporadically throughout the season

BLOOM COLOR: Pink, red, or white

LIGHT REQUIREMENT: Sun

HEIGHT × WIDTH: 4 to 8 feet × 4 to 8 feet

Special Features

Hummingbirds seek out the trumpet-shaped blossoms of weigela. You can count on this shrub to add a big burst of color to your garden in late spring. Many varieties continue to bloom intermittently throughout the rest of the summer. Most weigelas are medium-sized shrubs, but compact dwarf varieties are also available for the small-scale garden.

How to Grow

Plant weigela any time during the growing season in any well-drained soil. This shrub blooms best in full sun but will tolerate light shade. Water in dry weather until the plant is established.

Care and Maintenance

Remove dead tips in spring. Practice renewal pruning (see Appendix) in late winter or early spring. Any other pruning, if necessary, should be done immediately after the first flush of blooms fades. Pests and disease are seldom a problem.

Recommended Varieties

'Red Prince' was introduced by Iowa State University and is the best non-fading red. 'White Knight', also from Iowa State, is a superb white-flowering variety. Both grow 5 to 6 feet tall and about as wide. If

you're looking for a smaller shrub, check out the weigelas in the super-hardy Dance Series, from Canada. All are dwarf forms ranging in size from the 30-inch-tall 'Minuet', which has two-tone rose-and-purple flowers, to the 4-foot-tall 'Polka', which produces bright-pink flowers. Red-flowered 'Rumba', 'Samba', and 'Tango' complete the series. 'Variegata' is hardy to zone 5 and produces rose-colored flowers on plants with green-and-cream foliage.

'Variegata'

'Red Prince'

'Minuet'

'Rumba'

Winterberry

Ilex verticillata

OTHER COMMON NAMES:
Michigan Holly

ZONES: 4 to 9

FRUIT TIME: Fall and winter

FRUIT COLOR: Red or orange

LIGHT REQUIREMENT: Full sun or partial shade

HEIGHT × WIDTH: 3 to 8 feet × 3 to 8 feet

Special Features

Winterberry is aptly named, considering the unrivaled winter color provided by its bright berries. Unlike its first cousins, the evergreen hollies, winterberry loses its leaves in fall, all the better for displaying its fruit. The only threat to winter color is a raid by hungry cedar waxwings or robins. Winterberry is native to Midwestern swamps as far west as Missouri, Iowa, and Wisconsin and is ideal for planting in wet soil.

How to Grow

Winterberry looks spectacular when planted in small groups against a backdrop of evergreens. To produce berries, you'll need to include a male plant as well as some berry-producing females. Plants need a humusy, acid soil that is normal to wet. Dig shredded leaves, pre-moistened peat moss, compost, or other organic materials into the soil before you plant. Although winterberry thrives in partial shade, you'll get more berries and have less trouble with leaf-spot diseases if you choose a site in full sun. Plant in spring or fall when the soil is cool.

Care and Maintenance

Water in dry weather, particularly during the first year after planting. Mulch to keep the roots cool and to preserve soil moisture. Little pruning is needed when plants are young. Rejuvenate older plants by renewal pruning (see Appendix). It may be necessary to control suckers at the base of the shrub if witerberry threatens to grow too wide for its space.

GARDEN TIPS

◆ With winterberry shrubs in your yard, you have beautiful holiday decorations close at hand. The branches you cut and bring inside will brighten the decor without so much as a drink of water.

◆ Yellowing leaves indicate that your soil is too alkaline for winterberry. Acidify the soil by applying sulfur or aluminum sulfate according to package directions.

Recommended Varieties

For red berries, choice female varieties are 'Red Sprite', a 4-foot dwarf plant, and 'Winter Red', which matures at 6 to 8 feet and has exceptionally long-lasting fruit. 'Afterglow' is a compact 6- to 8-foot variety with orange-red berries. As for male varieties, you can use 'Jim Dandy' to pollinate 'Red Sprite' and 'Afterglow', and 'Southern Gentleman' to pollinate 'Winter Red'.

Related Species

The Meserve hybrids (*I. × meserveae*), also called blue hollies, are the best evergreen hollies for the Midwest. Females and their male pollinators that are hardy through zone 5 include 'Blue Princess'/'Blue Prince' and 'China Girl'/'China Boy'.

Witchhazel

Hamamelis virginiana

OTHER COMMON NAMES:
Autumn Witchhazel,
Common Witchhazel

ZONES: 4 to 8

BLOOM TIME: Late fall

BLOOM COLOR: Yellow

LIGHT REQUIREMENT:
Sun or partial shade

HEIGHT × WIDTH:
15 feet × 15 feet

Special Features

If you hate to say good-bye to the last flower of the season, plant a witchhazel. Its yellow blossoms begin opening in late fall at about the same time its golden-yellow autumn foliage begins to fall. The flowers' unusual straplike petals curl up to protect themselves when the weather is cold, then unfurl on sunny days. If you brave the weather to go outside, you'll appreciate the flowers' spicy fragrance. But even from a window you can enjoy the sight of these late-season blossoms. The seed capsules provide a feast that is enjoyed by cardinals and other birds. Witchhazels are huge shrubs that make a wonderful privacy hedge where space allows.

How to Grow

Witchhazels are adaptable and easy to grow, and they thrive in almost any kind of soil. To lessen pruning chores, be sure to allow enough room for these large shrubs to grow. Specimens will develop a nice, full shape if you plant them in full sun. Spring planting is best.

Care and Maintenance

Water in dry weather. Mulch to preserve soil moisture and keep the roots cool. Once established, witchhazel requires little effort on your part. Diseases and pests are seldom a serious problem. Damage by leaf gall aphids is primarily cosmetic. If desired, you can prune witchhazel to grow as a small tree.

GARDEN TIP

◆ Want to try your luck "witching" for water? A forked branch from a witchhazel was often used by American pioneers who were looking for the perfect spot to dig a well.

Related Species

Vernal witchhazel (*H. vernalis*) is somewhat smaller and denser, growing about 10 feet tall. Its blossoms are yellow to red and usually open in the dead of winter, often in February, or early March.

Autumn Witchhazel

Vernal Witchhazel

Yew

Taxus × media

OTHER COMMON NAME:
Anglojap Yew

ZONES: 4 to 7

FRUIT TIME: Fall

FRUIT COLOR: Red

LIGHT REQUIREMENT:
Shade or sun

HEIGHT × WIDTH: 2 to
20 feet × 4 to 20 feet

Special Features

With their soft, dark-green needles, yews are one of our most attractive evergreens. They're especially valuable to home landscapes because they're one of the few evergreens that will thrive in shade. Often pruned into a formal hedge, yews are especially lovely when allowed to retain their natural shape. If there is at least one male around, female yews will produce bright-red berries enjoyed by wildlife.

How to Grow

Save yourself some pruning by choosing a variety according to its mature size (see recommended varieties). Good drainage is a must for long-term survival. Plant in spring so that plants will be well established before winter. Yews planted in a site that is shaded from winter sun will be less apt to suffer from winter burn. If growing as a hedge, space yews with a columnar form, such as 'Hicksii', 4 feet apart.

Care and Maintenance

Mulch to maintain soil moisture and keep roots cool. Water an inch a week in dry weather. If there are no autumn rains, water deeply before the ground freezes to help prevent damage from winter drying. Yews are a favorite food of deer; if your yard is frequently browsed by deer, it may be best to plant something else. You can prune or shear yews any time without harming them. Pruning in early spring is ideal, though, because new growth quickly hides the cuts.

> ## GARDEN TIP
>
> ◆ Yews in the path of an automatic sprinkler system often suffer from root rot. The tips wilt and brown, and eventually the whole plant dies. There is no cure, but you can prevent the problem by placing yews out of sprinkler range or by planting them on a berm or in a raised bed.

Recommended Varieties

'Tautonii' is a good choice for Midwest gardens because it's exceptionally resistant to winter burn. Without pruning, this yew grows 3 to 4 feet tall. Other outstanding varieties, from shortest to tallest, include 'Everlow', 18 inches; 'Chadwickii', 3 to 4 feet; 'Wardii', 6 to 8 feet; 'Brownii', 8 or 9 feet; and 'Hicksii', 18 to 20 feet.

Related Species

Japanese yew (*T. cuspidata*) is an erect or spreading tree that may grow 25 or more feet tall. 'Capitata' has an upright shape that is often maintained as a 10-foot hedge. Low, spreading forms that perform well in the Midwest include 'Emerald Spreader', 30 inches tall; 'Dark Green Spreader', about 4 feet tall; and 'Densa', also about 4 feet tall.

Trees

Everyone loves trees. But not everyone enjoys the work they involve: raking autumn leaves, spraying for pests and diseases, pruning to manage growth, trimming around trunks, cleaning up after storms, watering in dry weather, and removing dead wood. If you'd like to enjoy trees without being a slave to them, the trick is in the selection. Plant a dwarf white pine instead of the full-sized version, and it will stay in bounds without pruning. Choose a disease-resistant crabapple and you can skip spraying. Plant a strong, wind-resistant tree such as the bur oak, and there will be no branches to gather up after a storm. Select a tree with small leaves, such as the baldcypress, and you won't even have to rake in autumn.

The best way to be sure you won't end up having to remove a dead tree is by matching the tree to your site. If you have a spongy soil that stays wet, choose a tree that likes it that way, such as swamp white oak. If your soil tends to dry out quickly, plant a drought-tolerant tree such as linden. Many trees also have a preference for either acid or alkaline soil; if you don't know which your soil is, it takes only a few minutes to find out with a soil test kit from the garden center.

If a tree dies for an unknown reason, choose a different kind for replacement. Some tree diseases remain in the soil, waiting to infect the next tree you plant. Better yet, get a diagnosis through your county's Cooperative Extension Service and be sure to choose a variety that won't succumb to the same problem.

Before you plant a tree, don't forget to check with utility companies to be sure you won't accidentally damage an underground line. The power company would also be happy if you'd "look up" before you plant. If you limit yourself to a tree no more than 25 feet tall, such as a serviceberry or American hornbeam, you can save your tree from the lopsided pruning that is often necessary to make room for electric wires. You might also save your supply of electricity if a storm breaks tree branches.

In most yards, the biggest hazards to a tree's health are string trimmers and mowers—but it needn't be that way. Trees fare far better if they're grouped together with shrubs and surrounded with shade-loving ground covers or perennials. If a tree *is* planted in the middle of the lawn, it will grow better and stay healthier if the soil around it is covered with a 4-inch layer of bark chips or other mulch rather than grass.

Not all tree decisions are made for practical reasons. Sometimes, nostalgia wins. A dogwood or willow, for example, is often beset by disease and insect problems—but if you have fond memories of a certain tree and want to grow one, it will be worth the trouble. The information in this chapter will help you decide. For advice on how to plant or prune, check illustrated Appendix for tips and illustrations.

Baldcypress

Taxodium distichum

ZONES: 4 to 10

LIGHT REQUIREMENT: Sun

HEIGHT × WIDTH: 50 to 70 feet × 20 to 30 feet

Special Features

The soft, feathery needles of this deciduous conifer turn golden-brown or copper colored in autumn before they fall. One-inch green or purple cones add an attractive touch. Baldcypress is narrow when young and develops a broad, flat crown with age. It is a strong, sturdy tree that is not prone to storm damage, making it ideal for planting in wind-swept sites. A native of swamps, it's a good choice for planting in wet soil where many other trees would drown.

How to Grow

Plant a balled-and-burlapped baldcypress in spring; plant container-grown specimens in spring or summer. Although it is native to areas with wet soil, the tree adapts readily to dry soil, too.

Care and Maintenance

Keep the tree watered well during its first year and during droughts. Mulch to keep soil cool and moist. Once established, baldcypress usually needs little care. Pests and diseases are seldom serious, and you won't even have to rake the small needles when they fall in autumn. Prune out any blighted twigs. If the needles look pale in hot, dry weather, check for spider mites by thumping a branch over a piece of white paper. Moving specks on the paper confirm mites, which can often be controlled by hosing the needles off with water from the garden hose or with a spray of insecticidal soap.

GARDEN TIP

◆ If you plant a baldcypress in the front yard, be prepared in autumn for people to ask you why your evergreen is dying. A conifer that drops its needles is still a bit of an oddity in the home landscape.

Baldcypress

Bur Oak

Quercus macrocarpa

ZONES: 3 to 8

LIGHT REQUIREMENT:
Sun

HEIGHT × WIDTH: 70 to
80 feet × 70 to 80 feet

Special Features

Rugged and majestic, the bur oak grows slowly into a spreading shade tree. After the lustrous, dark-green leaves fall, the tree's statuesque form adds its beauty to the winter landscape. It is especially striking when the corky bark is covered with a dusting of snow. A native of Midwest grasslands, the bur oak is a survivor: It's the one tree that has withstood prairie fires, windswept plains, and competition from grasses. The large acorns provide welcome food for wildlife.

How to Grow

Bur oak is a tough tree that adapts to soils that are wet or dry, or even solid clay. It's also a good choice for areas with alkaline soil. Choose a young tree that is no more than 8 feet tall. Plant in spring. If the taproot is circling the bottom of the container, be sure to untangle it before planting.

Care and Maintenance

Water deeply once or twice a week in dry weather the first season after planting. To avoid attracting the sap-feeding beetles that spread oak wilt fungus, prune oaks when they're dormant, or wait until midsummer to do the job. Dead areas on leaves— usually a problem only if the season is wet—are caused by another kind of fungus, called anthracnose. Disfiguring but not serious if it doesn't happen every year, anthracnose usually requires no control. Raking and removing fallen leaves will help curtail future infections. You can also ignore the abnormal growths, called galls, that may appear on oak branches. They are caused by tiny flies or wasps and do little damage.

> ## GARDEN TIP
> ◆ Shredded oak leaves make a wonderful mulch for any kind of plant. Because they're slightly acidic, they're particularly beneficial for mulching plants that like acid soil, such as azaleas, blueberries, and white pines.

Related Species

There are dozens of different kinds of oaks that thrive in the Midwest. Some, including bur oak, belong to the white oak group. Slow growing and strong, they have built-in resistance to oak wilt disease. Others belong to the red oak group, which includes many trees with outstanding fall color. Members of this group grow more quickly but are not as strong.

White oak (*Q. alba*), the state tree of Illinois, is king of the white oak group. It grows best in slightly acidic soil and often turns a pretty wine-red in fall. Swamp white oak (*Q. bicolor*) is an excellent tree for the home landscape. It is easy to transplant and quicker to grow than many oaks, and it thrives in both wet and dry soils, and in clay.

The northern red oak (*Q. rubra*) is king of the red oak group. It thrives in well-drained, acid soil and turns a beautiful bright red in autumn. Black oak (*Q. velutina*), which is closely related to the red oak but slightly smaller at maturity, is more tolerant of soils that are dry, sandy, or clay. In areas with alkaline soil, the widely planted pin oak (*Q. palustris*) suffers from yellowing leaves and decline. A better choice for these areas is scarlet oak (*Q. coccinea*), a close relative.

Colorado Spruce

Picea pungens

ZONES: 3 to 7

LIGHT REQUIREMENT: Sun

HEIGHT × WIDTH: 30 to 60 feet × 15 to 25 feet

Special Features

The stiff branches and pyramidal shape of the Colorado spruce are a familiar sight in landscapes across the Midwest. Although the needles vary from green to blue, trees with blue needles are by far the most popular. Spruces are generally easier to grow than firs in this region.

How to Grow

Plant container-grown spruces any time during the growing season; plant balled-and-burlapped specimens in spring. Choose a site with well-drained soil. Trees will tolerate light shade but develop a nicer shape in full sun. To help prevent fungus disease, allow adequate space for good air circulation.

Care and Maintenance

Water in dry weather and mulch to conserve soil moisture. If the autumn is dry, water deeply before the ground freezes to help protect the needles from winter browning. Hose down the needles of young trees in hot, dry weather to prevent infestations of spider mites. If you want to prune a spruce to control its size or shape, cut each branch back to a live bud in spring when the new growth is soft. To avoid spreading diseases, prune in dry weather. If needles turn brownish purple and fall from lower branches, a fungus disease called needle cast is the probable culprit. To control it, spray Bordeaux mixture in late spring; repeat the spray a month later. If a few scattered branches die, inspect the branches for girdling caused by cankers. Cut and remove affected branches in dry weather.

Recommended Varieties

The Colorado blue spruce (var. *glauca*) is the best known of the Colorado spruces. Color is sometimes variable, so examine the selection for the color you want or buy a named variety, such as 'Hoopsii'. Smaller versions of Colorado spruce include 'Fat Albert', a semi-dwarf with a good blue color, and 'Montgomery', a beautiful silver-blue dwarf that grows as a low bush, about 3 feet high and 5 feet wide.

Related Species

White spruce (*P. glauca*) ranges in size from the beautiful and dense Black Hills spruce (var. *densata* 'Bailey') to the familiar dwarf Alberta spruce (var. *conica*). Weeping forms are also available. Serbian spruce (*P. omorika*) is a graceful tree with a tall, narrow shape. 'Nana', the dwarf Serbian spruce, is one of the best small evergreens for a Midwest garden. It grows slowly to a height of about 8 feet. 'Nidiformis', the bird's nest spruce, is a dwarf form of Norway spruce (*P. abies*). It owes its common name to the natural depression that forms in the center of the bush.

GARDEN TIPS

◆ A mature spruce takes a good-sized chunk out of most city yards, and pruning to control size is usually a losing battle. If you don't have room for a full-sized tree, substitute one of the fine dwarf selections.

◆ The tiny needles of dwarf spruces tend to collect in the center of the tree. Clean them out in spring to help your trees stay healthy.

Crabapple
Malus varieties

ZONES: 4 to 6

BLOOM TIME: Spring

BLOOM COLOR: Pink, red, or white

LIGHT REQUIREMENT: Sun

HEIGHT × WIDTH: 6 to 30 feet × 6 to 30 feet

Special Features

No other tree is as spectacular in flower as the crabapple. Many varieties also have brightly colored fruits that persist for months, adding color to the winter garden and providing food for birds. The foliage of some crabapples is colorful in autumn. Wherever you'd like to plant a tree, there's sure to be a crabapple to fit. They come in sizes ranging from 6-foot shrubs to 30-foot trees, with many different shapes to choose from: round, narrow, vase-like, spreading, or weeping.

How to Grow

Plant container-grown trees any time during the growing season. Crabapples adapt well to any type of soil as long as it is well-drained.

Care and Maintenance

Some crabapples are notorious for developing spotted leaves that drop by mid- to late summer. The easiest solution is to choose disease-resistant crabapples (see recommended varieties). To control disease on susceptible crabapples, rake up and destroy infected foliage. If your tree is especially prone to disease, you may want to consider spraying fungicide once a week from spring through June. Many gardeners, though, find it both easier and less expensive in the long run to replace the tree with a disease-resistant crabapple. In late winter, prune crabapples as necessary to remove branches that are damaged or crossed. Remove any water-sprouts—weak, vertical shoots that sprout in the center of the tree—or suckers that sprout at the base of the trunk as soon as you see them.

GARDEN TIP

♦ If the thought of messy fruits cluttering the ground in autumn keeps you from planting a crabapple tree, think again. Birds love the small, persistent fruits of many of the newer varieties. If any fruits do fall to the ground, they quickly disappear into the grass or mulch.

Recommended Varieties

'Donald Wyman', Sugar Tyme®, and Red Jewel® are outstanding white-flowering crabapples. The first has a round shape and grows about 20 feet tall and wide. The other two grow more upright and are a little shorter. 'Adams' has red buds that open to pink flowers and reddish-green foliage. The tree has a rounded shape and measures about 20 by 20 feet. 'Prairifire' produces eye-catching red flowers in spring and red-orange foliage in fall. It has a rounded shape and matures at a height of about 20 feet. All these crabapples have persistent red fruit and have demonstrated exceptional resistance to disease in research trials.

'Donald Wyman'

Flowering Cherry

Prunus serrulata

ZONES: 5 to 7

BLOOM TIME: Spring

BLOOM COLOR: Pink or white

LIGHT REQUIREMENT: Sun or partial shade

HEIGHT × WIDTH: 20 to 30 feet × 15 to 30 feet

Special Features

These small trees from Japan are beautiful in flower and produce autumn color, too. Like most other cherries and plums in the huge *Prunus* genus, they are usually short-lived. To many gardeners, though, the beauty—however fleeting—is worth the planting.

How to Grow

Plant container-grown specimens any time during the growing season, being sure to select a site with well-drained soil.

Care and Maintenance

Water in dry weather. Mulch to preserve soil moisture and keep the roots cool. These steps reduce stress and lessen the chances of attack by borers, cankers, or virus diseases. If tent caterpillars or webworms attack, prune out and destroy the nests. Watch for young caterpillars the following spring and spray with Thuricide® or other product that contains *Bacillus thuringiensis*.

Recommended Variety

'Kwanzan' is one of the showiest cherries, with pendulous pink flowers in spring. Leaves emerge coppery-bronze, turning green in summer, then reddish-copper in fall.

Related Species

Two outstanding cherries, both hardy to zone 4, are Sargent (*P. sargentii*) and Higan (*P. subhirtella*) cherries. Weeping forms of Higan cherries with double pink flowers

> **GARDEN TIP**
>
> ◆ Flowering cherries are at their best when planted in a shrub border and surrounded by spring-flowering bulbs.

are especially attractive. Chokecherry (*P. virginiana*) is a suckering native shrub that is one of the most shade tolerant of the cherries. 'Shubert' is a popular purple-leaf variety. Another plant with colorful leaves is purpleleaf sandcherry (*P. × cistena*), a hybrid with reddish-purple foliage. One of its selections, 'Big Cis', grows quickly into a small tree. Chokecherry and sandcherry do particularly well in cool climates, thriving as far north as zone 3.

Purpleleaf Sandcherry

Higan Sandcherry

'Shubert'

Flowering Dogwood

Cornus florida

ZONES: 5 to 8

BLOOM TIME: April or May

BLOOM COLOR: White, pink, or red

LIGHT REQUIREMENT: Partial shade

HEIGHT × WIDTH: 15 to 25 feet × 15 to 30 feet

Special Features

A flowering dogwood in bloom is a spectacular sight. The state tree of Missouri, this small understory tree also stages a show in autumn, with both red berries and red foliage. The fruits persist into winter, lasting until devoured by hungry birds.

How to Grow

Your chances of getting your flowering dogwood through the winter will be enhanced if the tree's parents grew in your same zone and in similar soil. In areas where the tree is borderline hardy, white-flowering dogwoods are usually more apt to survive the winter than those with pink or red blossoms. Plant a container-grown dogwood in spring, placing the root ball slightly higher than it was in the nursery to prevent root rot. The ideal location will have good air circulation and shade from high, overhanging branches. Flowering dogwood grows best in a moist, acid soil. Dig compost or other organic matter into the soil before planting.

Care and Maintenance

Water in dry weather. Mulch to keep the roots cool and preserve soil moisture. Providing a stress-free environment will help your tree fend off borers, fungus diseases, and other common problems of dogwoods. Other steps you can take to protect your dogwood include removing diseased branches, raking up fallen leaves, and avoiding high nitrogen fertilizer. Pruning, if needed, should be done after blooms fade. Apply a

GARDEN TIP

♦ Annual removal of the oldest stems of 'Cardinal' and other shrubby dogwoods grown for their showy stems will keep the shrubs looking their most colorful.

general purpose fertilizer in spring, or maintain soil fertility by spreading a 2-inch layer of compost and replenishing the mulch annually.

Recommended Varieties

'Cloud 9', a white selection, is one of the hardiest of the flowering dogwoods. White 'Cherokee Princess' and rose-red 'Cherokee Chief' are also good choices for the Midwest. 'Stellar Pink' and white-flowering 'Constellation'—both disease-resistant crosses of Kousa (*C. kousa*) and flowering dogwoods—are also hardy to zone 5.

Related Species

Corneliancherry dogwood (*C. mas*) is worth growing for its yellow blossoms in early spring. You can grow it as a large shrub or prune it to a single trunk. 'Golden Glory'—a good upright variety—makes an attractive 20-foot-tall screen. Corneliancherry dogwood is hardy to zone 4. Pagoda dogwood (*C. alternifolia*) is the hardiest of the tree dogwoods, surviving to zone 3. It is about 20 feet tall and has layered branches that look something like a Japanese pagoda. Although it often grows in a clump, you can prune it to a single-trunk tree, if desired.

Redosier (*C. sericea*) dogwoods are shrubby, with bright-red stems. Named varieties range in size from 2 to 8 feet tall, from dwarf 'Kelseyi', to mid-sized 'Isanti, to 'Cardinal', the tallest. For a red-stemmed shrub with variegated leaves, choose from two tatarian dogwoods (*C. alba*): Ivory Halo®, 5 to 6 feet tall with a compact shape; or 'Argenteo-marginata', which grows to 10 feet tall.

Flowering Pear

Pyrus calleryana

ZONES: 5 to 8

BLOOM TIME: April or May

BLOOM COLOR: White

LIGHT REQUIREMENT: Sun

HEIGHT × WIDTH: 25 to 35 feet × 15 to 30 feet

Special Features

Beautiful white blossoms in spring, dark-green leaves in summer, and red or yellow fall color make this small, fast-growing tree a good choice for home landscapes. Birds are attracted to the marble-size fruits. Although it is usually not long-lived, the pear's beauty makes it one of the most popular of flowering trees.

How to Grow

Plant a container-grown pear in spring or summer; plant a balled-and-burlapped specimen when the tree is dormant. Choose a site with well-drained soil.

Care and Maintenance

Water in dry weather, particularly during the first year after planting. 'Bradford', the most widely planted flowering pear, tends to produce narrow crotches and closely spaced limbs that break apart in ice or snow storms. To prevent damage, begin corrective pruning when the tree is young. Before the tree leafs out in spring, remove some of the branches, favoring wide crotches wherever possible. Limbs or twigs that look like they were burned in a fire are infected with fireblight. During the winter, prune out and remove affected branches, cutting a foot beneath visible damage.

Recommended Varieties

'Redspire', which has a narrow, pyramidal shape, and 'Aristocrat', which has a more open habit, are both more resistant to storm damage

GARDEN TIP

♦ The blossoms of the flowering pear are lovely to look at but not to smell. A spot close to your patio or bedroom window probably isn't the best site for this tree.

than 'Bradford'. Chanticleer® has a compact, narrow form with a uniformly branched crown that is also highly resistant to breakage. This superior variety is also resistant to fireblight and is one of the most cold hardy of the flowering pears.

'Aristocrat'

Chanticleer®

'Redspire'

Ginkgo

Ginkgo biloba

OTHER COMMON NAME:
Maidenhair Tree

ZONES: 4 to 8

LIGHT REQUIREMENT:
Sun

HEIGHT × WIDTH: 40 to
70 feet × 30 to 40 feet

Special Features

The ginkgo's bright-green, fan-shaped leaves grow in clusters of three to five. Their unique shape resembles the tiny leaflets of a maidenhair fern, which is why ginkgo is sometimes called the maidenhair tree. In autumn the foliage turns a beautiful golden color. When young, the ginkgo tends to be spindly, with few branches. With age, however, it slowly develops into a picturesque shade tree. Its form is variable, often more upright than spreading.

How to Grow

Plant a balled-and-burlapped ginkgo in the spring; plant a container-grown specimen any time during the growing season. A young tree is easier to transplant than a large specimen. Any kind of soil is acceptable as long as it is well drained.

Care and Maintenance

Water regularly in dry weather during the first year after transplanting. Ginkgo is one of the most trouble-free shade trees in the Midwest and is unlikely to suffer from any pests or diseases. It is prone to storm damage, though, if an early ice or snow storm catches it before the leaves drop. Remedial pruning may save the tree, provided no more than a third of the trunk's diameter has been torn away.

Recommended Varieties

Because the 1-inch, yellow-orange fruits produced by a female ginkgo are messy and smelly, a male tree is the best choice. To be sure you're getting a male, buy a named selection, such as 'Autumn Gold'.

'Autumn Gold'

Green Ash

Fraxinus pennsylvanica

ZONES: 3 to 8

LIGHT REQUIREMENT: Sun

HEIGHT × WIDTH: 50 to 60 feet × 30 to 40 feet

Special Benefits

Green ash grows quickly into a spreading shade tree, often thriving where few other trees will grow. Leaves turn yellow in fall. Because male varieties are seedless, they make the best choice for the home landscape: seed clutter is eliminated and the yard isn't plagued with volunteer seedlings.

How to Grow

Plant a balled-and-burlapped ash in spring; plant a container-grown tree in spring or summer. The green ash adapts well to almost any conditions but grows faster in rich, moist soil.

Care and Maintenance

Prune when the tree is young to encourage strong branch angles (see Appendix), thus minimizing breakage in storms later on. Water in dry weather and maintain a 4-inch layer of mulch around the tree to reduce stress. Healthy trees resist attack from borers and scale insects as well as cankers, ash yellows, and leaf spot diseases. Remove any dead branches. If oystershell scale is severe, remove heavily infested branches and spray remaining branches with a refined horticultural oil such as SunSpray® in May.

Recommended Varieties

'Patmore' is an excellent seedless variety with a fine form that requires little or no pruning.

Related Species

White ash (*F. americana*) is a large, stately tree with dark-green leaves that turn gold, maroon, or purple in autumn. Both 'Autumn Purple' and the more compact 'Autumn Applause' are seedless and will light up your yard in early autumn with their purple or wine-red foliage. 'Fallgold', a black ash (*F. nigra*), is seedless, too, and has long-lasting, golden-yellow color.

'Autumn Applause'

'Fallgold'

'Autumn Purple'

Honeylocust

Gledistsia triacanthos var. *inermis*

OTHER NAME: Thornless Honeylocust

ZONES: 4 to 9

BLOOM TIME: May or June

BLOOM COLOR: Green

LIGHT REQUIREMENT: Sun

HEIGHT × WIDTH: 30 to 60 feet × 30 to 60 feet

Special Features

The graceful, fernlike foliage of the honeylocust is a familiar sight in Midwestern cities. Honeylocust is a fast-growing, Midwest native, though the trees offered in nurseries lack the wicked thorns usually found on trees in the wild. The late spring flowers are inconspicuous but fragrant. Seedless varieties eliminate the clutter of fallen pods.

How to Grow

Honeylocust is easy to transplant any time during the growing season. The tree tolerates all soils, whether wet, dry, or compacted. It also tolerates heat and road salt, so it's a good choice for planting near a city street.

Care and Maintenance

Water in dry weather until well established. When the tree is young, prune in the dormant season to maintain a central leader and eliminate weak angles (see Appendix). Check the limbs for localized infections, called cankers, and remove any you find. If leaf buds fail to open in spring or are deformed, plant bugs are to blame. There's usually no cause for alarm; new leaves will open soon. If feeding is unusually heavy, tips of twigs may die. If you want to control the bugs, spray a lightweight horticultural oil such as SunSpray® Ultra-Fine Spray Oil in mid-spring. An attack by mimosa webworms is usually more serious. These caterpillars skeletonize leaves, at times turning an entire tree brown by late summer. Rake up and destroy fallen leaves in autumn to get rid of the cocoons. Insecticides are most effective if sprayed in early summer when newly hatched caterpillars are first detected. If locust leaves yellow or brown, then drop by mid- to late summer, suspect honeylocust spider mites. To check for their presence, hold a white sheet of paper beneath a branch and tap the leaves. If you see tiny specks moving on the paper, spider mites are confirmed. Insecticidal soap will control them in future years but must be applied early in the season to maintain your tree's appearance.

GARDEN TIPS

◆ Honeylocust is a good lawn tree because it casts only filtered shade, allowing grass to grow beneath its branches. When the small leaflets fall, they won't smother the grass.

◆ If honeylocusts already abound in your neighborhood, consider planting something else. Horticulturists worry that the enormous popularity of this tree might pave the way for a disaster like those that virtually destroyed American elms and chestnuts.

Recommended Varieties

'Skyline' and 'Shademaster' are outstanding varieties that produce few pods. If you like the look of branches tipped with bright, golden leaves in spring, plant 'Sunburst'. It, too, produces few seedpods, but it is more susceptible to cankers than green-leafed varieties.

Hornbeam (American)

Carpinus caroliniana

OTHER COMMON NAMES: Ironwood, Musclewood, Blue Beech

ZONES: 3 to 9

BLOOM TIME: Spring

BLOOM COLOR: Green

LIGHT REQUIREMENT: Shade or sun

HEIGHT × WIDTH: 20 to 30 feet × 20 to 30 feet

Special Features

The American hornbeam, a Midwestern native, is an understory tree that is ideal for small yards. It is beautiful in all seasons: Red leaves emerge in spring along with drooping green catkins that are similar to birch flowers. Dark-green summer leaves often turn to orange or yellow in autumn. In winter, the smooth, slate-gray bark, fluted trunk, and graceful form add interest to the landscape. Clusters of small, nut-like fruits attract birds. American hornbeam is sometimes grown as a multi-stemmed tree. It grows slowly and takes time to adjust after planting, but like many Midwestern natives, it's tough and long-lived once established.

How to Grow

American hornbeam is ideal for planting in a shady site, but it will tolerate full sun as long as the soil is moist. Not all specimens are equally hardy, so gardeners in the northern part of the region should determine the tree's origin before they buy. Plant in spring to give the tree more time to get established. Although native to bottomlands, hornbeam adapts to both wet and dry sites.

Care and Maintenance

Water when the weather is dry during the first year after planting. No control of diseases or insects is required. Pruning is seldom necessary.

GARDEN TIP

♦ Similar names make it easy to confuse American hornbeam with another tough native tree, the American hophornbeam (*Ostrya virginiana*). Both are members of the birch family, and both sometimes go by the name of ironwood. The hophornbeam grows taller and is less tolerant of growing in wet soil. Its flaky bark is a marked contrast from the smooth bark of the hornbeam.

Hophornbeam

Kentucky Coffeetree

Gymnocladus dioicus

ZONES: 4 to 8

BLOOM TIME: Late May or early June

BLOOM COLOR: Green, inconspicuous

LIGHT REQUIREMENT: Sun

HEIGHT × WIDTH: 50 to 70 feet × 40 to 50 feet

Special Features

Native to river valleys throughout the Midwest, the Kentucky coffeetree grows slowly into a handsome, mid-sized tree with an open, spreading shape. Dark-green leaflets line up in compound leaves 3 feet long, giving the tree a soft, fern-like appearance in summer. In spring, the leaves are tinged with pink, purple, or red, turning bright yellow—if conditions are right—in autumn. Winter, though, is when the Kentucky coffeetree really shows off, revealing its bold skeleton and rough, scaly bark. Stout, leathery pods cling to the branches of female trees. Inside the pods are large, round seeds that were used by pioneers to make a coffee substitute, giving the tree its common name.

How to Grow

Although the Kentucky coffeetree grows best in deep, fertile soils, it adapts readily to almost any conditions and is a particularly good choice for planting in alkaline soil. Young trees are quicker to establish than older specimens. Container-grown trees can be planted any time during the growing season.

Care and Maintenance

Established trees are drought resistant and need no pampering after the first year. Pests and diseases are seldom a problem, but raking may be: the long stems and pods, which fall at different times, create a lot of lawn litter. Breakage from storms is usually minimal. When pruning is necessary, do it in late winter or early spring.

GARDEN TIP

◆ Flowers and grass are easy to grow beneath a Kentucky coffeetree. The tree's leaves are slow to emerge in spring, allowing time for spring-flowering bulbs and early wildflowers to bloom; and because the tree casts shade that is filtered rather than dense, shade-tolerant grasses will also thrive.

Kentucky Coffeetree

Lacebark Elm

Ulmus parvifolia

OTHER COMMON NAME:
Chinese Elm

ZONES: 5 to 9

LIGHT REQUIREMENT:
Sun or shade

HEIGHT × WIDTH: 30 to
50 feet × 30 to 40 feet

Special Features

Because of its other common name—Chinese elm—this tree is often confused with Siberian elm (*U. pumila*), a weedy tree prone to breaking in storms and attracting elm leaf beetles. But the lacebark is a strong, medium-sized tree with built-in resistance to pests and diseases. It's beautiful, too, with glossy, dark-green leaves, a graceful shape, and interesting bark that has orange, gray, and brown mottling.

How to Grow

Lacebark elm is a tough tree for difficult urban sites and adapts to almost any soil, even soil that is compacted. It does well in sun or shade and is easy to transplant any time during the growing season.

Care and Maintenance

Water in dry weather the first season after transplanting, and mulch to retain soil moisture. Once the tree is established, you won't have to do much to maintain it. Any pruning (see the Appendix for guidelines) is best done before leaves emerge in spring.

Recommended Varieties

'Dynasty' has a rounded shape and orange-yellow fall color. Athena® is particularly outstanding in winter, thanks to its colorful mottled bark.

Related Species

Gone are the days when majestic American elms (*U. americana*) lined the streets of Midwest cities. Dutch elm disease—first identified in this country in the thirties—left few survivors. The few trees that did manage to survive are now facing a new threat as elm bark beetles spread a stronger strain of the fungus. If you have one of the survivors, you may be able to save your American elm by removing and chipping any infected branches as soon as you see wilting leaves. A new injection that fights the fungus with another fungus may also help save your tree. Plant breeders at the University of Wisconsin, the Morton Arboretum in Lisle, Illinois, and the U.S. National Arboretum in Washington, D.C. are working to develop elms that have the American elm's elegant vase shape but that can also resist Dutch elm disease and elm yellows, a serious disease spread by leafhoppers. Watch for new introductions. Disease-resistant hybrids already available include 'Homestead', 'Regal' and Accolade®.

> ### GARDEN TIP
>
> ◆ If you're looking for a tree that mimics the vase shape of the American elm, plant a Japanese zelkova (*Zelkova serrata*), another member of the elm family. The leaves of this large shade tree are deep green in summer and purple, red, or yellow in autumn. It is hardy through zone 5.

Athena®

Linden (American)

Tilia americana

OTHER COMMON NAME: Basswood

ZONES: 3 to 8

BLOOM TIME: June

BLOOM COLOR: Pale yellow

LIGHT REQUIREMENT: Sun or shade

HEIGHT × WIDTH: 40 to 80 feet × 30 to 50 feet

Special Features

Lindens are excellent shade trees for this region. They have a tall pyramidal shape with a medium-to-slow growth habit. Red buds open in spring to large, heart-shaped leaves. The June flowers are inconspicuous but fragrant, filling the air with the scent of citrus. Fall color doesn't rank high on linden's list of virtues, but sometimes the foliage turns a pretty yellow.

How to Grow

Linden is an adaptable tree. It will grow faster if it's planted in moist, well-drained soil, but it usually survives in any site. You can plant a container-grown linden any time during the growing season.

Care and Maintenance

An established linden tolerates drought, but you can prevent leaf scorch if you water during dry periods. Prune shoots at the base of the tree to maintain a single trunk. Lindens have few problems with pests or diseases. If aphids congregate on leaves of young trees, simply hose them off with water. Lace-like insects called lacebugs sometimes cause brown blotches or yellowing of leaves; control by spraying insecticidal soap when they first appear in early summer. Lindens often require more attention to pruning than other shade trees because they tend to develop multiple leaders and crowded branches. Prune in winter, maintaining a central leader and well-spaced side branches.

> ## GARDEN TIP
>
> ◆ The dense shade beneath a linden makes it difficult to grow grass or other plants. It's better to maintain a layer of bark chips or other mulch, spread 4 inches deep on the ground eneath the branches.

Recommended Variety

'Redmond', the most popular American linden, matures with a uniform pyramidal shape. 'Boulevard' has unusual ascending branches, a strong central leader, and a narrow shape, making it ideal for sites where room for spreading branches is limited.

Related Species

Littleleaf linden (*T. cordata*) is smaller than most American lindens. The leaves are smaller, too, as the name implies. 'Greenspire', a littleleaf variety, has dark-green foliage and maintains a strong central leader. 'Shamrock'® is similar but has stouter branches, slightly larger leaves, and a more open canopy. Silver linden (*T. tomentosa*) makes a superb shade tree for Midwest yards. It's especially beautiful when its silver-backed leaves shimmer in the wind and when the foliage turns yellow in autumn. Silver linden is also exceptionally tolerant of heat and drought, and it is less prone to breaking under the weight of ice or snow.

Magnolia

Magnolia hybrids

ZONES: 4 to 9

BLOOM TIME: Spring

BLOOM COLOR: Pink, wine-red, white, or yellow

LIGHT REQUIREMENT: Partial shade

HEIGHT × WIDTH: 10 to 30 feet × 10 to 30 feet

Special Features

Magnolias for the Midwest are not the evergreen trees of the South, but they are lovely just the same. The large flowers, which are sometimes fragrant, open early, often before the bold leaves appear. Some magnolias stage a repeat performance, with more blooms in summer; some have fruits with exposed red seeds that are attractive in autumn. After the leaves fall, the smooth, silvery bark and fuzzy buds add winter interest. Magnolias' small size is just right for most home landscapes.

How to Grow

Choose a spot out of direct sun in order to delay spring flowers, which are apt to be zapped by cold weather if they open too early. A site with moist, well-drained, acid soil is ideal. Add compost, shredded leaves, or other organic materials to the soil before you plant. If your soil is alkaline, acidify it with ground sulfur or aluminum sulfate according to package directions. Magnolias are fussy about being moved, so choose a container-grown plant rather than a bareroot tree. Plant in spring, being careful not to break any of the fleshy roots.

Care and Maintenance

Water in dry weather. Add a layer of mulch to conserve soil moisture and help keep the roots cool. Mulch also eliminates the need for cultivating the soil to control weeds, thus protecting the magnolia's shallow root system. Pruning cuts on thick branches are slow to heal, so train your young tree to the shape you want while the branches are still small. Early summer is the best time for pruning. Remove any suckers at the base if you want to grow your magnolia as a single-trunk tree. Fertilize with an acid fertilizer according to package directions but stop by midsummer so that new growth will have time to toughen up for winter. If the mulch layer is wearing thin, add more before winter.

GARDEN TIP

◆ Plant your magnolia against a backdrop of evergreens. With the evergreens to block the wind, the flowers will show off beautifully— and they'll last longer, too.

Recommended Varieties

'Elizabeth' and 'Butterfly' are two outstanding yellow-flowered selections that are hardy in the Midwest to zone 5, and possibly to zone 4 with protection. 'Wadas Memory' is another hardy hybrid, with fragrant, white, 6-inch blossoms. Little Girl hybrids, including 'Ann', 'Jane', 'Betty', and 'Ricki', perform well in zones 4 to 6, blooming in various shades of purple or purple-red. Two Loebner magnolias, white 'Merrill' and pink 'Leonard Messel', are equally hardy. If you live in zone 5 or 6, you can successfully grow the well-known saucer magnolia (*M. × soulangiana*), which has large, tulip-shaped blossoms of white and pink.

Related Species

Star magnolia (*M. stellata*) grows naturally as a multi-stemmed shrub. Its flowers often bloom while winter lingers. The pink buds of 'Royal Star' open to white, daisylike flowers that measure 4 to 5 inches across. Star magnolias are hardy to zone 4.

Pussy Willow

Salix caprea

ZONES: 4 to 8

BLOOM TIME: Late winter, early spring

BLOOM COLOR: Silver

LIGHT REQUIREMENT: Sun

HEIGHT × WIDTH: 15 to 20 feet × 12 to 15 feet

Special Features

The soft, furry flower clusters opening in late winter is reason enough to plant a pussy willow. Whether grown as a small tree or a large, multi-stemmed shrub, the plant grows quickly but is often short lived.

How to Grow

Plant any time, but be sure to select a spot where the soil stays moist. Willow roots wreak havoc on sewer or water lines, so plant your willow at a safe distance from them.

Care and Maintenance

Water in dry weather and mulch to retain moisture. Willows are beset by a host of problems, including cankers and borers. If your tree declines, though, you can easily renew it by cutting it to the ground. You'll soon be rewarded with healthy new shoots.

Recommended Variety

'Pendula' is a weeping form that makes a lovely accent.

Related Species

Corkscrew willow (*S. matsundana* 'Tortuosa') has curiously twisted branches that make it an interesting conversation piece. It's hardy to zone 4 and grows 20 to 30 feet tall. Niobe weeping willow (*S. alba* 'Tristis') is a graceful weeping tree that grows 50 feet tall and about as wide. 'Prairie Cascade', a hybrid weeping willow from the Morden Research Center in Canada, grows 35 to 45 feet tall and is hardy to zone 3.

GARDEN TIP

◆ Cut an armload of willow branches in late winter and put the stems in a vase of water. In a couple of weeks, the catkins will open, giving you an early taste of spring.

'Prairie Cascade'

'Pendula'

'Tortuosa'

'Tristis'

Redbud

Cercis canadensis

ZONES: 4 to 9

BLOOM TIME: Early spring

BLOOM COLOR: Rosy-purple or white

LIGHT REQUIREMENT: Partial shade

HEIGHT × WIDTH: 20 to 30 feet × 25 to 35 feet

Special Features

When driving down any Midwest street in early spring, it's easy to pick out the rose-purple flowers of redbuds in full bloom. The same distinctive color shows up at the forest edge, where this understory tree thrives in the wild throughout much of the Midwest. It is a small, spreading tree with a medium rate of growth, growing wider than it is tall. Redbud is sometimes sold in a clump, three trunks to a container. The clusters of flowers appear before the reddish-purple, heart-shaped leaves emerge. Foliage is usually dark green in the summer, turning a dull yellow in autumn. After the leaves fall, a mature tree is still an asset, with dark, scaly bark and flat, persistent seed pods.

How to Grow

Not all redbuds are equally hardy, so be sure to buy a cold-hardy strain. Plant in spring in a site with afternoon shade and moist but well-drained soil.

Care and Maintenance

Water in dry weather, and mulch to retain soil moisture. Prune in spring to remove any dead wood. Pull out volunteer plants or transplant them in spring to a site you prefer. Avoid high nitrogen fertilizer, which may encourage more leafy growth at the expense of flowers. To reduce problems with canker— a fungus that shows up as a sunken area on bark and eventually kills the branch— avoid wounding the tree. Prune out dead branches 4 or 5 inches below visible damage and sterilize your pruners with rubbing alcohol after each cut. If leaves on a branch wilt, then die, but you see no sign of cankers, suspect verticillium wilt, a soil-borne fungus. Some trees can recover if affected branches are pruned out and stress on the tree is reduced. If the tree dies, replace it with a small tree that is resistant to the fungus, such as American hophornbeam.

GARDEN TIPS

◆ For a spectacular spring show, plant redbuds with flowering dogwoods, serviceberries, or daffodils.

◆ If you're spreading a weed-and-feed product on the lawn, be sure to make a wide swath around a redbud. This tree is particularly sensitive to damage from herbicides.

Recommended Varieties

'Royal White', a "whitebud," has extra large, white blossoms. 'Forest Pansy' is an outstanding purple-leafed variety for gardens in the southern half of zone 5 and south.

'Forest Pansy'

River Birch

Betula nigra

ZONES: 4 to 9

LIGHT REQUIREMENT: Sun

HEIGHT × WIDTH: 40 to 50 feet × 30 to 40 feet

Special Features

Often grown as a clump of three trunks, the river birch's main attraction is its peeling, pinkish-tan bark. This fast-growing tree has other virtues that are less obvious: natural resistance to the bronze birch borers that cut short the life of most other birches in our region, and a flexible trunk that seldom breaks when the tree is bent under the weight of ice or snow. Yellow autumn color, although not dependable, is nice when it happens.

How to Grow

River birch prefers a slightly acid soil and will register its dislike of alkaline soil by turning yellow. Choose a spot where the soil stays moist and tree roots are shaded from the hot afternoon sun. This birch is more tolerant of clay soil than most others. It is easy to establish and can be planted any time during the growing season.

Care and Maintenance

Take care not to let the soil dry out, particularly during the tree's first season. Mulch to conserve soil moisture and keep roots cool. As the tree grows taller, you may want to gradually remove a few of the low, pendulous branches to show off the attractive bark. Late summer is the best time for the job.

Recommended Varieties

Heritage® offers an attractive, lighter bark that is a mixture of cream and salmon. Fox Valley® is a dwarf that grows only 10 to 12 feet tall.

GARDEN TIP

◆ The bark of a young river birch at the nursery isn't extraordinary, but be patient: in a year or two the beautiful, peeling bark will be evident.

Related Species

'Whitespire'—a variety of the Asian white birch (*B. platyphylla*) selected by Dr. Ed Hasselkus at the University of Wisconsin—has more resistance to borers than other white birches. 'Crimson Frost'—a hybrid of the Asian white and European white birches—has reddish-purple foliage all season and cinnamon-colored bark. Cut-leaf weeping birch (*B. pendula* 'Dalecarlica') has distinctive, cut leaves and a white bark. In areas with alkaline soil, sweet birch (*B. lenta*) performs better than most other birches. It is borer resistant and has reddish-brown bark and nice yellow autumn color.

'Whitespire'

'Crimson Frost'

Serviceberry

Amelanchier arborea

OTHER COMMON NAMES:
Juneberry, Shadblow,
Downy Serviceberry

ZONES: 4 to 9

BLOOM TIME: Early spring

BLOOM COLOR: White

LIGHT REQUIREMENT:
Sun or partial shade

HEIGHT × WIDTH: 15 to
25 feet × 10 to 25 feet

Special Features

Serviceberry is a small understory tree that can also be grown as a large shrub. This Midwestern native is beautiful in all seasons: White blossoms open in early spring, just before the redbuds bloom. Red summer fruit turns black as it matures and is quickly gobbled up by birds. Fall color is variably red, gold, orange, or yellow. In winter, the smooth, gray bark and interesting branch structure add interest.

How to Grow

Plant in well-drained soil any time during the growing season. Add compost or other organic material if your soil is clayish or sandy. Allow plenty of space for good air circulation to help prevent mildew. Protect young trees from rabbits with a circle of poultry netting or similar barrier.

Care and Maintenance

Water in dry weather. To grow serviceberry as a tree, keep it pruned to a single trunk. If you choose to let the plant grow naturally, little pruning is necessary. Spotted foliage and blighted shoots are signs of a rust disease that alternates between junipers and red cedars one year, and serviceberry, apple, or flowering quince the next. Remove and destroy the orange growths from the junipers or cedars in spring, if practical; or refrain from growing serviceberries within a half-mile of red cedars or Rocky Mountain junipers.

GARDEN TIPS

◆ If you can beat the birds to the berries, they're wonderful in jams, pies, or muffins.

◆ Serviceberry is at its best planted in a shrub border with spring-flowering bulbs against a backdrop of evergreens.

Recommended Varieties

Apple serviceberry hybrids (*A. × grandiflora*) have been selected for their outstanding fall color. 'Cole's Select' is a spreading variety that grows 20 feet tall. It is often sold in clump form. 'Autumn Brilliance' and 'Princess Diana' are disease-resistant, 25-foot-tall varieties.

'Autumn Brilliance'

'Cole's Select'

Smoketree

Cotinus coggygria

OTHER COMMON NAME: Smokebush

ZONES: 5 to 8

BLOOM TIME: July and August

BLOOM COLOR: Smoky-pink

LIGHT REQUIREMENT: Sun

HEIGHT × WIDTH: 10 to 15 feet × 10 to 15 feet

Special Features

The puffs of "smoke" that cover smoketree in summer are really pink, hairy plumes that grow on the flower stalks. As the smoke clears in fall, the blue-green leaves often turn purple, red, or yellow. Smoketree can also be grown as a bush with multiple stems.

How to Grow

Smoketree thrives in any well-drained soil. Plant container-grown plants in spring or summer.

Care and Maintenance

Prune dead tips of branches in early spring. Keep mulch pulled back to discourage rot. Occasionally, a smoketree will succumb to verticillium wilt. There is no cure and the infection remains in the soil, so don't replace the smoketree with another.

Recommended Variety

'Daydream' puts out lots of pink "smoke."

Related Species

American smoketree (*C. obovatus*) grows somewhat taller. The "smoke" isn't as showy but the dependable fall color— a mixture of reds, yellows, and oranges—is spectacular. This tree, which thrives in zones 4 to 8, is also somewhat hardier than the common smoketree.

GARDEN TIP

- Purple-leaf varieties such as 'Royal Purple', 'Nordine', and 'Purple Supreme' are grown primarily for their colorful foliage. Cutting the plant back to the ground in spring sacrifices the "smoke" but forces more colorful shoots to grow. Even zone 4 gardeners can grow a smokebush this way; although cold kills the top, the roots are hardy.

(c. obovatus)

'Nordine'

'Royal Purple'

'Nordine Green'

Sugar Maple

Acer saccharum

OTHER COMMON NAME:
Hard Maple

ZONES: 4 to 8

LIGHT REQUIREMENT:
Sun or shade

HEIGHT × WIDTH: 50 to
75 feet × 30 to 60 feet

Special Features

Sugar maple is one of the best shade trees for the Midwest. It dresses for autumn in a magnificent combination of gold, orange, and red. This native tree grows slow but strong, and its winged fruits provide food for birds.

How to Grow

Plant in moist, fertile soil that is well-drained. Sugar maple adapts to sun or shade. It does not do well in compacted soil, such as that often found in new neighborhoods. Choose a site where nearby application of winter de-icing salt is unlikely.

Care and Maintenance

Water during dry weather to help prevent leaf scorch. Corrective pruning, such as removing narrow crotches (see Appendix), is best done in late winter or early spring before leaves emerge. Plant ground covers or mulch the ground beneath your maple; dense shade and surface roots make growing grass impossible.

Recommended Variety

'Legacy' is one of the best sugar maples for the Midwest, thanks to leaves that resist tearing or scorching in hot, drying winds.

Related Species

Black maple (*A. nigrum*), another Midwest native, looks very similar to sugar maple but is thought to be more tolerant of heat and drought. 'Greencolumn' is a choice variety that was selected in central Iowa by the late Bill Heard, founder of Heard Gardens in Johnston. It has a fine, upright form and dependable yellow-orange fall color. Red maples (*A. rubrum*) such as Red Sunset® make lovely shade trees. They have a rounded shape and gorgeous red fall color. Red maples do best in a slightly acid soil, so if your soil is neutral or alkaline, a better choice may be one of the Freeman maples (*A. × freemanii*), such as Autumn Blaze®. Part red maple, part silver maple, Freeman hybrids often have the best characteristics of both parents.

Japanese maples (*A. palmatum* or *A. japonicum*) are wonderful small ornamental trees that come in many colors and forms. Unless you live in zone 6 or have a protected niche in zone 5, however, they're not for you. For colder parts of the Midwest, try any of a number of other small maples: The amur maple (*A. tataricum* ssp. *ginnala*) is often grown as a multi-stemmed, 15-foot shrub. It has bright-red, winged seeds in summer and colorful autumn foliage. The Shantung or purpleblow maple (*A. truncatum*) is a 25-foot, rounded tree that leafs out in purple, turns glossy green, then changes to yellow or orange in fall. Miyabei maple (*A. miyabei*) is a 40-foot tree with dark-green foliage in summer and yellow leaves in autumn.

GARDEN TIP

- Don't be too quick to remove lower limbs from a young maple. The branches perform a valuable service in shading the trunk when it's young and tender, thus preventing damage from winter sunscald. Let the tree grow a few years before taking off a few of the lowest limbs.

Washington Hawthorn

Crataegus phaenopyrum

ZONES: 4 to 8

BLOOM TIME: June

BLOOM COLOR: White

LIGHT REQUIREMENT: Sun

HEIGHT × WIDTH: 20 to 30 feet × 20 to 25 feet

Special Features

Small enough to plant beneath a power line, Washington hawthorn is ornamental year-round: Spring leaves are reddish-purple, turning glossy green by early June and highlighted by clusters of white flowers. Red fruits ripen in early fall and are soon joined by colorful autumn foliage of orange or scarlet. The shiny red fruits persist throughout the winter...or until eaten by hungry birds.

How to Grow

A good urban tree, Washington hawthorn will settle for soil that is rich or poor, wet or dry. You can plant a container-grown tree any time during the growing season.

Care and Maintenance

Prune hawthorns in late winter before leaves emerge, thinning the crown by removing any water sprouts (weak vertical shoots) or crossing branches. Remove any suckers growing at the base of the tree. A number of pest and disease problems beset hawthorns.

The most frequent one is hawthorn rust, a fungus disease that alternates between hawthorn one year, and red cedar or juniper the next. Leaves develop orange or brown spots on their upper surfaces and often drop early; fruit may be disfigured.

GARDEN TIP

- Plant your hawthorne where no one is likely to run into it: the thorns are wicked, growing up to 3 inches long.

Control requires removing the alternate host, if practical, or spraying a fungicide once a week for a month, beginning when the flower buds open. A dormant oil spray before leaves open will control scale insects. Prune and destroy dying branches to control borers or fireblight. Infections from leaf-spot fungi can be lessened by raking up and destroying fallen leaves in autumn.

Related Species

Thornless cockspur hawthorn (*C. crusgalli* var. *inermis*) has the flower, fruit, and fall color without the thorns. 'Winter King' is a popular variety of green hawthorn (*C. viridis*) that is known for its outstanding display of half-inch red fruits. It has fewer thorns than the Washington hawthorn, and its leaves are much less susceptible to rust.

'Winter King'

Thornless Cockspur Hawthorn

White Fir

Abies concolor

OTHER COMMON NAME:
Concolor Fir

ZONES: 4 to 7

LIGHT REQUIREMENT:
Sun or partial shade

HEIGHT × WIDTH: 30 to
50 feet × 15 to 30 feet

Special Features

One of the best firs for the Midwest, this beautiful evergreen has soft needles of blue-green or silver-green. The tree grows slowly into a stately pyramid. Dwarf and weeping forms are also available.

How to Grow

A site with full sun is best, but white fir will also tolerate partial shade. Plant in rich, moist, well-drained soil. Improve clay soil by adding compost or other organic materials before planting. Allow adequate space for good air circulation to help prevent disease.

Care and Maintenance

Water in dry weather and mulch to conserve soil moisture. If autumn weather is dry, water deeply before the ground freezes to help protect the needles from winter browning. If browning does occur, delay pruning damaged tips in spring to give any live buds a chance to grow. If you've allowed enough space for your fir to mature, pruning won't be necessary. If you want to prune to control size or shear into a formal shape, though, do it in spring when the new growth is soft. You can prune back to any live bud without harming the tree.

If the central leader is broken in a snow or ice storm, here's what to do: Make a slanted cut just below the break, leaving a smooth surface that will heal more quickly. Then use yarn to tie a dowel to the top of the remaining trunk. Choose a side branch at the top of the tree, bend it upward to be the new leader, and tie it to the dowel. Shorten other side branches at the tree's top so they won't compete with the new leader. A few scattered dead branches are usually the result of girdling by cankers. Cut and remove infected branches in dry weather.

> ## GARDEN TIP
>
> ◆ When is a fir not a fir? When it's a Douglas fir (*Pseudotsuga menziesii*). Not in the same genus, or group, as true firs, Douglas fir thrives in the Midwest in zones 4 to 6. Plant it in a sheltered but sunny site.

Recommended Variety

If you don't have room for a full-sized fir in your yard, substitute dwarf 'Compacta'.

Related Species

Caucasian fir (*A. nordmanniana*) is another beautiful fir that can tolerate the temperature extremes of our region, thriving in zones 4 to 6. Its needles are dark green.

'Compacta'

Caucasian Fir

White Pine

Pinus strobus

ZONES: 3 to 7

LIGHT REQUIREMENT:
Sun or partial shade

HEIGHT × WIDTH: 50 to
80 feet × 20 to 30 feet

Special Features

White pine is noted for its long, soft, blue-green needles which are gathered together in bundles of five. It is a relatively fast-growing evergreen with a narrow pyramidal shape. Weeping and dwarf forms are also available.

How to Grow

Although white pine grows best in full sun, it is a bit more tolerant of shade than most other pines. It prefers acid soil and is not a good candidate for planting in the alkaline soils of the western half of the Midwest. Choose a site with good drainage: white pine won't tolerate wet feet. The ideal site is protected from wind and not near an area where de-icing salts may be applied in winter. Container-grown trees can be planted any time during the growing season.

Care and Maintenance

Water regularly during the first year after transplanting, and thereafter during dry spells. Mulch to retain soil moisture. If autumn rains have been skimpy, lessen damage from winter drying by watering deeply in fall before the ground freezes. If you want to control the size or shape of a pine, the time to do it is in spring when the new shoots, called candles, are expanding. Just pinch each candle with your fingers. Branches of mature trees become brittle and may snap off under the weight of snow or ice. Prune broken branches just outside the branch collar (see Appendix). Pine sawflies, wormlike insects that devour needles of mugo, Scotch, and other pines in spring, are seldom a problem on white pine.

GARDEN TIPS

◆ Because of disease problems, most Midwest horticulturists no longer recommend planting Austrian or Scotch pines.

◆ Check pines several times for pine sawfly larvae between the time when redbud and bridalwreath spirea bloom. These wormlike insects feeding in clusters and can quickly defoliate a young pine. To get rid of them in a hurry, simply shake each infested branch over a bucket of hot water.

Recommended Varieties

'Pendula' has a beautiful, weeping form. 'Nana' is a slow-growing, compact dwarf.

Related Species

Mugo pines (*P. mugo*) are variable in size. Prune trees growing in confined areas every spring by pinching the new shoots (see illustrated Appendix). Lacebark pine (*P. bungeana*) is hardy to zone 5 and has a beautiful trunk with peeling, mottled bark.

'Nana'

'Pendula'

Vines

Vines do for a garden what ribbons do for a package. Whether scaling a trellis or arbor, or scrambling over a fence or stump, vines are the perfect finishing touch. They knit together all the other elements of the garden.

Vining plants also allow you to bring flowers right up to eye level, where the blossoms can be enjoyed at close range. You won't even have to stoop to sniff fragrant flowers such as those of honeysuckle or sweet autumn clematis. You'll also delight in the hummingbirds attracted to blooms of vines such as trumpet vine and cardinal climber. And you'll savor the fall colors of Boston ivy or Virginia creeper.

Vining plants are useful, too. Use them to hide trash cans, downspouts, utility poles, or any other ugly necessities. Or depend on vines to provide welcome shade for a patio, deck, or garden bench.

Vines such as wisteria are heavyweights that require a sturdy support. Annual vines such as sweet peas and cardinal climber are delicate enough to climb a string.

The type of support needed also depends on how a particular vine climbs. Twiners, such as morning glory and honeysuckle, spiral around their supports as they grow. This type of vine can easily wrap itself around netting, lattice, string, wire, or a slender pole. Claspers, such as clematis and porcelain berry, have specialized stems called tendrils that fasten the vine to its support. A trellis made of wire or nylon netting makes climbing easy for this type of vine. Clingers, such as trumpet vine and ivy, have aerial roots or "holdfasts" that adhere to just about any flat surface. This type of vine is ideal for growing on flat surfaces, such as walls made of brick or stone. But it can't attach to netting or string.

Vine-covered walls are a wonderful way to unify house and garden, but be sure you don't allow the vines to damage your home. If you have wood siding, protect the wood from rot by leaving several inches of space for air to circulate between the wood and a vine-covered trellis. When it comes time to paint the house, you'll find it convenient if the top of the trellis is attached by hooks, especially if the trellis holds perennial vines. It's then a simple matter to unhook the trellis and lay it on the ground out of the way, vines and all.

If your house is made of brick or stone, you can grow vines right on the walls. But check the mortar and, if necessary, repair it before you plant. Although vines can't hurt sound mortar, those with aerial roots, such as English ivy, may worsen the situation if the mortar is already crumbling. Aerial roots can also dislodge roof shingles, so keep this type of vine pruned below the roofline.

In this chapter, you'll find a sampling of the easy-to-grow vines that will thrive in your Midwest garden, along with tips to help you choose the right one for your site.

Boston Ivy

Parthenocissus tricuspidata

ZONES: 3 to 8

LIGHT REQUIREMENT:
Sun or partial shade

LENGTH OF VINE: 50 feet

Special Features

The glossy, maplelike leaves of this clinging vine turn red-orange in autumn. Blue-black berries ripen in late summer on mature vines, furnishing food for wild birds.

How to Grow

Plants tolerate almost any soil, though they grow best in humusy soil that has been enriched with organic materials. Plant in sun or shade; expect the best autumn color from plants growing in full sun.

Care and Maintenance

Water in dry weather. Prune as needed to keep the vine within bounds or to remove tips suffering from winter dieback.

Related Species

Virginia creeper (*P. quinquefolia*) is a native vine that grows

GARDEN TIP

♦ Boston ivy is a good choice for the colder parts of the Midwest where English ivy is not hardy.

from New England to the Midwest. It turns fiery red in fall, with small purple fruits that are much loved by birds. Engelman ivy (*P. quinquefolia* var. *engelmannii*) is a smaller, more refined variety suitable for home landscapes. It's hardy in zones 3 to 9.

Virginia Creeper

Engelman Ivy

Clematis

Clematis hybrids and species

ZONES: 3 to 8, variable by variety

BLOOM TIME: Variable, late spring to fall

BLOOM COLOR: Blue, lavender, pink, purple, red, violet, white, yellow, or bicolor

LIGHT REQUIREMENT: Sun

LENGTH OF VINE: 5 to 30 feet

Special Features

Among perennial vines, clematis reigns as queen. You can choose from varieties that have giant flowers up to 10 inches across or from those that have masses of tiny blooms. Some flowers are shaped like flat disks, others like clusters of dangling bells. Some bloom in spring, some in summer, and a few produce flowers in autumn. Some are blessed with a heavenly fragrance. Even the wispy seedpods of this vine are attractive.

How to Grow

The ideal site for clematis is shaded at ground level, with a trellis or other support that the vine can climb to reach the sun. Clematis also needs a site with well-drained soil. After removing the plant from its container, untangle any circling roots. Dig a hole deep enough to set the plant one or two inches deeper than it was growing in its pot. Add compost or other organic materials. Water, then mulch to preserve moisture and keep the roots cool.

Care and Maintenance

Water whenever the top inch of soil feels dry. Replenish the soil by adding a 2-inch layer of compost and fresh mulch once a year. If it's a spring bloomer, wait until the blooms fade, then prune only as much as necessary to keep the plant in bounds. Prune other varieties in early spring before new growth begins, cutting summer bloomers back by half and vines that bloom late in the season back hard, to 3 feet or less. If large numbers of gray blister beetles, also called potato bugs, threaten to devour all the foliage, handpick the beetles into a can of warm, soapy water. Clematis wilt, a fungus disease that thrives in wet soil and may girdle stems, sometimes attacks large-flowered varieties, causing the vine to wilt and die. Cut and remove any dead stems. Don't be too quick to give up—new shoots will usually appear, either during the current season or the following year.

GARDEN TIPS

◆ To grow clematis on a post or split-rail fence, just fasten a piece of nylon or wire netting to the wood so the tendrils will have something to cling to.

◆ A tree or large shrub also makes a good support for clematis. Plant the vine a foot or two from the base of the tree or shrub. Loosely tie the clematis to the trunk to help it start its climb.

Recommended Varieties

A well-known favorite is Jackman clematis (*C. × jackmanii*), which has violet-purple blossoms. Other popular varieties are 'Henryi', which has pure-white flowers and 'Nelly Moser', whose mauve-pink blossoms are striped with deep carmine. All are hardy to zone 4.

Recommended Species

Anemone clematis (*C. montana*) produces fragrant white or pink flowers in spring. Golden clematis (*C. tangutica*) has yellow, nodding bells in summer. Sweet autumn clematis (*C. terniflora*) is covered with a profusion of fragrant, 1-inch white flowers in late summer or early fall. All are hardy to zone 5.

English Ivy
Hedera helix

ZONES: 5 to 9

LIGHT REQUIREMENT:
Partial to full shade

LENGTH OF VINE: 20 to
30 feet

Special Features

English ivy is an adaptable and easy-to-grow clinging vine that
also makes an elegant ground cover. The thick, evergreen leaves
are attractive in all seasons. After plants mature, those in the
warmest parts of the Midwest produce persistent black berries.

How to Grow

English ivy is at its best growing on a brick or stone wall; or plant
it as a ground cover on a slope and take advantage of its ability to
control erosion. To help the plants survive the Midwest's hot summer and cold winters, the American Ivy Society recommends
removing up to half the plant's leaves before you plant. Then
dig a planting hole deep enough to bury both the roots and the
bare stem.

Care and Maintenance

In hot, dry weather, water plants to prevent leaf scorch, being sure
to water early enough in the day so that the foliage is dry before
dark. Pick off scorched leaves to improve the plant's appearance.
Wait until the leaves are dry to pick off any leaves infected by one
of the leaf-spot diseases. Be sure the soil is moist in the fall before

the ground freezes. If scale insects are a problem, spray plants with dormant oil in spring before new growth begins. Prune whenever necessary to keep the plants within bounds.

Recommended Varieties

There are a number of different kinds of English ivy available. Unfortunately, without the protection of a dependable snow cover, the survival of many of them is "iffy" in the Midwest. Three of the hardiest English ivy choices for this region include 'Baltica', 'Bulgaria', and 'Wilson'.

GARDEN TIPS

◆ You can enjoy some of the beautiful but less hardy varieties of English ivy by growing them indoors as houseplants. Be sure to hose off the foliage frequently with water in the kitchen sink to prevent damage from red spider mites.

◆ English ivy plants may take years to grow, but be patient. Remember the old adage: "First it sleeps, next it creeps, then it leaps."

'Baltica'

Honeysuckle

Lonicera hybrids

ZONES: Variable, some hardy to zone 3

BLOOM TIME: June, sporadically throughout the summer

BLOOM COLOR: Pink, purple, red, white, yellow, or multicolored

LIGHT REQUIREMENT: Sun or partial shade

LENGTH OF VINE: 15 to 30 feet

Special Features

The tubular flowers of most honeysuckles are deliciously fragrant. The fleshy berries are relished by birds. This adaptable, twining vine is easy to grow.

How to Grow

Plant in any kind of soil with good drainage. The ideal location for most kinds of honeysuckle is a spot where the roots are shaded but the top of the vine will be exposed to full or partial sunlight.

Care and Maintenance

Apply mulch or add low-growing plants to shade the roots. Provide netting or lattice for support. Prune to keep the vines within bounds in early spring before new growth begins.

Recommended Varieties

The red flowers of 'Dropmore Scarlet' (*L.* × *brownii*) bloom from June to frost and attract hummingbirds to the garden. This honeysuckle is hardy to zone 3, making it one of the best for northern gardens. Sadly, its flowers don't have much fragrance. The blossoms of goldflame honeysuckle (*L.* × *heckrottii*), on the other hand, are blessed with a heavenly

GARDEN TIP

♦ To renew a tangle of overgrown honeysuckle vines, cut plants back to about a foot from ground level.

fragrance. The carmine-red buds open to flowers that are rosy-red outside, yellow inside. This variety is hardy to zone 4.

Related Species

Hall's honeysuckle (*L. japonica* 'Halliana'), although sometimes invasive in the Midwest, is nevertheless a useful and beautiful evergreen ground cover for steep slopes. (Just keep it away from the base of young trees and other small plants it could twine around and suffocate.) The highly fragrant white flowers turn to yellow as they mature, creating a beautiful sight in June, often with a repeat performance later in the season. Hall's honeysuckle is hardy in zones 5 to 9.

Hall's Honeysuckle

Goldflame Honeysuckle

Morning Glory

Ipomoea species

ZONES: Annual

BLOOM TIME: Summer through early fall

BLOOM COLOR: Blue, crimson, lavender, pink, violet, white, or bicolor

LIGHT REQUIREMENT: Full sun, partial shade

LENGTH OF VINE: 8 to 20 feet

Special Features

Morning glories' trumpet-shaped blossoms and heart-shaped leaves are well known and much loved. The flowers open in morning and close at the end of the day.

How to Grow

Morning glories are easiest to grow from seed planted outdoors after the last expected spring frost. Space seeds 8 to 12 inches apart and cover them with ¼ inch of fine soil. For earliest bloom, you can also sow seeds inside 3 to 4 weeks before the last frost. Plants resent root disturbance, so sow the seeds in individual peat pots. Plant in well-drained, lean soil. Morning glories bloom best in full sun but tolerate partial shade.

Care and Maintenance

Furnish netting, a trellis, or other support for the vines to twine up. Guide the plants to the support, if necessary, to get them started. Let soil dry out between waterings, and don't fertilize. Remove dead foliage after it has been killed by autumn frost.

Recommended Varieties

You can buy seeds of many different kinds of morning glories. Two old-time favorites that are still popular are 'Heavenly Blue' (*I. tricolor*), which was one of the first named varieties and is favored for its sky-blue, 5-inch blossoms; and 'Scarlet O'Hara' (*I. nil*), winner of a 1939 All-America Selections award, which is adored for its 4-inch wine-red flowers.

Related Species

If you enjoy being outdoors on summer evenings, be sure to plant moonflower (*I. alba*). Its huge 6-inch blossoms open at night, emitting an appealing fragrance similar to cloves. If you love hummingbirds (and who doesn't?), you'll want to include cardinal climber (*I. × multifida*) in your garden plan. Bountiful red blossoms shaped like small trumpets cover the handsome green foliage of these dainty vines.

> ## GARDEN TIPS
>
> ◆ Water is slow to penetrate the hard seed coats of morning glory and its relatives. To speed up germination, soak the seeds in warm water overnight before planting, or nick the seeds with a knife or file.
>
> ◆ For round-the-clock snow-white blossoms, try combining moonflower with a white variety of morning glory such as 'Pearly Gates'.

Porcelain Berry Vine

Ampelopsis brevipedunculata

OTHER COMMON NAMES:
Turquoise Berry, Porcelain
Vine

ZONES: 5 to 8

FRUITING TIME:
September, October

FRUIT COLOR: Blue, lilac,
purple, turquoise, and white
berries

LIGHT REQUIREMENT:
Sun or partial shade

LENGTH OF VINE: 10 to
20 feet

Special Features

Exquisite clusters of delicate-looking, pea-size berries look as if
they're made of porcelain, with multiple colors appearing in a
single cluster. Some kinds have variegated leaves with white
markings that make a handsome foil for the fruit.

How to Grow

Porcelain berry vine is easy to grow from seeds, but if you want a
variegated form, select a container-grown specimen. The vine
thrives in shade but needs sun for best production of berries. A
spot with morning sun and afternoon shade is ideal. Plant in well-
drained soil. Provide a support such as a nylon or wire netting for
the vine's tendrils to grasp.

Care and Maintenance

Water in dry weather. Add compost or a slow-release fertilizer in
spring. Prune to keep in bounds or to remove winter-killed wood

in early spring. Pull out any unwanted seedlings that sprout where the berries drop.

Recommended Variety

'Elegans' is less invasive than the species. It also has beautiful variegated foliage, with pink markings in spring that gradually change to white as the season progresses.

GARDEN TIP

♦ Although usually listed as hardy only to zone 5, porcelain berry vine also thrives in zone 4 gardens as far north as the Twin Cities. The secret? Although the top growth dies back to the ground during severe winter weather, the vine grows rapidly and fruits on new wood, so nothing is lost.

'Elegans'

Sweet Pea

Lathyrus odoratus

ZONES: Annual

BLOOM TIME: Late spring, early summer

BLOOM COLOR: Every color except yellow

LIGHT REQUIREMENT: Sun or partial shade

LENGTH OF VINE: 1 to 6 feet

Special Features

Sweet pea's delicate sunbonnet-shaped flowers are old-fashioned favorites, beloved for their sweet fragrance and pretty colors. Often the older varieties with simple, smaller flowers and pale colors have the sweetest fragrance, while newer types offer large, sometimes ruffled blossoms and bright colors.

How to Grow

Sweet pea is a cool-season annual that grows best when planted as soon as the frost is out of the ground, just like edible peas. Although the plants need sunshine to bloom, hot temperatures are their undoing, so in this region they are best planted in a spot that receives morning sun and afternoon shade. Plant the seeds 2 inches deep and 6 inches apart in the garden. For earlier blooms, start seeds six weeks sooner indoors. Soak the seeds for a few hours before planting to speed sprouting. Sweet peas resent root disturbance, so plant each seed in an individual peat pot and cover with 1/3 inch of soil.

Care and Maintenance

As soon as the plants are 10 inches tall, pinch out their tips to encourage branching. Mulch to keep the roots cool and conserve soil moisture. Provide a trellis or other support that the tendrils can grasp. Water in dry weather, making an effort to keep the foliage dry. Don't fertilize. Cut all the flowers you want for bouquets and remove other faded flowers before they set seed to encourage continued blooming. If you find aphids (check the underside of tender new leaves for clusters of tiny insects), remove them with a forceful spray of water from the hose or spray with insecticidal soap. You may also need to install a temporary barrier to prevent rabbits from nibbling tender young seedlings to the ground.

GARDEN TIPS

- Mix powdered legume inoculant with the seeds before planting them in the garden. The powder contains beneficial bacteria that will help your sweet peas bloom more and grow more vigorously.

- "Plant" some twiggy branches with your sweet peas for the vines to climb as they grow; or plant a few seeds at the base of a shrub and let the shrub support the vines.

Recommended Varieties

Sweet peas are often sold in mixed colors, like 'Royal Family', a mix of large flowers in solid colors. Two old-fashioned varieties, 'Old Spice' and 'Painted Lady', are favored for their powerfully sweet perfume.

Related Species

Perennial pea (*L. latifolius*) is hardy to zone 4. It's easy to grow from either seed or young transplants and comes in pink, red, and white. The plants, which bloom from July to frost, often start flowering right as summer's heat puts an end to the planting of annual sweet peas. Although just as pretty as the annual vines, perennial pea regrettably has no scent.

Trumpet Vine
Campsis radicans

OTHER COMMON NAME:
Trumpet Creeper

ZONES: 5 to 9 (4 with protection)

BLOOM TIME: July to September

BLOOM COLOR: Orange-scarlet, yellow, or red

LIGHT REQUIREMENT: Sun or partial shade

LENGTH OF VINE: 30 to 40 feet

Special Features

Clusters of large trumpet-shaped flowers are a magnet for hummingbirds. Handsome and vigorous, this exceptionally easy-to-grow vine clings to walls, trees, or trellises with aerial rootlets. Trumpet vine spreads by both suckering roots and seeds. It is ideal for screening large areas.

How to Grow

Trumpet vine grows best in moist, humusy soil, but you can help control its aggressive nature if you plant it in soil that isn't overly rich. Dig a hole as deep as and twice as wide as the vine's container. Place the crown (the place where the roots and top meet) 1 inch below the soil surface. Cut the top back to about 8 inches. Provide a sturdy support for the vine to climb.

Care and Maintenance

Prune in early spring as needed to shorten and thin the vine, or to remove dead wood. The vine flowers on the current season's growth, so you won't sacrifice any blossoms if you prune drastically at this time. Although insects and diseases sometimes attack, they almost never do enough damage to require control. Mulch plants grown north of zone 5 for winter protection after the ground freezes.

Recommended Varieties

Common trumpet vine has orange-scarlet flowers. There is also yellow trumpet vine ('Flava'), an apricot hybrid called 'Mme. Galen' (*C.* × *tagliabuana*), and red-flowered 'Crimson Trumpet'.

GARDEN TIPS

♦ Use the bare, woody trunk of an older trumpet vine as a natural trellis for dainty annual vines such as cardinal climber or sweet peas.

♦ If you're growing trumpet vine on the side of the house, keep the top pruned back below the roof line; otherwise, the vine might dislodge the roof shingles.

'Flava'

'Mme. Galen'

Wisteria

Wisteria floribunda

OTHER COMMON NAME:
Japanese Wisteria

ZONES: (4) 5 to 9

BLOOM TIME: April to May

BLOOM COLOR: Pink, violet, or white

LIGHT REQUIREMENT: Sun

LENGTH OF VINE: 20 to 30 feet

Special Features

Flowers in drooping clusters up to 18 inches long appear in spring just as the leaves begin to emerge. These showy, fragrant flowers make wisteria one of the most magnificent of all flowering vines.

How to Grow

If you're eager for blooms, start with a grafted plant; seedlings may take ten years or more to flower. Plant in moist, well-drained soil that has been enriched with compost or other organic materials. Choose a spot that's sheltered from wind. Provide a super-sturdy fence, arbor, or pergola for support, because a mature wisteria can easily crush a flimsy structure. Keep your wisteria watered until it's well established, and mulch to conserve moisture.

Care and Maintenance

If yours is a grafted plant, remove any suckers that grow from below the graft. Withhold nitrogen fertilizer to encourage blooming. Prune any overhanging limbs if necessary to give your wisteria full sun. Prune a non-blooming vine no more than necessary to keep the plant in bounds. Once it flowers, limit pruning to pinching back side shoots each years after the blooms fade.

Related Species

If your Japanese wisteria is prevented from flowering by cold injury, consider growing the American version (*W. frutescens*) instead. Unlike Japanese wisteria, American wisteria blooms from June to August on new wood. Its lilac-colored flower clusters are fragrant and showy, though not as big as those of its Japanese counterpart.

> ## GARDEN TIP
>
> ◆ If you've done everything right and waited patiently, and yet your wisteria still won't bloom, try root pruning: slice down through the soil with a sharp spade, as if you were beginning to dig up the plant.

American Wisteria

The Water Garden

No matter what size water garden you choose, you'll need a flat spot for it. To get the best performance from blooming plants, the site should be sunny for at least six hours a day. Safety is another consideration. Be sure your new water garden isn't a hazard for young children, and check local zoning restrictions before you begin.

Most city water is too alkaline for plants and fish. When you fill your pool, use a pH test kit to determine the water's alkalinity, then add a neutralizer if necessary to bring the reading to near neutral (7 to 7.5). You probably already have a good neutralizer on hand: white vinegar, added at the rate of one-half gallon per 5 gallons of water, will bring the pH reading down.

You can install a filter to keep the water clean, or you can put nature to work for you: Discourage the ugly green scum of algae by filling your pool with enough plants to cover one-half to two-thirds of the water's surface. Be sure to include some floating varieties, such as water hyacinth and water lettuce; their roots feed on sediments in the pool. Add a few snails to consume algae.

Oxygenator plants will also help keep the water clean, as well as provide oxygen for fish in the pool. The kind of plants sold in the pet department for aquariums will work fine. Plant several bunches in flower pots and set the pots on the bottom of the pool. Use one pot for every 2 to 3 square feet of water surface. Pond Shade®, a product made from non-toxic dyes, helps control algae by filtering the sunlight. It also tints the water a pretty shade of blue. Pond Shade® is safe for fish and plants, and will do no harm if your dog or cat drinks from the pool.

Another way to help your water stay clear is by adding some beneficial bacteria. A powdered form is available in such products as Nature Clear™. When added to the water on a regular schedule, these bacteria clear the water and eliminate the slime on the side of the pool—and they do it without chemicals or danger to fish.

Mosquitoes won't breed in your pool's water as long as you have some goldfish or guppies. Allow one small fish for every five gallons of water. If you don't want to bother with fish, you can solve the mosquito problem by floating a Mosquito Dunk® in the water. The ring slowly releases a form of *Bacillus thuringiensis* that infects mosquito larvae. Like the *Bt* used in vegetable gardens to control cabbage worms, this product is also environmentally friendly.

Once spring has arrived and your pool is filled with water, the real fun begins: choosing your plants. The next few pages showcase some of the best choices for a Midwest water garden, along with tips on helping them thrive.

Bog Plants

Special Features

Plants that thrive at the water's edge in nature's own pools will make the perfect "frame" for your water garden, too. These bog plants come in an endless variety. Some have colorful blooms, while others have eye-catching foliage. Some are winter-hardy, while others are tender tropicals that must be protected from frost.

How to Grow

Plant bog plants in plastic pots that allow for good air circulation. Lattice-type crates lined with burlap or other porous material work well. Use garden soil, not potting soil. After planting, spread a half-inch layer of sand or pebbles over the soil so it will stay in place when the pots are submerged. Place bog plants in the water garden with their crowns 1 to 2 inches below the surface of the water. Set them on a shelf at the edge of the pool or use bricks to elevate the pots to the proper level (see Appendix).

Care and Maintenance

Fertilizing the plants is necessary to produce a maximum number of blooms, but it's important not to use too much: excess nitrogen in the water encourages algae growth. Use fertilizer tablets made especially for water plants. Press the tablets into the soil, following package instructions. Divide hardy varieties when they become crowded. In winter, you can set hardy bog plants on the bottom of the pool as long as the pool is at least 2 feet deep. If it isn't, wrap the potted plants in a tarp and store them in a cool corner of the basement, or plant them in the ground in fall. To overwinter tropical bog plants, treat them as houseplants. Place them in bright light, and keep their saucers filled with water.

Recommended Hardy Bog Plants

Pickerel rush (*Pontederia cordata,* pictured at left) has shiny, heart-shaped leaves and spikes of blue flowers from mid to late summer. It is hardy through zone 4 and thrives in sun or partial shade.

Yellow water iris (*Iris pseudacorus*) has large yellow blooms in spring. It requires full sun and is hardy through zone 4.

Recommended Tropical Bog Plants

Water cannas (*Canna* species) resemble their dry-land counterparts, but unlike conventional cannas, they grow best in standing water. They thrive in sun or partial shade and produce red or yellow blooms all summer. Elephant's ear, or taro (*Colocasia* species), has huge, dramatic leaves. Some varieties have violet-colored stems. Miniature umbrella palm (*Cyperus involucratus* 'Gracilis') has whorls of spiked foliage in an umbrella shape. It grows to 2 feet tall, making it perfect for a patio pond. There is a 4-foot-tall version that works well in bigger ponds.

Yellow Water Iris

Umbrella Palm

Free-Floating Plants

Special Features

No other plants are as easy to grow as free-floating water plants. When you get home from the garden center with your plants in a water-filled plastic bag, just take them out of the bag and drop them in your pool. That's it—no soil, no fertilizer, no planting.

Floaters are a valuable asset in the water garden. Although they're quite attractive, they do more than just float around looking pretty. Their roots help keep the water clean by feeding on sediments in the pool, and their leaves shade the water surface, thus reducing algae.

Floaters are tender tropical plants, and they love hot weather. Put them in your pool in late spring or early summer after the water temperature reaches 70 degrees Fahrenheit. In midsummer, they'll grow so fast you'll have to "weed" the extras, but when cool, fall weather arrives, the plants will decline. Free-floating plants are very difficult to overwinter indoors because they require bright light and warm temperatures. Most people prefer to add them to the compost heap in fall and start with new ones each year.

Recommended Floaters

Water hyacinth (*Eichhornia crassipes*, pictured above) has shiny, cuplike leaves that grow in rosettes, making the plant attractive even before it blooms. Once blooming begins, water hyacinth produces lovely 6-inch, lavender-blue spikes non-stop until fall. You can grow water hyacinth in partial shade, but plants bloom best in full sun. New rosettes grow on stolons produced by the mother plant. In the South, water hyacinth clogs waterways and is banned. There are no such problems in our region, however, because plants cannot survive our Midwest winters. Water lettuce (*Pistia stratiotes*) looks

GARDEN TIP

♦ Adding free-floaters to your water garden will help your fish raise a family. The tangle of roots provides an ideal environment for spawning.

something like a small cabbage head and has velvety, pale-green leaves. It grows like a weed—new babies form on all sides, then break off to start colonies of their own. The only work you need to do to grow water lettuce is to pull out the unwanted extras. When you can't give any more away, add the extras to the compost pile. Water lettuce thrives in sun or partial shade.

Water Lettuce

Water Lilies

Special Features

Water lilies are the highlight of the water garden, and no wonder! Their exquisite flowers bloom in a rainbow of colors, surrounded by lush lily pads that float on the water's surface. There are two major groups of water lilies, each with its own set of advantages and disadvantages.

The flowers of tropical lilies bloom more, holding their heads up out of the water. In addition to the pinks, reds, whites, and yellows of hardy lilies, tropical lilies also bloom in blue and purple. They are often fragrant, and some are night bloomers, making them ideal if the only time you get to sit in your garden is in the evening. Tropical lilies, however, cannot withstand cold. They cannot be put in the water until its temperature reaches 70 degrees Fahrenheit, which in the Midwest means waiting until June. When you consider that they last only a single season, these lilies are also expensive.

Hardy lilies, on the other hand, will not only survive for years, but multiply. Plants begin growing in early spring, long before it's safe to put tropical lilies in the garden. Unlike those of tropical lilies, however, hardy lily blossoms float on the water's surface and are not as prominent. All hardy lilies open during the day and close at night.

How to Grow

Pot your plants in plastic pots that allow for good air circulation. Lattice-type crates lined with burlap or other porous material work well. Use garden soil rather than potting soil. After planting, spread a half-inch layer of sand or pebbles over the soil so it will stay in place when the pots are submerged. Place a water lily in the water garden so that its crown is about 6 inches below the water's surface. If necessary, use bricks to elevate the pot to the proper level (see Appendix).

GARDEN TIP

♦ To keep water lilies looking their best, trim off each bloom stalk at its base as soon as the flower fades; remove any yellowing leaves.

Care and Maintenance

Fertilizer is necessary for maximum blooms, but it's important not to use too much: excess nitrogen in the water encourages the growth of algae. Once a month during the summer, push the kind of fertilizer tablets that are made for water garden plants into the soil. Hardy water lilies grow rapidly and must be divided every year or two to keep the plants from becoming too crowded. You can divide plants any time during the growing season, but spring is the best time for the job. Remove each plant from its pot and divide the crown into three or four sections. Replant one in fresh soil, and share the extras with friends.

Hardy water lilies can be overwintered in one of two ways: If your water garden is at least 2 feet deep, take the plants off their brick perches and set the pots on the bottom of the pool. If you have a small water garden, such as a tub or a barrel, wrap potted water lilies in a tarp and store them in a cool corner of the basement for the winter. Tropical water lilies are difficult to overwinter and are best grown as annuals.

Tropical Pink

White Hardy

Wildflowers

When it comes to weather, the Midwest is a region of extremes. Plants here have to be able to take everything Mother Nature dishes out: searing summers, bitter-cold winters, violent storms, floods, droughts, and strong winds. In Clarkson, Nebraska, the folks at Bluebird Nursery—one of the nation's largest wholesalers of perennial plants—sum it up this way: "If they'll grow in Nebraska, they'll grow anywhere!" A corollary for gardeners: if they grew here before we came, they'll grow here today! The wildflowers that once dotted our prairies and woodlands had hundreds of years to adapt to our soils and weather extremes—so chances are good they'll thrive in your yard, too.

With few exceptions, the plants described in this chapter actually do best when the going gets tough. They need little, if any, fertilizer. Once established, many can sail through a drought without extra water. In fact, if you pampered our natives with rich, moist soil, most of them would only grow weak and flop over on their neighbors.

Besides being easy to grow, Midwest natives are charming, too. Now that wildflowers are all the rage, we wonder why it took so long to start planting these beauties in our gardens. In some cases, it was probably because they were once so common in the roadside ditches and along woodland trails. In other cases—such as goldenrod, for example—we didn't recognize some of our taller natives as valuable garden

plants until they'd gone to finishing school on the other side of the Atlantic and returned to us better behaved.

There are two ways to enjoy wildflowers in your yard. You can treat them just like any other perennial and grow them in a mixed-flower border. Or you can plant a collection of native wildflowers in a patch of their own and allow them to naturalize.

It's less expensive to plant a large wildflower patch if you start with seeds. To eliminate as many weeds as possible, till the ground shallowly several times at two-week intervals before you plant. If your wildflower patch is small, you'll get quicker results by starting with plants. Nowadays, you can buy beardtongue, blazingstar, cardinal flower, and many others as bedding plants in spring and summer.

Once established, a wildflower patch is nearly care-free. Most of our natives can grow for years without division. Mowing the plants after fall frost is often the only maintenance needed.

A garden filled with wildflowers is never dull. As some flowers fade and other kinds take their place, the patch is a kaleidoscope of changing colors. As easy to grow as they are beautiful, Midwest wildflowers can't be beat for Midwest gardens.

Aster

Aster species

OTHER COMMON NAME:
Hardy Aster

ZONES: 4 to 9

BLOOM TIME: Late
summer through fall

BLOOM COLOR: Blue,
pink, purple, red, or white

LIGHT REQUIREMENT:
Full sun, partial shade

HEIGHT × WIDTH: 12 to
48 inches × 15 to 36 inches

Special Features

Masses of these yellow-centered, daisylike flowers light up the
autumn perennial border. Butterflies adore the blossoms, which
make long-lasting cut flowers. You can choose from dozens of different types, ranging from short asters that are ideal partners for
chrysanthemums to tall ones that combine beautifully with ornamental grasses.

How to Grow

Plant in well-drained soil of average fertility. Space plants 12 to
20 inches apart. Transplant container-grown plants any time. You
can also grow asters from seeds sown in early spring.

Care and Maintenance

Water in dry weather. Fertilize sparingly. To control height, you
can cut back tall varieties by one half in late spring, or pinch back
growing tips several times in late spring or early summer as you
would chrysanthemums (see illustrated Appendix). Tall varieties
may require staking. Divide plants every two years in spring to

help the plants stay vigorous and under control.

Asters are susceptible to mildew, though some varieties offer mildew resistance. To help control this fungus, allow each plant room for good air circulation and keep the soil moist. Clean up infected plant debris. If cultural control methods fail, apply a fungicide every 10 to 12 days.

Related Species

Smooth aster (*A. laevis*) puts on a spectacular fall show of pale lavender-blue flowers on 2- to 4-foot-tall plants. The azure or sky-blue aster (*A. azureus*) is slightly shorter, with brilliant-blue flowers. A small aster ideal for the rock garden is *A. fendleri*, which is native to the plains of Nebraska and Kansas. Plants grow only 4 to 12 inches tall and have light-lavender flowers. 'My Antonia', a white variety, is an attractive new selection from GreatPlants, a joint program of the Nebraska Statewide Arboretum and the Nebraska Nursery and Landscape Association.

Despite their name, New England asters (*A. novi-angliae*) dot the Midwest, too. Though they are usually tall plants that require staking, some varieties are well-behaved beauties. One of the most loved is 'Alma Potschke', a 2-foot-tall, mildew-resistant variety with brilliant-pink blossoms. Another is 'Purple Dome', which has deep-purple flowers on sturdy 18-inch plants. New York asters (*A. novae-belgii*)—sometimes called Michaelmas daisies—are also popular in Midwest gardens. A particular favorite is 'Professor Anton Kippenberg', which produces mounds of blue-violet flowers on foot-tall plants.

GARDEN TIPS

- Cut and remove above-ground growth in the garden after fall frost. The cleanup helps control disease and prevents reseeding of less-desirable varieties. If your asters are naturalized in a patch with other wildflowers, though, just mow the entire patch and leave the cut plants where they fall.

- Avoid growing asters in overly rich soil—extra nutrients make asters weak and floppy.

Beardtongue

Penstemon species

ZONES: Variable from 2 to 9, depending on species

BLOOM TIME: Late spring or early summer

BLOOM COLOR: Pink, scarlet, violet, or white

LIGHT REQUIREMENT: Full sun or partial shade

HEIGHT × WIDTH: 16 to 48 inches × 12 to 30 inches

Special Features

Tall spikes filled with tubular snapdragonlike flowers create a spectacular display in the garden. The blossoms are great for cutting and are attractive to hummingbirds, too.

How to Grow

All penstemons demand well-drained soil. The plants, which tend to be short-lived, survive longest when grown in sandy, dry soil of low to average fertility. Space plants 1 to 2 feet apart, depending on variety, or sow seeds outdoors on the soil surface in early fall.

Care and Maintenance

Cut plants back after flowering to improve appearance. Drop the dried flowers in the garden to reseed; this will provide a small but continuous supply of new plants to replace the often short-lived originals. After the ground freezes in fall, spread evergreen boughs or other loose mulch for winter protection. Division is seldom needed, but if you want to attempt it, divide plants in spring.

Related Species

Penstemons comprise a large group of native wildflowers. One of the best for the Midwest is the foxglove penstemon (*P. digitalis*), which grows 2 to 4 feet tall and produces elegant clusters of

> ### GARDEN TIP
>
> ◆ Don't coddle beardtongues. They can take drought and heat but will decline in rich, moist soil.

white or light-rose flowers. An outstanding variety is 'Husker Red', a University of Nebraska introduction that earned the 1996 Perennial Plant of the Year award from the Perennial Plant Association. It begins and ends the year with attractive red foliage and takes the show in June with showy white flowers. Shell-leaf penstemon (*P. grandiflorus*) boasts large, 2-inch lavender flowers on 3-foot-tall plants. 'Prairie Snow', another introduction from Dale Lindgren at the University of Nebraska, is a superb selection with pure-white flowers. Common beardtongue (*P. barbatus*) produces scarlet flowers with a yellow-bearded lower "lip." The narrow leaves are glossy green, and plants grow up to 3 feet tall. 'Prairie Splendor', a new hybrid from the University of Nebraska breeding program, blooms for a month in magnificent shades of lavender, pink, rose, and white. The plants grow to slightly over 2 feet tall.

'Husker Red'

Common Beardtongue

Black-Eyed Susan

Rudbeckia fulgida

OTHER COMMON NAME:
Gloriosa Daisy

ZONES: 3 to 8

BLOOM TIME: July to
October

BLOOM COLOR: Yellow
or gold

LIGHT REQUIREMENT:
Full sun

HEIGHT × WIDTH: 24 to
36 inches × 24 to 36 inches

Special Features

If you want to light up your sunny garden, you can't beat these profuse 3-inch, golden-yellow daisies. The easy-care plants bloom non-stop for months, and the blossoms make great cut flowers. If you allow the season's last flowers to dry in the garden, the central cones will often remain intact, adding their subtle beauty and attracting birds to the winter garden.

How to Grow

Plant in fertile, well-drained soil. Space plants 12 to 24 inches apart, depending on variety. Plant container-grown plants any time through the growing season, or sow seeds on the soil surface in spring.

Care and Maintenance

Tall varieties may require staking. Pests and diseases are usually not a problem with most perennial types. If aphids are numerous, simply hose off the tiny insects with a strong jet of water from the garden hose. Divide plants in spring every four or five years as necessary to maintain vigor.

Recommended Varieties

'Goldsturm', 1999 Perennial Plant of the Year, is the undisputed star, producing golden-yellow flowers, prominent dark cones, and dark-green leaves that turn a pretty bronze in autumn. A long-lived, hardy perennial, it is seldom bothered by pests or diseases, and the sturdy, 2-foot-tall plants never need staking.

GARDEN TIPS

♦ In addition to hardy perennials, there are also biennial and annual types of black-eyed Susans. As long as you allow some plants to reseed in the garden, though, you're not apt to lose these bright beauties.

♦ Mildew or stem rot is occasionally a problem with annual and biennial types. There are usually volunteers waiting to take their place, so just remove the affected plants.

Related Species

'Herbstonne' (*R. laciniata 'Autumn Sun'*) is a great choice if you want a tall, back-of-the-border perennial. It grows nearly 6 feet tall. The flowers have drooping yellow petals and attractive green centers. Although their stems are sturdy, these plants often require light support to stand up through summer storms. 'Indian Summer' (*R. hirta*), winner of a 1995 All-America Selections award, has huge semidouble flowers that measure 6 inches or more across. It is a good variety to grow from seeds. *R. hirta* is not long-lived and is best grown as an annual.

Blanket Flower

Gaillardia × grandiflora

ZONES: 3 to 9

BLOOM TIME: June to September

BLOOM COLOR: A combination of bronze, red, and yellow

LIGHT REQUIREMENT: Full sun

HEIGHT × WIDTH: 12 to 36 inches × 12 to 24 inches

Special Features

Big, multicolored, daisylike flowers make a colorful addition to the sunny border. Blanket flower blossoms are also good candidates for bouquets. When the flowers fade, globe-shaped seedheads remain.

How to Grow

Plant in well-drained soil that has no more than average fertility. Plant container-grown specimens any time during the growing season, spacing plants 12 to 15 inches apart. You can also grow gaillardias from seeds scattered outside on the soil surface in spring.

Care and Maintenance

Stake tall varieties. Pests and diseases seldom cause any serious problems. Plants tend to be short-lived, but dividing every 2 to 3 years in spring will help them stay vigorous. Make sure the soil slopes away from the plants' centers, or crowns, to provide excellent drainage during the winter. Mulch lightly for winter protection after the ground freezes.

Recommended Varieties

If you want a care-free perennial, plant foot-tall 'Goblin' or 8-inch-tall 'Baby Cole'. Dwarfs that never need staking, both have red petals with yellow tips.

GARDEN TIP

◆ Start a colorful summer-long show by sowing seeds of annual blanket flower (*G. pulchella*) indoors 4 to 6 weeks before the last frost. Transplant outdoors after the weather warms. These easy-care, drought-tolerant plants are ideal candidates for planting in sunny containers.

'Baby Cole'

'Goblin'

Blazing Star

Liatris spicata

OTHER COMMON NAME:
Spike Gayfeather

ZONES: 3 to 9

BLOOM TIME: July to September

BLOOM COLOR: Rose-purple

LIGHT REQUIREMENT: Full sun

HEIGHT × WIDTH: 24 to 36 inches × 18 to 24 inches

Special Features

Use these tall bottlebrush blossoms for a beautiful vertical accent in the flower border. The flowers on these unique spikes open from the top down (the reverse of the way most spikes open). Butterflies love them, and so do flower arrangers: blazing star blossoms are long lasting in both cutflower and dried arrangements.

How to Grow

Plant in well-drained soil. Blazing star performs better in sandy or average soils than in clay. Space plants 12 to 18 inches apart, or sow seeds in fall or early spring.

Care and Maintenance

Although established plants are drought tolerant, they need watering in dry weather to look their best. Remove dead flowers to improve appearance. Plants require little care, and diseases and pests seldom bother them. If mildew develops in humid weather, thin plants to improve air circulation. Tall varieties may require staking. Division is seldom necessary.

GARDEN TIP

◆ If you want to increase your plants, dig and divide the corms in fall.

Recommended Variety

'Kobold' is one of the best for the perennial border. These compact plants grow about 2 feet tall and produce deep rose-purple flowers.

'Kobold'

Boltonia

Boltonia asteroides

ZONES: 3 to 8

BLOOM TIME: September to October

BLOOM COLOR: White

LIGHT REQUIREMENT: Full sun or partial shade

HEIGHT × WIDTH: 36 to 60 inches × 36 to 48 inches

Special Features

Great clouds of white 1-inch daisies cover these bushy plants in autumn. The flowers resemble perennial asters, but unlike asters, boltonia is mildew resistant and does not require staking.

How to Grow

Plant container-grown plants in well-drained soil of average fertility any time during the growing season. Space plants 18 inches apart. Avoid rich garden soil and shady sites.

Care and Maintenance

Established plants are drought tolerant and normally require little care. There's no need to remove spent blossoms; boltonia keeps blooming until frost without deadheading. Cut back after frost only if plants are flopping. For best results, divide clumps every two years in spring. If your soil is "clayish," you can get by with less-frequent division.

Recommended Varieties

'Snowbank' is an outstanding garden performer that produces extra-sturdy stems and the profuse white flowers that give the variety its name. If you'd rather have pink flowers, try 'Pink Beauty'. It blooms a few weeks earlier and grows shorter; it also tends to flop without staking and is not quite as vigorous.

GARDEN TIPS

- ◆ You can control boltonia's height by cutting plants back to 12 inches in late spring.

'Snowbank'

'Pink Beauty'

Bugbane

Cimicifuga racemosa

OTHER COMMON NAMES:
Black Snakeroot, Black
Cohosh

ZONES: 3 to 7

BLOOM TIME: July and
August

BLOOM COLOR: Ivory
white

LIGHT REQUIREMENT:
Partial to full shade

HEIGHT × WIDTH: 48 to
60 inches × 24 to 36 inches

Special Features

Bugbane's graceful flower spikes are a standout in the shady garden at a time when few other plants are blooming. These easy-care, long-lived plants have broad, handsome leaves and provide a strong vertical accent.

How to Plant

Plant in well-drained soil that is enriched with compost or other organic materials. Space plants 3 feet apart.

Care and Maintenance

Feed with slow-release fertilizer in spring. Water in dry weather, and mulch to conserve soil moisture. Pests and diseases are seldom a problem. Although plants have sturdy stems, light staking may be necessary to keep blooming plants upright through summer storms. Division, best done in spring, is rarely necessary.

Related Species

If you want to stretch the flower season into late fall, include several other species of bugbane in your shady border. *Cimicifuga japonica* blooms from August to September, and 'White Pearl' (*C. simplex*) blooms from September to October. 'Atropurpurea' (*C. ramosa*) is an extraordinarily beautiful purple-leafed variety that blooms in fall.

GARDEN TIPS

♦ Give bugbane a little time to get established. After two or three years of growth, it will be magnificent.

♦ For best blooms, plant bugbane where it gets morning sun and afternoon shade.

'White Pearl'

'Atropurpurea'

Butterfly Milkweed
Asclepias tuberosa

OTHER COMMON NAMES: Butterfly Flower, Butterfly Weed

ZONES: 4 to 8

BLOOM TIME: July to September

BLOOM COLOR: Orange-red

HEIGHT × WIDTH: 24 to 36 inches × 15 to 24 inches

Special Features

Monarchs and other butterflies are drawn irresistibly to these brightly colored flower clusters. The attractive reddish seedpods that appear after the blooms have faded are lovely in dried arrangements. The narrow, dark-green leaves of butterfly milkweed make it a handsome addition to the perennial border.

How to Grow

Butterfly milkweed performs best in soil that is light, sandy, and well drained. The plants require little fertilizer. Space specimens 12 to 18 inches apart in spring or summer, or sow seeds in early spring or fall.

Care and Maintenance

Established plants are drought tolerant and require little care. Because the plants are slow to appear in spring, mark their location to prevent accidental disturbance. You can remove dead flowers to encourage rebloom, but leave later flowers on the plant to form attractive seedpods. If you want volunteer seedlings, let some seeds mature in the garden. Aphids occasionally congregate on the leaves, but the tiny insects are easy to wash off with a strong jet of water from the garden hose. Established plants have difficult-to-transplant taproots, and division is not recommended.

Related Species

Swamp milkweed (*A. incarnata*) has attractive deep-pink flower clusters and thrives in any moist soil. The plants grow about 48 inches tall. Like butterfly milkweed, swamp milkweed attracts butterflies.

GARDEN TIP

♦ To enjoy adult butterflies, you have to be willing to allow their caterpillars to feed on foliage in your garden. These larvae often riddle the leaves of milkweed, which is one of their favorite foods. Try planting other flowers in front of your milkweeds to conceal the leaf damage, and you'll be rewarded with both flowers and butterflies.

Swamp Milkweed

Cardinal Flower

Lobelia cardinalis

ZONES: 3 to 9

BLOOM TIME: July to September

BLOOM COLOR: Bright red

LIGHT REQUIREMENT: Partial shade

HEIGHT × WIDTH: 24 to 36 inches × 24 inches

Special Features

A favorite of hummingbirds, cardinal flower's showy spikes provide welcome color in the woodland garden from midsummer to fall.

How to Grow

A wet spot where water frequently stands is the perfect place to plant cardinal flower. Add compost or other organic materials to help retain moisture. Space plants 12 to 18 inches apart, or sow seeds outdoors in late fall.

Care and Maintenance

Don't let the soil dry out. Remove flower stalks when blossoms fade. Add a light mulch for winter protection after the ground freezes, but be sure to remove the mulch promptly as soon as new growth begins in spring. Divide plants every two or three years in spring to help maintain their vigor.

Related Species

Great blue lobelia (*L. siphilitica*) has showy deep-blue flowers in late summer.

GARDEN TIP

♦ Cardinal flower is often short-lived but will reseed dependably in bare, moist soil.

Great Blue
Lobelia

False Indigo

Baptisia australis

OTHER COMMON NAME:
Blue Wild Indigo

ZONES: 3 to 9

BLOOM TIME: May and
June

BLOOM COLOR: Purple

LIGHT REQUIREMENT:
Full sun or partial shade

HEIGHT × WIDTH: 36 to
48 inches × 48 to 60 inches

Special Features

This shrubby blue-green plant shows off with 12-inch spikes of pea-shaped flowers in late spring. The flowers, which attract butterflies, are followed by large black seedpods that are great for dried arrangements.

How to Grow

Plant as a single specimen or space 3 feet apart. You can also start false indigo from seed planted in late fall or early spring. Plant in well-drained soil of average fertility.

Care and Maintenance

Plants are drought tolerant once established. In the garden, false indigo may require staking to keep from flopping on its neighbors as the season progresses. If rabbits feed on young plants, circle them with a cylinder of chicken wire. Division, which is seldom necessary, is made difficult by the plant's deep taproot.

Related Species

If you don't have room for the shrublike false indigo, try the miniature version (*B. minor*), which is similar but grows only 15 to 24 inches tall. Wild white indigo (*B. lactea*) is a white-flowered prairie native.

GARDEN TIP

◆ Pop a three-legged wire peony hoop over false indigo in spring to add support throughout the season; or, if you don't mind sacrificing the decorative black seedpods, cut growth back by half after blooms fade.

Wild White Indigo

False Indigo (miniature)

Goldenrod

Solidago hybrids

ZONES: 3 to 9

BLOOM TIME: August to September

BLOOM COLOR: Bright yellow or gold

LIGHT REQUIREMENT: Full sun

HEIGHT × WIDTH: 24 to 30 inches × 15 to 24 inches

Special Features

Goldenrod's dense, brightly colored plumes or flat-topped flower clusters are a cheerful sight in late summer and have earned goldenrod its place as the state flower of Nebraska. The blossoms are great for cutting or drying. New hybrids are stocky and sturdy, making them ideal for the perennial border.

How to Grow

Plant in well-drained soil of average fertility. Space plants 18 inches apart. Goldenrod species are also easily grown from seeds planted in early spring or late fall.

Care and Maintenance

Water in dry weather. Avoid excessive fertilization, which makes for weak, floppy growth. Division of plants, though seldom necessary, should be done in spring. Mildew sometimes occurs, but it is seldom serious—simply cut and remove any infected foliage. If you don't want your plants to reseed in the garden, remove spent flowers before the seeds ripen.

Recommended Varieties

Well-behaved hybrids like 'Cloth of Gold' or 'Crown of Rays' are good garden performers. The first grows about 18 inches tall, the second to 24 inches.

> ## GARDEN TIP
>
> ◆ Despite the persistent myth, you can't truthfully blame goldenrod for your hay fever. Go ahead and enjoy its bright beauty in your autumn garden.

Related Species

The native stiff goldenrod (*S. rigida*) can grow up to 5 feet tall and is perfect for naturalizing.

'Crown of Rays'

'Cloth of Gold'

Jack-in-the-Pulpit

Arisaema triphyllum

ZONES: 3 to 8

BLOOM TIME: April to June

BLOOM COLOR: Green, brownish purple, or a striped combination of both

LIGHT REQUIREMENT: Shade

HEIGHT × WIDTH: 12 to 24 inches × 6 to 12 inches

Special Features

Jack-in-the-pulpit's unique flower grabs attention with a showy hood (the pulpit) hovering over a tonguelike column (the jack, or preacher). In late summer, clusters of bright red berries add welcome color to the woodland garden and provide food for wildlife.

How to Grow

Choose a moist site, and enrich the soil with compost or other organic materials before planting. Set out young plants 8 to 10 inches apart in spring. You can also grow jack-in-the-pulpit from seeds sown in fall. Gather ripe berries, squeeze out the seeds, and plant immediately, barely covering the seeds with soil.

Care and Maintenance

Established plants are drought tolerant, but if you want to keep them actively growing throughout the summer, you'll need to water in dry weather; plants will otherwise go dormant. Jack-in-the-pulpit resents disturbance and should not be divided. Slugs are occasionally a problem; use baited traps or surround plants with a barrier of coarse sand or copper strips. Rust may also infect plants. If you see the telltale orange bumps on the undersides of leaves, remove the affected plant before the fungus spreads.

GARDEN TIP

- ◆ Jack-in-the-pulpit is the perfect solution for a deeply shaded site with poorly drained, "clayish" soil.

Joe-Pye Weed
Eupatorium purpureum

ZONES: 3 to 8

BLOOM TIME: July to September

BLOOM COLOR: Pale purple or rose

LIGHT REQUIREMENT: Full sun or light shade

HEIGHT × WIDTH: 36 to 72 inches × 36 to 48 inches

Special Features
The showy flat-topped flower clusters of Joe-pye weed are a magnet for butterflies. The bold plants make a magnificent back-of-the-border planting.

How to Grow
Choose a site where the soil stays moist. Set plants 3 feet apart in spring or summer, or sow seeds in autumn.

Care and Maintenance
Mulch plants to conserve soil moisture. Water in dry weather. Plants sometimes require staking, particularly if they're growing in too much shade or in overly rich soil. Thin for good air circulation to help prevent mildew. Cut and remove infected plant parts if necessary. Divide plants in spring every third year or when the clumps become crowded. Cut the plants back to the ground in fall after frost.

Recommended Varieties
The sturdy reddish-purple stems of 'Gateway' grow 5 to 6 feet tall and are topped with mauve flower clusters. 'Chocolate' has striking bronze-purple foliage and creamy-white flowers.

Related Species

Hardy ageratum (*E. coelestinum*), or mist flower, has blooms of lavender-blue that are similar to those of the well-known annual ageratum. These 2- to 3-foot-tall plants thrive in full sun or light shade. White snakeroot (*E. rugosum*), an excellent plant for the dry woodland garden, has white flower clusters on 3-foot-tall plants.

GARDEN TIPS

♦ To control the height of Joe-pye weed, shear plants back by half in early June.

♦ All three species of *Eupatorium* can be invasive if allowed to set seed. If desired, prevent volunteer plants by removing faded flowers before the seeds mature.

White Snakeroot

Hardy Ageratum

Purple Coneflower

Echinacea purpurea

ZONES: 3 to 9

BLOOM TIME: July to October

BLOOM COLOR: Pinkish-purple

LIGHT REQUIREMENT: Full sun, partial shade

HEIGHT × WIDTH: 24 to 36 inches × 24 inches

Special Features

Bright-colored petals surround the bristly orange cones of these showy, 4-inch daisylike flowers. One of the most spectacular of all our native plants, purple coneflower is also exceptionally easy to grow. It is tolerant of both heat and drought. The blossoms attract butterflies and make great cut flowers.

How to Grow

Plant container-grown plants any time during the growing season in lean, well-drained soil. Space plants 18 to 24 inches apart. If growing from seeds, plant purple coneflowers in fall or early spring.

Care and Maintenance

Remove dead flowers to improve appearance, promote continued blooming, and prevent volunteer seedlings in your garden. Plants are nearly pest-free and need no coddling. Occasionally, a plant is distorted, with light-green leaves and a branching top. Flowers are small or lacking. Discard the plant before leafhopper insects spread this virus-like disease to healthy plants. Divide every 3 or 4 years in spring.

Recommended Varieties

'Magnus', named Perennial Plant of the Year in 1998 by the Perennial Plant Association, has deep-rose flowers. Unlike most coneflowers, which have flowers shaped like umbrellas, the petals of 'Magnus' don't droop. 'White Swan' (also called 'Alba') is a creamy-white variety.

GARDEN TIPS

♦ If left standing, purple coneflower's central cones add winter interest and attract finches to the garden.

♦ Plants may require staking if grown in too much shade or in soil that is too rich.

Related Species

Pale purple coneflowers (*E. angustifolia* or *E. pallida*) are stunning in a patch of wildflowers, often growing slightly taller than the more common purple coneflower. Their large blossoms have skinny, drooping, pale-pink petals. The yellow coneflower (*E. paradoxa*) has yellow petals and brown cones. Though a native of the Ozarks, it is hardy to zone 3.

Pale Purple Coneflower

'Magnus'

Trillium

Trillium grandiflorum

OTHER COMMON NAME:
Great White Trillium

ZONES: 4 to 7

BLOOM TIME: April and May

BLOOM COLOR: White fading to pink

LIGHT REQUIREMENT: Shade

HEIGHT × WIDTH: 10 to 16 inches × 12 to 18 inches

Special Features

Trillium's large flowers open in early spring and are a welcome sight in the woodland garden. The name "trillium" means triple, and everything about this plant comes in threes, from its three-petaled blossoms to its whorls of rich-green leaves. Trilliums combine beautifully with other early wildflowers such as Virginia bluebells and jack-in-the-pulpit.

How to Plant

Choose a shady site where the soil remains moist. Enrich the soil by adding compost or other organic materials. Plant in spring, spacing plants 12 inches apart. Trillium's fleshy rhizomes can also be planted in fall. If you want to grow trillium from seed, you must be patient: it may be five years or more until the plants bloom.

Care and Maintenance

Mulch to conserve soil moisture, and water in dry weather. Refrain from picking any leaves: as long as they're green, the leaves are needed to strengthen the rhizomes for future blooms. Pests and diseases are seldom a problem, and plants don't require division.

Related Species

Prairie trillium (*T. recurvatum*) produces purple, red, or yellow-green blooms. Despite its common name, this plant prefers woodlands to prairies. Snow trillium (*T. nivale*) is the earliest trillium to bloom in the Midwest, with white flowers that open in March. Plants grow no more than 6 inches tall.

GARDEN TIPS

♦ Refrain from collecting trilliums in the wild. Past collecting has seriously depleted this Midwest treasure.

♦ Surround trilliums with shade-loving plants such as ferns. The ferns will fill the void when trilliums retreat into summer dormancy.

Snow Trillium

Prairie Trillium

Virginia Bluebells

Mertensia virginica

ZONES: 3 to 8

BLOOM TIME: April and May

BLOOM COLOR: Sky blue

LIGHT REQUIREMENT: Partial to full shade

HEIGHT × WIDTH: 12 to 24 inches × 12 to 18 inches

Special Features

Pink buds open to clusters of sky-blue bells in early spring. Large blue-green leaves add to the plant's attraction. Despite their name, Virginia bluebells are also a treasured native of the Midwest.

How to Grow

Plant in spring in rich, moist soil enriched with compost or other organic materials. Plants bloom and grow best with morning sun and afternoon shade. Space plants 12 inches apart. Once they have bloomed, Virginia bluebells pull a disappearing act for the rest of the season. Pair them with ferns or other woodland natives to fill the void left by their summer dormancy.

Care and Maintenance

Mulch to conserve soil moisture, and water in dry weather until the plants enter their summer dormancy. Pests and diseases require no treatment. Virginia bluebells never require division, but if you want to increase the number of plants, divide in spring. In favorable conditions, some volunteer plants may grow from dropped seeds.

Appendix

PLANTING

Plants are sold three ways: bare-root, balled-and-burlapped, and in containers.

Bare-Root Plants

Bare-root trees, shrubs, and perennials are usually planted only in the spring. Before planting, soak the roots in a bucket of water for 2 to 24 hours (but no longer). Make a mound of soil in the middle of the planting hole and spread the roots evenly over the mound. Fill the hole with soil, firm it with your hands, then water thoroughly.

Balled-and-Burlapped Plants

Large trees and shrubs are sometimes sold balled-and-burlapped. Set the plant in the hole, then remove all the ties from around the trunk and loosen the burlap. Cut away as much of the burlap as you can. Fill the hole with soil, firm it with your hands, and water thoroughly.

1. Remove plant from container.

Container Plants

Container plants can be planted any time during the growing season. Before you take a plant out of its container, cut away any roots that are growing through the drainage holes. Then check to see whether or not the roots are growing in a circle; if they are, loosen them with your fingers or a knife.

Set the plant in the hole at the same depth it was growing in its container, then backfill with soil removed from the hole. Firm the soil with your hands and water thoroughly.

2. Loosen roots.

3. Set plant in planting hole.

Digging the Planting Hole

To plant a tree or shrub, dig a hole as deep as the rootball and at least twice as wide.

Too Deep

Correct

Too Shallow

Strawberries are usually sold bare root. The placement of the crown is critical. The correct position is shown in the middle drawing. The roots should be spread out in a natural position.

When a **perennial** is placed in its planting hole, the crown (where the top meets the roots) should be level with the ground.

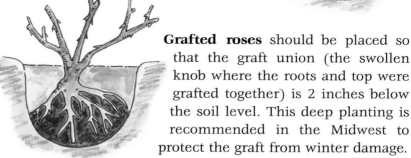

Grafted roses should be placed so that the graft union (the swollen knob where the roots and top were grafted together) is 2 inches below the soil level. This deep planting is recommended in the Midwest to protect the graft from winter damage.

Water Gardens

Place **water lilies** in a pool so the soil surface in their containers is about 6 inches below the water's surface. If necessary, use bricks to elevate the container to the proper level. Bog plants should be placed on a ledge or elevated on bricks so that the soil surface of their containers is 1 to 2 inches below the water's surface.

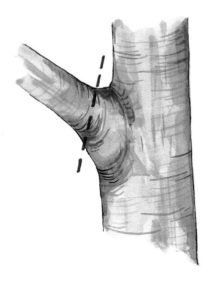

Deciduous Trees

Most trees and shrubs require only a little annual pruning to keep them healthy. Previous guidelines for proper pruning recommended making cuts flush with the tree trunk, but that turned out to be overdoing it. The tree needs the "collar"—a swollen area at the base of each branch—to help repair the damage done by pruning. Make the cut just outside this swollen area.

Don't "top" a tree; instead, remove a branch at the point where it joins another large-diameter branch or the trunk itself.

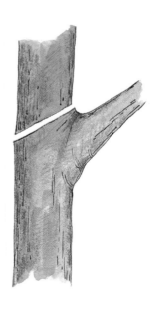

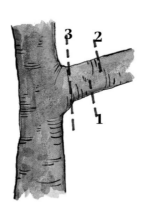

3-Step Pruning Method

When you must remove a large branch, take the time to use the 3-step method so that the weight of the branch won't tear the tree's bark.

Shrubs

To keep shrubs in peak form, cut one-third of the oldest stems back to ground level in late winter (renewal pruning). If you want to shorten any remaining stems of spring-blooming shrubs like lilac or forsythia, wait until after the blooms fade (heading back).

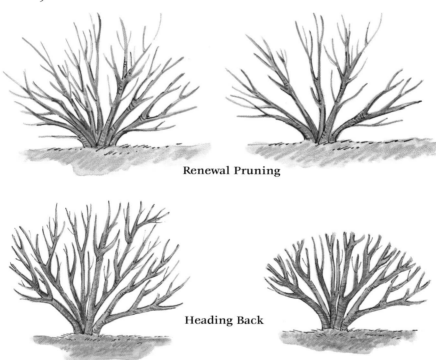

Renewal Pruning

Heading Back

Evergreens

To control the size or shape of a **pine,** simply pinch off the new shoots, called candles, with your fingers. To control the size or shape of a **fir** or **spruce,** prune back to any live bud in spring when the growth is soft.

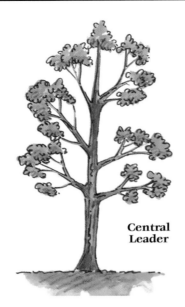

Fruit Trees

Central Leader

Open Center

Apple and **pear tree**s are usually pruned with a central leader. **Plums** and **peaches,** and sometimes **cherries,** are pruned by the open center system. Remove suckers and water sprouts. Remove branches that have narrow crotches, branches that grow towards the tree's interior, broken or diseased branches, and branches that are rubbing against other branches.

Grapes

Grapes fruit only on year-old wood, so remove canes that have already produced fruit. Maintain a central trunk with four canes,

or "arms," and four short spurs (each with a bud or two), which will become next year's arms. Shorten the current year's arms to about a dozen buds each.

Perennials and Annuals

Many flowering plants, such as **chrysanthemum** and **petunia,** can be "pinched" to increase fullness or encourage new growth. Just use your fingers to pinch off growing tips.

Roses

Modern roses such as **hybrid teas** should be pruned in spring just before new growth begins. **Old-fashioned roses** that bloom only in June should be pruned after the blooms fade. Plan pruning cuts to open up the center of rose bushes for better air circulation.

DIVIDING PERENNIALS

Most perennials require division, usually every three to five years. When blooms decline, it's time to divide. You can easily pull many perennials, such as **aster,** apart with your hands.

Others, such as **daylily,** form massive clumps. Put two garden forks back to back and pry the clumps apart.

After you dig up **iris** rhizomes, use a sharp knife to cut off sections. Each section should have its own fan of leaves. Discard the old centers and any soft or rotted spots in the rhizomes. Trim the fans back to about 6 inches. Spread the roots over a mound of soil and replant, being sure that the top of each rhizome is one inch below the soil's surface.

Some plants require support to keep from flopping on the ground. For an easy, old-fashioned way to prop up plants, simply push tree branches into the ground.

Using branches, or "pea stakes," for support was originally a method used for peas, but it works for any plant that needs support.

Many tall annuals and perennials require support when they're in bloom. You can buy collapsible plant braces or peony rings for the job.

Here's another way to support **peonies:** When the shoots are about 6 to 8 inches tall, lay a square of welded-wire fencing material over the plant. As the peony shoots push up through the openings, the wire holds the stems upright.

To make sturdy cages for standard **tomato** varieties, start with a 5 ½-foot length of 6-inch mesh concrete-reinforcing wire for each cage. It will make an 18-inch diameter cylinder. Clip the bottom ring, leaving prongs to slip into the ground. Fasten the cylinder together with twisted wires if you want to be able to take it apart for winter storage.

GLOSSARY

Alkaline: describes soil that lacks acidity, often because it has limestone in it

Annual: a plant that lives its entire life in one season

Balled-and-burlapped: describes a tree or shrub that is dug up in the field and whose roots and soilball are then wrapped with burlap

Bare root: describes a plant with no soil around its roots

Canker: an infection on a woody stem that is characterized by a sunken area

Cold hardiness: term used to describe a perennial plant's ability to survive the winter cold in a particular region

Compost: decomposed organic material that has a crumbly texture and is used as a soil conditioner and source of plant nutrients

Corm: the bulblike structure of some plants (such as crocus or gladiolus)

Crown: the base of a plant at, or just beneath, the surface of the soil, where the roots meet the stem

Deadhead: to remove faded flowers from a plant to improve its appearance and stimulate further flowering

Dieback: the death of a plant stem, starting at the stem's tip

Division: the practice of digging and splitting apart a perennial plant to control its size and/or improve its vigor and flowering

Dormant: describes a plant that has temporarily ceased active growth and is in a resting period

Established: describes a plant that has recovered from transplant shock and resumed growth

Evergreen: a plant that does not lose its foliage in autumn

Frond: the leaflike part of a fern

General-purpose fertilizer: fertilizer with a balanced proportion of three key nutrients: nitrogen, phosphorus, and potassium

Graft union: a swollen area on a trunk or woody stem where the top part of one plant has been joined to the root system of another plant, as for roses and fruit trees

Harden off: to gradually expose plants to outside growing conditions

Humus: decomposed organic material; an important component of soil

Hybrid: a plant that results from a cross between two related plants with different characteristics; the offspring produced by breeding plants of different varieties or species

Mulch: a layer of material such as wood chips, shredded leaves, or grass clippings that is spread on bare soil in order to discourage weeds, reduce erosion, conserve moisture, and/or moderate soil temperature

Naturalize: to grow in a random, informal pattern as plants do in their natural habitat

Node: the place on the stem from which a leaf grows

Organic material: plant or animal residues such as leaves, fruit or vegetable peelings, grass clippings, manure, peat moss, pine needles, dead plants, compost, and bark chips

Peat moss: organic matter that is derived from peat sedges or sphagnum mosses (sphagnum peat moss is often used to boost soil acidity)

Perennial: a plant that lives more than one season

Pinch: to remove a growing shoot by pressing it between thumb and forefinger

GLOSSARY

Pollination: the transfer of pollen grains by wind or insects from the male part of a flower to the female part of a flower

Rhizome: a swollen stem structure that lies horizontally just beneath the soil surface

Rootbound: describes a plant that has been confined in its container too long, forcing the roots to wrap around themselves (successful transplanting requires untangling and trimming away some of the matted roots)

Selection: a plant variety chosen for its desirable characteristics

Self-seeding: describes plants that produce seeds which mature in the garden, then drop to the ground and grow with no assistance from the gardener

Slow-release fertilizer: a fertilizer that releases its nutrients gradually (it may be either organic or synthetic)

Species: a group of plants with many shared characteristics

Sucker: a new growing shoot produced by an underground root

Top-dress: to apply compost or fertilizer to the surface of the soil

Tuber: a type of underground storage structure, such as a potato

Variegated: describes leaves that are streaked, edged, blotched, or mottled with a contrasting color

Variety: a plant with specific features that differ from those of the species to which it belongs (in this book, the term is also used to describe cultivated varieties, technically known as *cultivars*)

INDEX

INDEX

INDEX

Earl May

ABOUT THE AUTHOR

Jan Riggenbach is known and loved throughout the Midwest for her down-to-earth gardening information. Every week for twenty-five years, she has chronicled her garden discoveries and experiences in newspapers across the region.

Over the years, thousands of readers have written to tell Jan that her syndicated column, "Midwest Gardening," is the first thing they read in their local newspapers.

Now Jan has compiled "the best of the basics" in this *Midwest Gardener's Handbook*, published in cooperation with Earl May Garden Centers.

In addition to her newspaper column, Jan writes the garden column for *Midwest Living* magazine, seasonal features for major newspapers, and occasional articles for national garden magazines including *Organic Gardening* and *National Gardening*.

Most of Jan's writing is based on her own experiences (good and bad) with choosing and growing hundreds of plants in her own southwest Iowa garden. Those experiences are reflected in the detailed information in this book.

Jan's writing has earned her The Exemplary Journalism Award for Home Garden Communication, from the National Garden Bureau, and other awards from the Garden Writers' Association of America, National Gardening Association, American Community Gardening Association, Professional Plant Growers' association, and the Environmental Protection Agency.

Jan is a strong believer in gardening as therapy for people facing health problems. She is a registered horticultural therapist, helping hospitals, nursing homes, and other institutions set up special gardening programs.